Gerard McBurney

London July 19th 96

Edison Denisov

Contemporary Music Studies

A series of books edited by Peter Nelson and Nigel Osborne, University of Edinburgh, UK

Edison Denisov

by

Yuri Kholopov

and

Valeria Tsenova
Moscow Conservatoire

Translated from the Russian by Romela Kohanovskaya

 harwood academic publishers
Australia • Austria • Belgium • China • France • Germany • India
Japan • Malaysia • Netherlands • Russia • Singapore • Switzerland
Thailand • United Kingdom • United States

Copyright © 1995 by Harwood Academic Publishers GmbH.

Harwood Academic Publishers
Poststrasse 22
7000 Chur, Switzerland

British Library Cataloguing in Publication Data

Kholopov, Yuri
  Edison Denisov. — (Contemporary Music
  Studies, ISSN 0891-5415; Vol. 8)
  I. Title II. Tsenova, Valeria
  III. Kohanovskaya, Romela IV. Series
  780.92

  ISBN 3-7186-5425-3 (hardcover)
          3-7186-5426-1 (softcover)

CONTENTS

INTRODUCTION TO THE SERIES

The rapid expansion and diversification of contemporary music is explored in this international series of books for contemporary musicians. Leading experts and practitioners present composition today in all aspects — its techniques, aesthetics and technology, and its relationships with other disciplines and currents of thought — as well as using the series to communicate actual musical materials.

The series also features monographs on significant twentieth-century composers not extensively documented in the existing literature.

NIGEL OSBORNE

LIST OF PLATES

Frontispiece: Edison Denisov at home in Moscow (Photograph: Valery Plotnikov)

1. Zagreb, May 1969: Makoto Shinohara, Ursula and Heinz Holliger, Alfons Kontarsky and Klaus Huber
2. With Luigi Nono in a Moscow electronic studio in the mid-1960s
3. With Gennady Rozhdestvensky, Moscow 1988
4. With Pierre Boulez, Moscow, 1967
5. With Ursula Koubler-Vian (1980s)
6. With Pierre Boulez, Moscow, 1990 (Photograph: Viktor Bazhenov)
7. Scene from *Confession* (Theatre Estonia), 1984
8. Scene from *Confession* (Theatre Estonia), 1984 (Photograph: Vladimir Krasnoperov)
9. Scene from *l'Ecume des jours* (Perm Theatre of Opera and Ballet), Moscow, 1989
10. Scene from *l'Ecume des jours* (Opéra de Paris), 1986 (Photograph: Michel Jzabo)
11. At home (Photograph: Monroe Warshaw)
12. With Yuri Kholopov and Alfred Schnittke, Moscow, 1984

Edison Denisov at home in Moscow (Photograph: Valery Plotnikov)

FOREWORD

Edison Denisov belongs to a generation of composers who came to the fore in the post-Stalinist era and were destined to change the course of Russian music. This generation includes the Moscow-born Andrei Volkonsky, Alfred Schnittke and Sophia Gubaidulina, and some more talented composers from other Russian cities. It would be hard to find a more impressive case of 'running against the stream' in the history of Russian music. An artist invariably reflects in his creations the pace of his times. That '...wie die Zeit vergeht...' (Stockhausen) manifests itself in the very spirit of his art and the artistic conceptions underlying his most remarkable works. Modern Russian art, music included, has been naturally involved in the current spiritual movement unfolding both in this country and the world at large, revealing its prevailing trends. It is another matter in what way these trends are reflected. That post-war generation of composers grew up in an atmosphere of totalitarianism raging behind the Iron Curtain, under the upsurge of the 'personality cult' and the enforced precepts of so called 'socialist realism'. Their reaching maturity coincided with persecutions of the best writers, poets and theatrical figures in the late 1940s, the party resolutions on music, and the struggle against 'formalism' and 'cosmopolitanism'.

This generation took the challenge and embarked on its own way. For all its individual differences, during the period from the 1950s to the 1970s, it was proceeding through some definite stages: from an unconscious, but mounting intellectual ferment to an open breach with the official ideological doctrines cultivated by the Composers Union, a state controlled body in the musical sphere, towards more and more daring and independent artistic conceptions. On the road to self-expression this generation was guided by the idea of spiritual freedom. It was not stated in their artistic programmes or 'platforms', for it was out of the question. Rather, on the contrary, it was disguised in musical experimentation or concealed behind some neutral declarations, which allowed it to stay away from the ruling ideological dogmas and cliches. To be able to profess an idea one had to follow it as a reference point, rather than demonstrate it openly and directly. One of the means of gaining spiritual freedom was to address oneself to the banned modern methods of musical composition. It eventually gave rise to the Russian avant-garde that emerged and developed in music in the late 1950s — early 1960s. Though outwardly it represented just a subsidiary of the Western avant-garde of the same historical period, this trend in Russia was motivated by somewhat different factors. In Western Europe the avant-garde constituted primarily an artistic, musical phenomenon. As for Russia, the natural urge to keep abreast of the times was interlinked here with the process of spiritual emancipation from the ideological pressures of the ruling system. The Russian avant-garde was progressing within the context of 'the struggle against avant-gardism'. The innovators in music were inevitably subjected to ideological criticism and accused of hidden political motives, though they were spared the sensational scandals that erupted around such 'dissidents' as Boris Pasternak and Alexander Solzhenitsyn.

The creative personality of Edison Denisov, one of the leading Russian avant-gardists, was shaping up under the above described conditions. In this respect his career is most characteristic. Starting in the Shostakovichian style, Denisov then took a sharp turn towards the New Music cultivated by Boulez and Nono. The employment of modern technical procedures proved to be a powerful means for releasing his creative potential which lay beyond the control of the ruling system. The revelation of an artist's attitude to the effect exerted by the environment is paramount to opposing it. Denisov's creative individuality, rooted in the past of Russian music and developed under the beneficial impact of such twentieth-century classics as Stravinsky, Bartók and Webern, got an opportunity to reveal itself to its best advantage in his avant-garde compositions written during the period from the 1960s to the 1980s, beginning with his cantata *The Sun of the Incas*.

The name of Edison Denisov has also been associated with a wide range of matters involved in the creative organization of music as an art of sound production. A change of generations naturally entails a drastic renovation of musical thinking, its genre systems, the logic of its musical language – melody, rhythm, harmony, counterpoint, thematic arrangement, colour effects, and the principles of musical forms.

The new image of modern Russian music is still little known in the West. As a matter of fact, it substantially differs from what it used to be in the times of Prokofiev and Shostakovich. This book is an attempt to disclose the inner world and the art of one of the prominent representatives of contemporary Russian culture.

Yuri Kholopov and Valeria Tsenova

CHAPTER 1

A BIOGRAPHICAL OUTLINE

1. CHILDHOOD AND SCHOOL YEARS

The Family

Edison Vasilyevich Denisov was born on April 6, 1929 in Tomsk, the first university city in the Asiatic part of Russia.[1] His father, Vasily Grigoryevich (1906–41) was a remarkable person. A radio physicist passionately in love with his vocation,[2] he was one of the pioneers of the large-scale movement of wireless enthusiasts, which emerged in the twenties in this country. Vasily Denisov invented a short-wave transmitter, the first of its kind in Siberia, conducted the first experiments in aviation radio communication, set up the first broadcasting station in Western Siberia, and devised a 'Magniton' device for musical accompaniment to silent films. The call-sign of his home radio station was known to radio-amateurs in many countries.[3] The composer's mother, Antonina Ivanovna Titova (b. 1905) was a doctor by profession. Upon graduation from the Medical Department at Tomsk University, she held various medical positions.

Neither of his parents had a musical education, nonetheless, the family was often engaged in music-making. Endowed with a good ear and a beautiful voice, Mother was fond of singing, while Father was a fairly good pianist. The parents wanted their son to go to a music school, but he flatly refused calling music a 'girlish pursuit'. At that time he was keen on some other things. From his earliest years Edik Denisov (as he was commonly known) was fascinated by mathematics, like his father. When he was just two years old, he showed interest in numbers and figures. Then, at the age of five, he got interested in chemistry. He learned to read very early and was always questioning his parents about what he read. Sometimes his mother got tired of his questions and had even to hide some books from him. When he was seven, he went to school.

School Years

At school Edik made a good progress, especially in physics, mathematics and German.

His interest in music arose unexpectedly for himself and his parents. Once, in the hostel for postgraduates of the Physics & Mathematics Department of Tomsk University where the Denisov family used to live, he heard the man living next door playing a mandolin. That neighbour became the boy's first music teacher; then Edik took up the clarinet and later the seven-stringed guitar, using a teach-yourself book. With his drive for music growing, he was now determined to make a serious study of it. Since he was already sixteen years old, the only way out was to enter the general music courses (GMC). It was hard to study, for he had to attend the evening courses and the family had no piano at home, so he had to study the piano late at night in a kindergarten.

While still at school, Edik Denisov set up a small ensemble, with himself playing the mandolin. During the last year of the war and the first post-war years this group used to appear in concerts in hospitals.

After he had attended the GMC for a short time, Edison Denisov passed the exams and entered the piano department at the Tomsk Music College.

University Years

Upon finishing a general-education school in 1946, Edison Denisov entered the Physics & Mathematics Department of Tomsk University.

Edison Denisov:

"I felt no particular attraction to either physics or mathematics. But since my father had a big library and I always liked his occupation, I decided that I should follow suit. And after I attended the university for some time, I came to realize that I was more interested in mathematics than in physics. I felt increasingly drawn to the most abstract domains of mathematics such as mathematical logic and topology."

A course of lectures read by Zakhar Ivanovich Klementyev, then an associate professor, who had evacuated to Tomsk from Leningrad, gave impetus to the young man's thorough study of mathematics. Denisov was impressed by the relationships delineated in Klementyev's lectures between mathematics and other fields of human knowledge, such as literature (the professor used to recite poetry during his lectures) and the arts. As a result, Denisov switched to the Mathematics Department of Tomsk University to attend Klementyev's classes.

Zakhar Klementyev:

"At the senior courses I used to read lectures on the more advanced and complex problems of mathematical analysis, such as the theory of functions and functional analysis. Edison Denisov was one of my most attentive students. I admired the clarity of his thinking, the easiness and natural spontaneity with which he mastered the most abstract ideas and intricate mathematical theories. During my seventy-year-long teaching career I met many talented persons endowed with special mathematical gifts, but Edison's abilities looked most extraordinary to me."

The Music College. First Works

Along with the university Edison Denisov attended the special piano classes at the music college. He had at his disposal a fairly big music library containing a number of compositions little known at the time, among them Shostakovich's opera *The Nose* and *Katerina Izmailova*.

Edison Denisov:

"I felt particular attraction to Russian music. I believe it was Glinka who captivated me most at that time and whose works I played more often than anyone else's. Especially his operas were invariably on my music-stand and every day I played something from these operas and tried even to sing".

His drive for composition first arose during his studies at the music college. There was no one in Tomsk to teach composition and therefore his early opuses proved to be imitative and far from the composer's future style. His earliest works, preludes for piano written during the period from 1947 to 1949, bore out the young composer's infatuation with lyrical poetry. Some preludes have epigraphs from Alexander Blok, Alexander Pushkin and Zinaida Gippius. These preludes also reflect a vigorous study of musical literature: three of them were written à la Scriabin, Chopin and Prokofiev.

His *Classical Suite* for two pianos (1948–49) falls into five parts — Prelude, Gavotte, Minuet, Intermezzo and Gigue, with the Gavotte orchestrated for chamber ensemble and representing the composer's first independent experiment in scoring.

The same period yielded several lyrical songs written on poems by Heine, Mickiewicz, Blok, Lermontov and Yesenin, in their style akin to the Russian art songs of the first half of the 19th century.

Of his early works, special mention should be made of his comic scene *Failure* (1949), based on Anton Chekhov, which is in fact a mini-opera for four vocalists. The humour and character delineation in this composition telling about an unsuccessful marriage are reminiscent of Dargomyzhsky and Mussorgsky.

A Mathematician or a Musician?

By 1950 when he graduated from the music college with honours and got a diploma of a teacher of the elementary music school, Edison Denisov found himself irresistibly drawn to music. The young man faced the most serious dilemma in his life: he had to make a choice between two careers — a mathematician's or a musician's, for it was hardly possible to serve 'two gods' at the same time.

He was considered a highly promising student at the university and his superiors hoped to see him on the teaching staff there. At the music college Edison also made a good progress and was reputed as a student endowed with the great musical gifts. Besides, the young man had a bent for composition. But there was no chance in Tomsk to get a qualified piece of advice as to his gifts as a composer. Before making his choice the young specialist had to obtain an authoritative opinion about his music. And Edison Denisov took a decisive and bold step: he sent his compositions for appraisal to a major master of the day — Dmitry Shostakovich.

Ex. 1   'Full Moon O'er the Meadow'

Dmitry Shostakovich:

"Dear Edik, I've received your letter. I'm glad that you are so bent on music and aspire to become a musician. But before you take such a serious decision (entering the Conservatoire) I would ask you to send me your compositions" (from the letter of February 28, 1950).[4]

Upon getting a permission from the venerable composer Edison Denisov sent him his pieces written independently during his studies at the music college — the *Classical Suite*, romances and his comic scene *Failure*.

Dmitry Shostakovich:

"Dear Edik, your compositions have astonished me... I believe that you are endowed with a great gift for composition. And it would be a great sin to bury your talent" (from the letter of March 22, 1950).

Shostakovich found not only time to answer to a complete young stranger from Tomsk, but sent him a detailed letter with an analysis of his works and displayed a keen interest in the career of the budding composer. Dmitry Shostakovich gave his opinion on each separate item. Most of all he liked Denisov's song on poems by Alexander Blok 'Full Moon O'er the Meadow' in which he distinguished its piano part (see Musical Example 1).

So it settled Denisov's future career. A regular correspondence sprang up between the young and the world-famous composers. Dmitry Shostakovich repeatedly expressed his desire 'to meet and have a talk' with the aspiring composer from Siberia. He also volunteered to show Denisov's compositions to some Moscow-based musicians, namely Vissarion Shebalin, Semyon Bogatyrev and Anatoly Alexandrov. In his view, it could be a tentative exam for the young composer. However, their judgement proved to be 'quite unexpected' for Dmitry Shostakovich. In his letter of May 20, 1950 he informed Denisov that the Moscow professors acknowledged his general musical capacity, a fairly high level of professionalism, but failed to see in him the hallmarks of 'genuine gift for composition'.

On Shostakovich's advice in the spring of 1950 Denisov came to Moscow and tried to enter the Conservatoire. But he failed to pass the exams. In addition to the negative opinion of the professors of the Moscow Conservatoire — Bogatyrev and Shebalin — about his endowments as a composer, he showed a poor knowledge of musical theory.

Nonetheless the first unsuccessful attempt failed to crush the aspirations of the young man from Siberia. He went back to Tomsk, graduated with honours from the university in 1951 as a specialist in 'functional analysis', passed his exams to attend the post-graduate courses and ... left for Moscow once again. On an agreement with the director of the music college at the Moscow Conservatoire he was allowed to take some lessons there to prepare himself for another attempt to enter the conservatoire.

This time thoroughly prepared by his studies at the college, in the summer of 1951, Edison Denisov became a student of the composition department at the Moscow Conservatoire.

2.   THE CONSERVATOIRE

The Post-1948 Period

The beginning of his composer's career coincided with the most difficult period in the national musical life. The Resolution adopted by the Central Committee of the Communist Party in 1948 unleashed a campaign of severe criticism levelled at the 'formalists' — Prokofiev, Shostakovich, Myaskovsky, Aram Khachaturyan, and a galaxy of Western composers. Even some of Pyotr Tchaikovsky's later works came to be regarded as ideologically alien (his songs, and separate items in his *Queen of Spades*). "The whole of the Soviet people" (the ideological cliche of the time) without exception condemned the 'errors' of composers and musicologists. The late forties and the early fifties witnessed devastating ideological indoctrination of the people and the 'brainwashing' of the intelligentsia. The menace of reprisals for the 'wrong' tastes or views was impending. The label of a 'formalist and cosmopolitan bowing down before the corrupt bourgeois West' was offhandedly pinned on the creators of 'formalist' works. A crowd of cynical and unscrupulous characters emerged from the bottom of the intellectual life, taking a sadistic pleasure in repeating such formulas and clichés and spitefully defaming the best achievements in modern music. It was out of the question to defend the 'formalists' out loud, for it was tantamount to opposing the party and the people. Igor Stravinsky became one of the most dangerous persons, since he was an 'emigré' which meant a 'betrayer' and 'traitor to the Motherland' who used to be executed by shooting some years earlier.

During the years following the adoption of that notorious Resolution the conservatoire students had to lock up themselves in a classroom to play a Shostakovich symphony or a Prokofiev sonata. Composer Roman Ledenyov whose interest in Hindemith was brought to somebody's notice (he once played a piece by Hindemith) was summoned to the Komsomol Committee of the conservatoire for an ideological slating. Composer Arno Babajanyan used to tell his friends how, already in the seventies, he still quivered whenever he heard the name of Hindemith.[5] Jazz music was banned. To play it, jazz musicians gathered together behind the closed doors in some flat in the suburbs, which was jokingly called a 'jazz shelter'.[6]

After Stalin's death (in 1953) Edison Denisov asked Dmitry Shostakovich whether the changes for the better could be expected. Shostakovich's reply was rather pessimistic: "Edik, the times are new, but the informers are still the same." The black shadow of 1948, despite the purifying effect of the 1958 Resolution on 'correction of the errors' committed by the 1948 Resolution, was hovering over Soviet music for many years to come.[7] Edison Denisov remained honest in his views. As early as in the mid-fifties he came to assert that the Resolution of 1948 on music had been 'wrong' and was persecuted for his attitude to it.

Under Vissarion Shebalin's Tutorship

Dmitry Shostakovich:
"You must study in Shebalin's class, for nowadays he is the only one who can teach the 'musical metier', or to be more precise the 'composition metier'. And this is the most important for you now" (from the letter of August 4, 1951).

On his mentor's advice Edison Denisov asked to be enrolled in the composition class of Vissarion Yakovlevich Shebalin who was to guide his musical education for eight years, including the conservatoire course and three years of postgraduate studies.

Edison Denisov:
"Vissarion Yakovlevich was not only a good composer and a true professional, but also a remarkable teacher. I owe him a lot and I'm very grateful to him for that. Shostakovich had been right Shebalin was a superb instructor in composition".

During his first years at the Conservatoire Denisov was inspired mainly by Shostakovich's music. The friendship between the famous master and the young composer went on.

Denisov composed several pieces 'à la Shostakovich', a piano trio included. Upon scanning them Shebalin pointed out that all of them had been written in a style to be alien to Denisov some time later. Once he said: "This composer is not in your line. With the time passing you will depart from him. I advise you to study Debussy more closely, for he is far more akin to you".[8] One can only wonder at the insight and intuition of the great teacher. Meanwhile the second-course student came out with a song-cycle entitled *Nocturnes*. Shebalin liked most songs from this cycle, particularly the one called 'A Flute on the River', observing that "this little song is to give rise to everything to be composed afterwards".[8]

Two songs from the cycle *Nocturnes* were published in March 1954 in the music supplement to the *Sovetskaya Muzyka* magazine. It was the first publication of the young composer's works.

The invaluable trait of Shebalin the teacher was his striving to familiarize his students with a wide range of music, modern compositions included. He was intent to make out of them versatile musicians with a broad scope and true knowledge of musical literature the conservatoire course of which could not meet their quests. According to the reminiscences of Shebalin's many pupils, they used to play four and eight hands the oratorios by Bach and Handel, symphonies by Haydn, Mozart, Schubert, Brahms, Mahler, Tchaikovsky and Glazunov. In 1955 Shebalin held a seminar in his class on all of Beethoven's symphonies and his *Missa Solemnis*. A detailed analysis was made of some operas by Mozart, Glinka, Tchaikovsky, Rimsky-Korsakov, Mussorgsky, and Debussy's *Pelléas et Mélisande*. They also played in the class the musical compositions banned for performance, such as *The Buffoon* and *Esquisse automnal* by Prokofiev and works of another 'formalist' — Shostakovich, whose symphonies and other opuses, often in MSS, were brought by Shebalin himself. In other words, it was music never performed anywhere and forbidden even to mention. Shebalin introduced his students to the recorded music which he, as a conservatoire professor, had a chance to order abroad, among them the compositions by Stravinsky, Hindemith, Schoenberg, Berg, Honegger, Dallapiccola and Petrassi. It was in Shebalin's class that Denisov for the first time heard the recording of Pierre Boulez's *Marteau sans maître* (The Hammer Without a Master) which made a strong impression on him (the score was not available). Shebalin said that this music was not to his liking and he did not understand it, though he felt it to be a talented work and he believed that the budding composers should know it as anything talented emerging around. As Denisov recalls, Shebalin's classes were permeated with an atmosphere of common sense, devoid of terror of a 'forbidden fruit' and blind worshipping of any innovation.

Shebalin encouraged his students to attend other classes too, emphasizing the benefits of a 'fresh approach'. Denisov spent many hours in the classes of Heinrich Neuhaus and Aram Khachaturyan. He was also often seen in the class of Nikolai Peiko. During his last years Shebalin felt ill for long periods and when he was 'out of action' Nikolai Peiko came to replace him. Peiko was an austere, biting, ironical and demanding teacher. Besides, Denisov studied instrumentation under Nikolai Rakov and the musical analysis under Victor Zuckerman. For more than three years he also attended Vladimir Belov's class at the piano department. Edison often appeared in concerts as a pianist performing, among other things, compositions of his colleagues.

The young composer was also engaged in intensive social activities. For several years running he headed the student scientific society at his department trying to cultivate little-known classical and modern music. Denisov believed in the importance of this work, for during the sessions of this society students could familiarize themselves with compositions of their colleagues, gain an understanding of music and appraise it properly.

Denisov's active attitude to life found another manifestation in his articles, comments and reviews published in the *Sovetskaya Muzyka* magazine. Those were mostly informative reportages, press notices of performances given by Soviet and foreign musicians, and reviews of the released recordings.

His challenging article, 'Once More on the Youth Education', appeared in Issue 7 of that magazine for 1956. The author boldly criticized the top officials of the Composers Union who failed to help the young musicians and attend their concerts and examinations, while the members of the composition chair sometimes appeared ridiculously overcautious in their actions. Thus, once a song to lyrics by Robert Burns was excluded from concert performance because of the following 'seditious' words: "Of a' the airts the wind can blaw, I dearly like the west" (on the assumption that 'the west' implied 'the bourgeois West' ideologically hostile to communism). In that article the young composer wrote that "it was high time to stop making fuss over each minor second and shout about the 'still persisting formalism' because of any occasional discordant note."[9]

In Search of Folk Music

Folkloristic expeditions as an indispensable practice for students of the Theory & Composition Department at the Conservatoire played a major part in Denisov's creative biography. Altogether, he took part in three expeditions.

In the summer of 1954 a small group of students, including the young composers Edison Denisov and Alexander Pirumov, left for the Kursk Region. The expedition was headed by Anna Vasilyevna Rudneva, a noted folklorist. The students visited two districts in the Kursk Region and recorded down a great number of drawn-out and wedding songs, and ditties. That was an unforgettable experience which gave rise to new artistic conceptions. According to Denisov, that expedition made him understand the true meaning of folklore which, as it turned out, had little in common with what you read about it in books or listened to on radio.[10]

On his second expedition, which took place the following summer, Edison Denisov went together with his friends Alexander Pirumov and Alexei Nikolayev. This time it was the Altai, an area little explored by folklore scholars and abounding in rich song traditions. During the three weeks the young composers spent there they once more were captivated by folk music in live performance in the native surroundings.

Edison Denisov went on his third expedition in the summer of 1956 upon graduation from the Conservatoire. Together with Alexei Nikolayev they visited the Tomsk Region.

These three expeditions not only enriched him spiritually and expanded the scope of his artistic perceptions. In practical terms they resulted in his choral arrangements and employment of folk motives in his compositions. A vivid evidence of a folk line in Denisov's creativity is his opera *Ivan the Soldier* which reflected not only his knowledge of folk music, but also the easiness with which he tackled traditional texts. The true creative reinterpretation of his folkloristic findings occurred in the 1960s and was fully realized in his vocal-instrumental cycle *Wails*.

Graduation from the Conservatoire. The Postgraduate Years

In the spring of 1956 Edison Denisov graduated from the Moscow Conservatoire.

The Minutes of the Session of the State Examination Commission.

June 1, 1956
Chairman of the commission: Professor D. D. Shostakovich
Compositions: *Ivan the Soldier*, Act 1 of the opera
           Symphony for full orchestra
           Nocturnes, a song-cycle
Mark: 'excellent' (unanimously)

In the August of 1956 Denisov became a postgraduate student at the Moscow Conservatoire. The same summer he was made a member of the Composers Union of the USSR.

June 6, 1956
To the Union of Soviet Composers
I strongly recommend Edison Vasilyevich Denisov for membership in the Union of Soviet Composers.
Edison V. Denisov is endowed with a great gift for composition. His works are distinguished for a good taste, vivid melodies, heartfelt lyricism, and a sense of musical dramaturgy. I must also stress that Edison Denisov possesses a sense of humour which is invaluable in a composer. Though he is still young, Denisov has reached a high level of professionalism. A talented composer, a highly educated and cultured person, Edison V. Denisov must be admitted to the membership of the Composers Union.

Dmitry D. Shostakovich[11]

Works Written During the Conservatoire Years (1951–59)

Quite a lot of compositions were produced by Edison Denisov during his conservatoire and postgraduate years. His works were performed at the Composers Club and in the philharmonic halls. In the fall of 1957 his Trio and some songs were first heard on the national radio.[12]

The works written during his conservatoire years bore the natural traces of his apprenticeship. The young composer was intensively assimilating the classical traditions and successfully recreated them in his music.

His compositions for various instruments of those years carried the imprint of the Shostakovichian style. It manifested itself, for instance, in his *Quartet No. 1* and his *Piano Trio in D minor* written while he was a third-year student. It is a model of traditional cyclic form and in its through idea and musical language it is reminiscent of Shostakovich's chamber ensembles: 1st movement is a sonata-like

Moderato with its tonal repercussions from the initial movement of Shostakovich's Symphony No. 5 /d – E♭ in the exposition, and d – D in recapitulation/; 2nd movement is a bulky Scherzo; 3rd movement is a leisured Largo; 4th movement is the eleven-part Rondo in D major with its serene development erupted (like in the Finale of Shostakovich's Symphony No. 8) by a dramatic climax from the first movement, framing the cycle in its thematic arrangement.

It would be hard to identify the shoots of Denisov's future style in the above and some other instrumental works written during the conservatoire studies in the academic style. But this academic approach should be appraised positively, for it implies not a lack of one's own style and original ideas, but constitutes a logically requisite stage in the evolution of any composer. A good assimilation of traditions is a token of true training and sound composition techniques.

Three suite-cycles for orchestra — *Musical Pictures, Children Suite* and *Little Suite* — proved a good workshop for polishing off some composition techniques. These suites represent a series of genre, characteristic pieces; their lively and ingenuous music is akin to Prokofiev. The short pieces in unextended form, which make up these suites, are marked for melodic finesse.

The largest instrumental composition of the conservatoire period was Denisov's diploma work — *Symphony in C major* in four movements, written in strict conformity with the traditional rules of form, instrumentation and tonality. It was completed in October 1955. Its two movements — the slow one and the finale — were performed in the Grand Hall of the Moscow Conservatoire at the graduation concert of the composition department in May 1956.

Departure from pure academicism based on a freer approach to folk music in the vein of Stravinsky began to show in his two-movement *Trio for Violin, Clarinet and Bassoon*. The composer made a synthesis of classical and folk polyphony, with combined counterpoint and canonic techniques going hand in hand with collateral-part polyphony. This trio, as well as some other compositions of the same period, reveal certain elements of the twelve-note composition procedure to which Denisov was intuitively drawn. In the finale you can occasionally discern some series of notes which are not to be repeated.

The same highly original synthesis of classical notation and some singular features of Russian folk polyphony is encountered in his *Sonata for Two Violins*. Its second movement — Variations on two folk themes — serve for the composer merely a source which he substantially revises. This movement develops basically on the principle of free variation characteristic of folk music, with a single line of movement from the initial opposition of the themes towards their unification. The third movement of the sonata is a double fugue of the Bartók type. The episode brings out a melody closely related to a folk one and at the same time presenting a remote version of the fugue's theme (Musical Example 2).

Denisov's vocal compositions turned out to be the most independent. Several song-cycles written during the conservatoire period revealed the highly original traits of the young composer's artistic perception. These cycles have a number of common features such as harmonic colourfulness, a careful treatment of the verse details, the priority of the vocal part, natural modulation, and a striving to convey the psychological atmosphere of each poem in music. Three directions of the young composer's current interests can be clearly distinguished in his vocal music: the first, Romantic, trend was brought forth by a wide-ranging study of the Romantic vocal repertoire. To this trend belong his two song-cycles — *Five Songs*

Ex. 2   Sonata for two violins, part III, *A* — theme, *B* — episode

on *Poems by Robert Burns*, the first composition written at the conservatoire, and *Youth Sufferings* on poems by Heine, a cycle written during his postgraduate studies; the second trend linked with Russian songs found its manifestation in his song-cycle *Native Land* on poems by Alexander Prokofiev; and the third trend was associated with musical imagery of the Orient. *Three Songs on Poems by Avetik Isahakian* reflected Denisov's preoccupation with the music of Aram Khachaturyan, which is evident from the songs' harmonic and melodic structures.

The song-cycle *Nocturnes* on poems by the Chinese poet Bo Tzu-i exerted the greatest influence on Denisov's subsequent works. This cycle expressed most of all the features to characterize his later music— the unassuming and easy piano part and a fragile intonation of the vocal line. Some 'chinoiseries' are also noteworthy — for example, the pentatonic scale in the last part, as well as quests for unique colour-effects frequently manifested in a combination of the chromatic system and natural harmony. The best song of this cycle distinguished by Shebalin is 'A Flute on the River' (Musical Example 3).

His opera *Ivan the Soldier*, which it took him nearly four years to compose,[13] in its style is reminiscent of the works written by Stravinsky during his Russian period (such as *Mavra* or *Renard*). It is a burlesque opera.[14]

Edison Denisov:

"Once I bought from a second-hand bookseller an old and thick edition of Afanasyev's fairy tales and became engrossed in reading. One of these tales made the basis of my opera. I wrote the libretto myself, which was quite a difficult task, for there were just three pages in Afanasyev's tale. I had to add a lot of text, including even some of my own verse and many texts from the folkloric records. There are no citations in this opera. I have

Ex. 3   "Nocturnes", No. 5 — 'A Flute on the River'

always shared Bartók's attitude to folklore: it should be studied and admired but never exploited and spoilt by arrangements."

The opera, cast in three acts and five scenes, presents quite a coherent composition abounding in recurrent images, scenes and musical items. The main arch making it an entity links Scenes 1 and 5. This is the common place of action (the Tsar's palace), the scene of the court trial: in Scene 1 it is the trial of the soldier who dared to fall in love with the tsarevna, in Scene 5 it is the failed execution of Ivan the Soldier (introduced is the character of a hangman looking for his victim) and, finally, a similar ending of these two scenes: the first ends in 'Glory' to the tsar and the last one — with a 'Toast' to the newlyweds.

The key, third, scene of the opera is the most extended and complex in structure. Denisov made use of the method encountered in 19th-century Russian operas of uniting the extended crowd scenes: the first section of Scene 3 is composed in the rondo form. It is a scene on the market-place, involving a great number of participants (with its recurrent popular theme).

The general compositional structure of the opera can be presented in the following way:

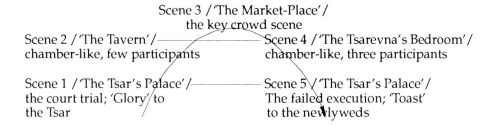

Scene 3 /'The Market-Place'/
the key crowd scene

Scene 2 /'The Tavern'/
chamber-like, few participants

Scene 4 /'The Tsarevna's Bedroom'/
chamber-like, three participants

Scene 1 /'The Tsar's Palace'/
the court trial; 'Glory' to
the Tsar

Scene 5 /'The Tsar's Palace'/
The failed execution; 'Toast'
to the newlyweds

Thematically the opera is based on folk music. The first thing that strikes the ear is the fresh and vivid intonation conveyed predominantly in simple forms (couplets and their variations). There are no too complex structures and scenes in this opera, everything being clear, laconic and unequivocal.

As a whole, the opera *Ivan the Soldier* is traditional in its harmonic language, expressive means and musical dramatic patterns. Nonetheless it has been written skillfully, revealing the composer's superb training. Its integrity and its easily perceived music were likely to ensure it a successful run on operatic stage.[15]

The First Press Reviews

The first to make a notice of Edison Denisov's music was the newspaper *Sovetsky Muzykant* (The Soviet Musician) released by the Conservatoire. Professor V. P. Bobrovsky from the chair of musical theory in his review of the concert in which the song-cycle *Nocturnes* was performed, along with other pieces written by the student composers, acclaimed Denisov's fine artistic taste but recommended that the young composer should not indulge in this genre and depart from modern themes (*Sovetsky Muzykant*, May 22, 1953, p. 2).

Almost all the reviewers of his music found it a bit too dry. And in the spirit of the times this sourness was ascribed to 'the influence of the Western modernist style of the 1920s' (*Sovetskaya Muzyka*, No. 1, 1959, p. 201). The composer was also constantly criticized for his too complicated musical language. Thus, his Trio for Violin, Clarinet and Bassoon (one of his most tonally smooth compositions) was called an 'unnatural' opus not distinguished for any significant musical idea (*Muzykalnaya Zhizn*, No. 21–22, 1958, p. 14).

All the reviewers unanimously criticized his most original work of those years — the Sonata for Two Violins. It was discarded as an 'alien work useless for the listeners' which should be kept at home as a sample of experimentation and which should not be hastily made public (*Sovetskaya Muzyka*, No. 5, 1960, p. 23). All the critical press comments were consonant with the general ideological tendencies prevailing in the late 1950s.[16]

3. ACQUISITION OF HIS OWN STYLE

Self-education

By the end of his postgraduate studies Denisov's composition thinking began to change. He came to realise that not everything he had been taught at the conservatoire was correct and adequate for complete musical education and he had to look for something else and new. According to his own words, all of a sudden he became aware that he knew and could do nothing and he had to begin his education from the scratch.

The years from 1959 to 1964 were mostly devoted to self-education. During that period Denisov produced few compositions. He was mainly engaged in a detailed analysis of music. He was determined to go through all the composers discarded from the conservatoire curriculum, forbidden to study and whose names were not even mentioned within the conservatoire walls.

First of all it was Stravinsky. Denisov made a thorough study of nearly all of his principal works. These studies resulted either in reports made at the Conservatoire and the Composers Union or in scientific papers.[17]

The second composer to be studied was Bartók whose music, according to Denisov himself, came as one of the greatest revelations in his life. In Bartók's compositions he discovered for himself a new soundscape and learned to erect a musical entity from the tiniest cell.

Then came Debussy, one of his most admired modern composers, and Hindemith. But the more Denisov studied the latter's works the less he liked them. Having spent a lot of time on their study, Denisov, in his own words, 'gave it up as a bad job'.

Denisov is firmly convinced that Hindemith's music is structural, rigid and hollow, and he often refers to Stravinsky's opinion that his compositions are 'as dry and unnourishing as pasteboard'.[18] Indeed Hindemith represented an artistic trend completely alien to Denisov's own quests. He was always drawn to another art and a different kind of music which, like a flower, was subject to constant change and motion. Certainly, Denisov may be too categorical in his judgement of Hindemith. Nevertheless, despite the obvious subjectiveness of his views, all the conclusions about his music have been drawn on the basis of its meticulous analysis.

And one more major 'node' in the formation of Denisov's own style is the music of the Second Viennese School. By the late 1950s he 'knew nothing about Webern, heard a little of Berg and failed to understand and accept Schoenberg'. But the fate willed him to meet the French pianist Gérard Fremy, a wonderful musician, who happened to be his neighbour at the conservatoire hostel. Denisov recalled how Gérard had first shown him Webern's string trio, and how he had failed to understand it and criticized his music saying that it was artificial and bad. But gradually, despite the outward resistance, he came to understand it and admitted that he had been wrong. As he more and more immersed in Webern's musical world, he grew captivated by it. He learned a lot from his detailed analysis of the works by Webern and Schoenberg (as for Berg, to quote his own words, he had failed 'to have time for him').[19]

Early in 1964, after he had in the main completed his composition training, Denisov felt himself fully equipped for personal freedom in composition and entitled to his own attitude to composers and their music. According to his own words, "I came to realize that from now on I could be my own self because I had already gained an understanding of what I needed in my life and art."

Opus One: *'The Sun of the Incas'*

From the press reviews of the mid-sixties:

> *"The Sun of the Incas* by the Soviet composer Edison Denisov made quite a sensation of the concert; can you imagine a Soviet musician writing serial music!"
>
> (*Carrefour*)

> "Edison Denisov's chamber cantata, *Sun of the Incas*, afforded interesting evidence that the Soviet Union can now produce not only space-ships to photograph the back of the moon but composers who can write in a variety of international modern styles without losing their place in the Composers' Union."
>
> (*Sunday Times*, Brighton)

The first composition in which Denisov came into his own was *The Sun of the Incas* on poems by Gabriela Mistral. He wrote it easily and within a short span of time.

Edison Denisov:

"For me this composition was very important since the whole period of my previous quests combined here with what had been inside me back during the conservatoire years and some touches of which were perceptible in my cycle Nocturnes. Besides, these were the verses that apparently urged me to sharpen up the colour-effects of the instruments. Here for the first time I made a wide use of the percussion group and the type of its treatment so characteristic of my later works."

It is this cantata that Denisov rates as his first opus after which he began feeling fully responsible for each note coming down from under his pen. And it was this cantata that changed in many respects the attitude to the composer for the better, in spite of the fact that it met with sharp criticism on the part of the Soviet officials and was repeatedly banned for performance.

The first performance of *The Sun of the Incas* took place in Leningrad on November 30, 1964; the vocal part was delivered by the singer Lydia Davydova under the baton of Gennady Rozhdestvensky. Up to the last day it was not clear whether it would be performed or not. A few days before the concert the Moscow authorities repeatedly telephoned the Leningrad Philharmonic demanding either to cancel the concert or withdraw *The Sun of the Incas* from the programme. And only the prestige of Gennady Rozhdestvensky saved it, for the philharmonic management did not wish to spoil then contacts with the outstanding conductor.

Gennady Rozhdestvensky:

"I remember that everything was prohibited and not allowed—the menace of a ban was hovering over the whole matter. I was left with the impression that Denisov's composition was a major achievement. It was a pioneering work and it always involved a great amount

of risk both for the composer and the performer. If you can't do anything, then it means that you violate some social relationships" (from a talk with the conductor on February 13, 1988).

After all, the premiere did take place. It was the first major performance of the composer's work that scored a big success with the audience.

Edison Denisov:

"In Leningrad two concerts were given, one after the other. After the performance the public applauded and called us onto the stage for many times. Rozhdestvensky counted the number of the calls and was delighted that we were called for 15 times before the audience. And he was even more pleased when during the second concert the hall was surrounded by the militia and three blocks away the tickets were sought after for a concert performance of a work by an unknown composer."

Following its first performance in Leningrad, the Universal edition publishers got interested in the cantata. And the score of this composition found its way to the West. In the summer of 1965 *The Sun of the Incas* was performed in Darmstadt (under the baton of Bruno Maderna), where the cantata figured as the first serial work by a Soviet composer to appear in the West.

Shortly after its performance in Darmstadt the world-renowned composer and conductor Pierre Boulez included *The Sun of the Incas* into the programme of the 'Domaine musical' concert of which he was a sponsor.

Pierre Boulez:

"Dear Mr Denisov. This is true that we are going to perform your cantata 'The Sun of the Incas' within 'Domaine musical'. It is on the programme planned for November 24 and to be conducted, as in Darmstadt, by Bruno Maderna. I'll hand over to him your remarks as regards the errors you have noted down in the Darmstadt recorded performance.

I'm very happy that we have been the first to include your work in our programme and I hope it to be the beginning of our future contacts. If it is possible we would be happy to receive you in Paris for the occasion" (from the letter of September 12, 1965).

The cantata *The Sun of the Incas* was performed in a magnificent concert hall by the best musicians in the programme along with Webern and Varèse. The numerous press reviews wrote with admiration and puzzlement about Denisov's composition, calling it the highlight of the programme, as an exquisite and poetic piece enriching Soviet music.

The Paris premiere became a milestone in Denisov's artistic career. He came to the notice of the world musical community, while his cantata from now on became one of the most popular and frequently performed of his compositions.[20]

There is a documental evidence that the cantata *The Sun of the Incas* was highly acclaimed by Igor Stravinsky to whom this composition of the young musician from Moscow was presented by the American composer Joel Spiegelman. The latter described his meeting with Stravinsky in his letter to Denisov (of May 16, 1966): "I spent four hours with Stravinsky. He is now old but very likeable. Despite his terribly many physical complaints (he is paralyzed and can hardly walk), his mind is still keen. I showed him *The Sun of the Incas* and he liked it very much. He told me that you were remarkably talented."[21] In the same letter Spiegelman writes that he showed this composition at the Juilliard School in New-York and Roger Sessions also praised it very much.

In contrast to the enthusiastic response *The Sun of the Incas* won in the West, the official opinion of the Soviet Composers Union was quite different. The details of its discussion in Moscow at the Composers Union were brought to light in the

Sovetskaya Muzyka magazine (No. 1, 1966, pp. 30–32). It was a most revealing case of so called 'creative discussion' with the composer subjected to biting criticism.

The common opinion, as it was recorded down by the *Sovetskaya Muzyka* magazine, was as follows: the cantata had failed to deeply touch the musicians and it was only its phonic aspect that presented some interest. 'Complete anarchy on the part of the composer' (Khrennikov), 'substitution of creativity by erudition' and doubts about Denisov's endowment with a true artistic gift (Shchedrin) — such were the terms in which *The Sun of the Incas* was treated.

The above discussion at the Composers Union and the campaign mounted against Denisov interrupted for many years to come the concert performances of his Opus. No. 1 in his homeland.

4.   RUNNING AGAINST THE STREAM

'The New Technique Is Not a Fashion'

The article under such title was written by Denisov on a commission of the Italian magazine *Il contemporaneo* (the monthly supplement to the newspaper *Rinàscita* published by the Central Committee of the Italian Communist Party) and appeared in its August issue for 1966.

In this short article written in a calm and tactful manner Denisov came out against the unhealthy 'sensations' created sometimes by the bourgeois critics trying 'to use the interest in the new Soviet music in their commercial interests' (cited from the MS original text of the article). These 'publicity speculations' were due to the fact that Soviet music was virtually unknown in the West at the time. And such situation prevailed through the fault of the concert organizations and the performers rarely promoting anything new. According to the author, "There are too few people in art to promote not themselves but somebody else's achievements." In his article Denisov stood out as one of these few exponents of Soviet music. He wrote: "A characteristic feature of the overwhelming majority of young composers in the Soviet Union is their striving to expand the framework of the musical language and not confine it to the tonal system exclusively." Denisov pointed out that many young composers used in their music the serial procedures, aleatory and sonoristics, among them Leonid Grabovsky, Rodion Shchedrin, Sergei Slonimsky, Andrei Volkonsky, Arvo Pärt and Alfred Schnittke. "The Soviet composers have lately been more and more engaged in experimentation, expanding the range of their musical language and employing the new types of techniques evolved in the 20th century, and this tendency should be regarded as a good pledge against the main danger threatening our music in the postwar years — that of academicism."

The latter statement made some people feel insulted. In their 'Retort' published in the *Sovetskaya Muzyka* (Issue 10, 1970, pp. 44–46) they argued that Denisov 'in defiance of the truth alleged that a majority of the young Soviet composers preferred serialism, dodecaphony and aleatory in their work' (p. 44). To all appearances, the officials at the Composers Union believed that 'serialism, dodecaphony and aleatory' should be perceived as swear-words.

Furthermore, Denisov introduced some young composers and gave a concise appraisal of their works. Thus, for the first time in a foreign publication there appeared the names of Andrei Volkonsky (who was the first, as Denisov writes, to employ the serial technique in the USSR), Alemdar Karamanov, Sergei Slonimsky, Boris Tishchenko, Arvo Pärt, Rodion Shchedrin, Sophia Gubaidulina, Nikolai Karetnikov, Valentin Silvestrov et al. Regardless of his personal sympathies and tastes, Denisov presented the best achievements of his colleagues. Paradoxically as it may seem, a great number of the mentioned names also aroused irritation in the official circles. The above cited 'Retort' pointed out: "He (Denisov) named the composers who later in the West were rated as 'Soviet avant-gardists'. The principle of uniting these composers in one list was purely formal ... disregarding their age and individuality, the value of their compositions and the degree of their craftsmanship" (*Sovetskaya Muzyka*, No. 10, 1970, p. 44). Hence Denisov was accused of the fact that it was him who prompted to supply the West with the names of 'Soviet avant-gardists' giving them 'distorted appraisals'. Apparently, the 'distortion' of his appraisal was explained by Denisov's challenging assertion that these composers made use not only of the tonal technique. According to the *Sovetskaya Muzyka* magazine, Denisov had also 'distorted' the picture when he qualified Volkonsky's *Suite of Mirrors* as one of the best achievements of Soviet music and compared its influence on the young generation in the USSR with that of Shostakovich's Fifth Symphony. 'Distortion', perhaps, was also in Denisov describing the above mentioned persons as 'talented, remarkably gifted, interesting and highly individual composers'.

His article had the following conclusion: "The young generation of Soviet composers turned to the new techniques not at all to follow the current 'fashion' but because the bounds of the tonal system proved too narrow to express the new ideas constantly raised by life itself."

In the mid-sixties the article 'The New Technique Is Not a Fashion' had the effect of an explosion. It was running against all the existing tenets of 'the Soviet official art' and clearly defined Denisov's musical and public standpoints. Following the appearance of this article, stormy events came rushing into his life. Such a challenge could not go unpunished.

The first to respond to the publication was the Secretariat of the Composers Union which decided to discuss it at its special session. One of the points on its agenda was 'On Violation of the Ethical and Civic Standards of Behaviour by Some Members of the Composers Union' (to be delivered by Tikhon Khrennikov).[22] It adopted the following resolution:

"The Secretariat regards the publication by the composer E. Denisov of his article in the Italian bourgeois mass media, containing the basically wrong statements on the current trends in Soviet music, as a brazen violation of the ethical and civic standards of conduct compulsory for each member of the Union. The Secretariat asks the officials of its Moscow Branch to examine this matter and report the results to the Secretariat of the Composers Union of the USSR." Signed by Tikhon Khrennikov, First Secretary of the Board, and Pyotr Savintsev, Secretary of the Board.

The matter was discussed at the session of the Moscow Branch; Denisov was not excluded from the Union membership (though it was impending). But the whole story had very unpleasant consequences,[23] since it prompted the bans imposed on the performance and publication of his scores. Thus Denisov came to belong to the category of 'banned' composers.

Another consequence of Denisov's publication in 'the bourgeois press' was his dismissal from his teaching job at the Moscow Conservatoire. In July 1967, when Denisov was on a leave, he got the following letter from the conservatoire: "Dear E. V. Denisov! The administration of the Moscow State Conservatoire informs you that owing to the insufficient teaching load at the instrumentation chair in the coming 1967/68 study year you are discharged from your teaching job at the conservatoire as of September 1, 1967." Signed by the Rector — Professor A. V. Sveshnikov.

Dismissal from the job for disobedience was an action from the Stalinist era and it naturally caused resentment among Denisov's students who declared that they would not stand for any other teacher in his stead.[24] Under their pressure, already after the study term had started, Denisov was reinstated in his job; the formal apologies were presented to him while the head of the chair called the whole matter a 'misunderstanding'. But it was obvious that this 'misunderstanding' had been carefully planned.

The above events unleashed persecutions of Denisov which went on up to the mid-eighties.

A *Propos* of One Interview

> To the Secretariat of the Composers Union
> from E.V. Denisov

Application

The *Sovetskaya Muzyka* magazine (No. 1, 1970) carried a 'Retort' which in a crude and unceremonious manner criticized my interview given to a correspondent of the Novosti Press Agency in December 1968 in Moscow and printed in the fall of 1970 in the magazines *Musik* (West Germany), *Muzsika* (Hungary) and *Hudebni Rozhgledy* (Czechoslovakia).

The interview was published abroad with major abridgements made without my consent ... The *Sovetskaya Muzyka* magazine not only fails to mention this fact but, moreover, for some reasons keeps off the Russian original, citing instead the double translation done at a low professional level and distorting the ideas expressed in my interview. The arbitrarily selected quotes, inadequately translated and abbreviated in 'proper' places, create a false idea of the content of my interview...

I would ask the Secretariat to read out the full text of my interview and express your opinion on the above mentioned facts.

> December 24, 1970

The anonymous 'Journalist',[25] the author of the 'Retort' published in the *Sovetskaya Muzyka*, regarded a selection of questions posed before Denisov in his interview as biased. The main focus had been placed on the so-called 'Soviet avant-garde'. Denisov had referred to the composers within the age brackets from

33 to 40, but stressed that the association of composers in the 'avant-garde' trend was most relative, for "Every one has been looking for something new, without seeking a special status for oneself. These composers felt discontent with the conventional patterns and in their quests were looking for new expressive means, new forms of work and artistic methods." According to Denisov, they were related only in one thing: they did not view tonality as the sole possible form of sound organization.

It was also irritating that Denisov had mentioned the wrong names: Andrei Volkonsky and Tigran Mansuryan among composers looking for modern expressive means; Stravinsky and the composers from the Second Viennese School as the ones who had exerted the strongest influence on Denisov himself and his colleagues, and only then Prokofiev, Shostakovich and Scriabin (the 'Journalist' seemed to believe that the first priority should have been given to the classics of Soviet music).

The 'Journalist' expressed his indignation over the current 'myth about Denisov' in the West as he alleged that "some figures and organizations abroad have long been trying to create a 'myth about Denisov' and present him as 'the leader of the Soviet avant-garde'" (*Sovetskaya Muzyka*, No. 10, 1970, p. 46). The magazine had no doubts that such 'myths' had been founded on the hidden anti-Soviet motives. In its view, many Western musicians were 'honestly deluded' showing an undeservedly heightened interest in Denisov.

The 'Retort' in the *Sovetskaya Muzyka* prolonged the chain of unpleasant events in the composer's life: in Voronezh the performance of his *Music for Eleven Wind Instruments and Kettledrums* was banned (on the grounds of this article), in Tbilisi a cable from the Soyuzconcert made the local managers to withdraw his cantata *Wails* from the concert programme, in Moscow the performance of his *Italian Songs* was cancelled, the Sovetsky Kompozitor Publishers suspended the publication of his cantata *The Sun of the Incas*.[26]

Finally, the campaign against Denisov unleashed because of the publication of his interview resulted in the Resolution of the Secretariat of the Composers Union of the USSR as of July 26, 1971. It condemned the practices of transferring scores or literary material abroad without the knowledge and consent of the Secretariat: "All the Union members should be warned that from now on any person to violate the present resolution shall incur strict disciplinary punishment up to the expulsion from the membership of the Composers Union of the USSR."

A Chronicle of Bans

Below we cite the facts that reveal the life of a composer who happened to fall into disgrace with the authorities. These facts were gathered together and recorded down by Denisov himself:

  – *During the plenary sessions of the Composers Union in the winter of 1966 the composer G. Wohlgemuth and the musicologist H. Richter were looking for me for more than a week. In the foreign commission they were told that 'Denisov was away from Moscow at the moment'. To their request to be provided with my telephone number they were told that I had no telephone at home.*

– The performance of The Sun of the Incas *on April 19, 1968 in Moscow (in a philharmonic concert) was banned. Whom by?*

– On September 14, 1967 Konstantin Iliev and Lea Koen from Bulgaria were looking for Volkonsky and myself in Moscow. The next day in Khrennikov's room at the Composers Club they were auditing the recorded music at 11 a. m. and asked to meet Denisov and Volkonsky. They were told that 'Denisov has left for the Warsaw Autumn Festival' and 'Volkonsky was away from Moscow'. At the moment I and Schnittke were in the next room copying our recordings. Iliev left for Bulgaria without meeting anyone he wanted to see.

– In the summer of 1967 when Victor Yeresko wanted to include my Variations for Piano *in his programme of a foreign tour he was told that Denisov's music was not to be performed abroad.*

– In November 1968 the cellist Natalia Gutman was told in the Mosconcert that she was not to play the works by Stravinsky, Denisov and Schnittke because their music was banned for performance.

– On September 18, 1970 I presented my Italian Songs, Three Pieces for Piano Four Hands *and* Romantic Music *to the Secretariat of the Composers Union. T. Khrennikov thus commented them: "All of this is just a waste of time" and nobody objected to him.*

– On March 7, 1971 the flutist Alexander Korneyev and the pianist Alexander Bakhchiyev were forbidden to play my Sonata for Flute and Piano.

– On November 4, 1971 Natalia Gutman was ordered by the Mosconcert not to play my Sonata for Cello and Piano.

– The Gosconcert banned the playing of my String Trio *to the 'Trio à cordes de Paris' during their tour in the USSR (November 12–29, 1972).*

A list of such facts could be continued. It was enough to make one phone call and Denisov's composition was crossed out from the programme or himself dismissed from a job or any activity.

There was a lot of bans and lies concerning not Denisov alone. The campaign of baiting was launched against all the composers of his generation who dared to run against the stream. One had to possess great willpower to withstand the onset of lies, hostility and envy. But Denisov has stood up to it all.

5. THE WEST GETTING TO KNOW DENISOV

Notwithstanding a great amount of obstacles, in the mid-sixties his music came out to the notice of the world musical community. From that time on, the world premieres of his major works took place in the West. One of the obvious reasons was certainly the long-time bans to play his music at home. But it was not only that. A fresh spurt of new Russian music which infused Denisov's compositions captivated the Western musicians.

Denisov found invaluable his contacts with the foremost Western composers, the so-called avant-gardists, such as Boulez, Nono, Stockhausen, Xenakis, Serocki, Ligeti, Dutilleux, Crumb, Dallapiccola and Donatoni. Many of them were pleasantly surprised to learn about the existence of interesting musical phenomena in Russia. Thus, Iannis Xenakis in his reply to Denisov's postcard wrote: "I was particularly happy to meet you and other young Soviet composers and musicians representing the new trends in your country" (from the letter of November 20, 1962). And here is what Karlheinz Stockhausen had to say: "Dear Mr Denisov, I was very happy to receive a letter from you. It overwhelmed me. I have always believed that the new music would eventually find its way to your country, for I often heard most Russians to be endowed with remarkable musical gifts" (from the letter of November 24, 1966).

The composers exchanged the scores, came to know one another and their works. A vigorous creative communication was going on which could be seen from their correspondence. Here are a few more extracts from their letters.

Luigi Dallapiccola: "Dear Mr Denisov, in my last letter I expressed my wish to familiarise myself with your music...and now I had a chance to hear your Sonata for Cello and Piano. My wife and me listened to it with great attention: we found the performance very good and followed your musical speech, so intimate (and singular), very much excited and aroused. And in these several lines I heartily congratulate you. Bravo!" (October 22, 1971).

George Crumb: "Dear Mr Denisov, thank you so much for sending me the recording of your Cello Concerto! Your work is very beautiful and represents a valuable addition to the cello repertoire. Congratulations!" (July 17, 1982).

Denisov was not only in brisk correspondence with Henri Dutilleux but also consulted him as to the proper intoning of the French text in his song-cycle *La vie en rouge*. After the performance of *The Sun of the Incas* in Paris Dutilleux wrote: "I attended the concert and can say that the work has won a very good response, acclaim and a lot of applause. Earlier I scrutinized the score and enormously liked its spirit, preciseness and free language" (March 8, 1972).

Luigi Nono became a close friend. His first letters to Denisov are dated back to the early 1964. In the mid-sixties Nono came to the Soviet Union with a team of Italian composers. Denisov met him on several occasions and they discussed various artistic problems. The fiery Italian was always sincere and fervent in his views on new compositions of his friend from Moscow.

His contacts with Pierre Boulez played a major part in Denisov's career. In the early sixties Boulez came to see the score of his cantata *The Sun of the Incas* and found it a talented work. Though the young Russian composer was absolutely unknown to him, he included this composition in the festival programmes in Darmstadt and Paris. From that time on, they were in intensive correspondence.

Boulez did his utmost to arrange Denisov's visit to Paris and attend the performance of *The Sun of the Incas* there. He followed all the instructions Denisov had given him to make it possible. In his letter of October 9, 1965 Boulez enumerates all his efforts: "A cable was sent to the Composers Union. Then a letter was sent to the embassy. The state secretary in culture was brought into action. I hope that thanks to all these efforts you would be able to come". However, Boulez's hopes were thwarted. Denisov was forbidden to go on this trip. Here is an extract from Boulez's letter of November 14, 1965 "I am furious, especially as this refusal comes from the lowest-ranking music officials, who themselves write music that 'would make dustbins vomit', as Varèse used to say. And what about the personal freedom, a question on which I cannot accept compromise; there is no reason why these officials, on a regal whim (like Louis XIV) forbid you purely and simply, and without any justification, to travel to hear your own work performed."

Boulez was not discouraged and went on with his efforts to get a permission for Denisov to visit Paris. But conservatism of the Soviet officials proved too strong. Denisov was not to attend the concert in Paris, as well as many other concerts in which his compositions were played in different countries of the world.

In January 1967 during the tour of the BBC orchestra in Moscow Boulez met Denisov in person. The friendship between two composers went on.

The foreign mass media started to write about Denisov. Of course, it was mainly press reviews of the concerts in which his compositions were played. The notices were favourable, with the reviewers stressing Denisov's highly original talent and musical style. One of the first serious publications on his music became Detlef Gojowy's article 'The Soviet Avant-Gardists' (*Das Orchester*, No. 1, 1970) in which he figured prominently along with Schnittke, Slonimsky, Gershkovich and Roslavets. The first musicological studies of Denisov's music also included the articles by Valentina Kholopova and Alfred Schnittke, which were published in the Polish magazine *Res Facta* in 1972.

6. 'THE KHRENNIKOV SEVEN'

With his popularity growing abroad, his music was still neglected at home. The following facts from the general campaign of bans illustrate the subordinate position in which the Soviet composers found themselves when the low-ranking officials could cut short their career and deny them an opportunity to develop international contacts. In most cases Denisov was left even unaware of the invitations coming from abroad to his name, while the officials took upon themselves to conduct correspondence on his behalf. Here is just one of such cases: Denisov was invited to Latin America to take part in the seminar of modern music. Of course, the composer never went there. A reply was sent to the society of modern music in Uruguay to the effect that Denisov was not a specialist in giving lectures and simply unable to make a report on the musical scene in the Soviet Union. Instead of Denisov the Composers Union offered to send another musician who could, in the official view, make a report 'at a much higher level'.

In other cases the officials resorted to downright lies. Thus, for instance, Denisov was invited by the 'Comedie des Alpes' theatre to provide a musical score to Mikhail Bulgakov's play *Ivan Vasilyevich*. The official letters had been sent to various departments and the company's manager had applied a lot of effort to get Denisov. The composer had no objections to this commission. But the answer from the Composers Union contained another telltale sample of the Soviet bureaucratic rhetorics: "Dear Sirs, we acknowledge the receipt of your letter offering E. Denisov to write incidental music to Bulgakov's play *Ivan Vasilyevich*. As the composer informed us, he was ready to accept your offer at first, but now he has got an unexpected and quite urgent commission which will take all his time free from his teaching job at the conservatoire." In this way they held sway over Denisov's destiny on many similar occasions. God knows how many such invitations were kept in the officials' rooms at the Composers Union! In those times all the composers adhering to honest views and unwilling to make compromises had to work in an atmosphere of lies and ignoring.

In the early seventies Denisov found his calling in a new type of activity. His efficiency and managerial abilities which had been noticed back in his student years found their realization in the two cycles of concerts he arranged and supervised at the Composers Union.

The first cycle was entitled '20th-Century Music'. It lasted for a short time. The authorities disapproved a stir around its concerts featuring the music by Alfred Schnittke, Sophia Gubaidulina, Tigran Mansuryan, and contemporary foreign composers. For the first time after a long interruption several compositions by Nikolai Roslavets and Leonid Polovinkin came to be played in the concerts of this cycle. The second cycle, 'New Works by Moscow Composers', under Denisov's supervision lasted up to the early 1990s. Denisov was truly noble in promotion of talented Moscow-resided composers virtually unknown to anybody and whose music was never performed anywhere. It should be noted that the regular concerts of these cycles sponsored by Denisov and arranged by him at the Composers' Union became a hallmark of the musical life in the 1970s and 1980s. It was next to impossible to get to many concerts, with the auditoriums being overpacked. It was the site for the new art to break out into the fore and lift the screen of artistic isolation.

Another curious fact from the composer's biography is associated with the studio of electronic music, which opened in Moscow in 1966. The ANS synthesizer, an electronic optical device, was invented by the Soviet scientist Yevgeny Murzin who dedicated his invention to Alexander Scriabin. It was installed in Scriabin's memorial flat. It was the sole place in Moscow where composers had a chance to immerse in the new world of electronic sounds. Quite a few interesting discoveries were made while this studio was functioning. Among those who worked there were Sophia Gubaidulina, Alfred Schnittke and Eduard Artemyev. It played a major part in Denisov's creative evolution, too. His *Birdsong* came as a result of his experimentation in electronic music he conducted there.

The electronic studio in Moscow lasted for approximately ten years; in the late seventies its work was declared useless and unpromising and it was closed. But it gave rise to Denisov's future quests in electronic music which he was to carry on in Paris in the early 1990s.

In the late seventies the expression 'The Khrennikov Seven' came to be widespread among musicians in this country. Those were seven composers whom Tikhon Khrennikov at the 6th Congress of Soviet Composers united into one group as those who could not be regarded as true exponents of Soviet music. That group comprised Yelena Firsova, Dmitry Smirnov, Alexander Knaifel, Victor Suslin, Vyacheslav Artemov, Sophia Gubaidulina and, the last on the list, Edison Denisov. The cause of pinning such label was the popularity these composers enjoyed abroad and, specifically, the performance of their works within the festival of Soviet music in Cologne in 1979. A boycott was imposed on the composers whose names had been mentioned by Khrennikov at that congress.

As a matter of fact, this boycott changed nothing in Denisov's life: as before his works were neither performed, nor published, nor recorded. Moreover, the bans on his music concerned not only the performance inside the country. The tentacles of the authorities from the Composers Union, the USSR Ministry of Culture and the Cultural Department of the CC CPSU (whence came a larger part of these bans) reached far beyond the borders of the homeland. The programmes of the tour concerts were easily changed, with many cancellations (withdrawing

Denisov's compositions) made known frequently a few hours before the departure of performers on a tour. Hence the musicians often found themselves in an awkward situation when they had to play the pieces not expected of them, but those dictated by the 'top' authorities.[27]

In the mid-seventies a team of young cinema-makers from Leningrad decided to shoot a film about Soviet music. This film, *Dialogues on Music*, had three parts (Part One covered the twenties and thirties, Part Two — the forties and fifties; the adviser on these two parts was M. Druskin, a musicologist from Leningrad; Part Three focused on the sixties and seventies, with Yuri Kholopov acting as an adviser). Some episodes in this film featured several Soviet composers in free and easy surroundings. The third film which aroused the most negative response on the part of the officials showed Alfred Schnittke, Arvo Pärt, Sophia Gubaidulina, Vladimir Martynov, Tikhon Khrennikov and Alexander Knaifel, their daily life and work, and concerts in which their latest compositions were performed. It was uncustomary to see so many shots of Edison Denisov who as the leading narrator appeared almost constantly on the screen. The film not as yet properly completed was shown to the representatives of the musical community who failed to accept the violation of subordination proportions and the conventional practices prescribing who, what and how much was to be spoken and written about, the more so, to be shown on the screen. The film was discussed at the USSR Composers' Union. As Denisov recalled it later, the most outspoken in their objections were the composers Karen Khachaturyan ("This film is a slander on our history"), Alexei Nikolayev who said that it would be monstrous to show this film to a wide public, while one of the Party leaders at the Composers Union, G. Voskanyan, brought even an ideological accusation declaring that 'only our enemies' in the West praised Denisov. After this discussion the film was 'nipped in the bud'. Even the suggestion that the film should be preserved at the cost of major amendments failed.

7. DENISOV THE TEACHER

Edison Denisov has been engaged in his teaching job at the Moscow Conservatoire immediately after his postgraduate studies. At first it was at the chair of musical theory. For some time he read lectures in musical analysis at the piano department and was an assistant professor in the special course of musical analysis under Professor Victor A. Zuckerman.

Victor Zuckerman:

"We worked together with Denisov reading a course of lectures in musical analysis at the musicological department. It was done against our will, on an order of Professor Sergei S. Skrebkov, who headed the chair of musical theory. He explained his action by the following reason: 'In a year or two Denisov will dry up as a composer and therefore he has to be prepared for teaching theoretical subjects'" (from a talk with Victor Zuckerman on March 31, 1988).

Perhaps, for the same reasons the disagreeable 'avant-gardist' Denisov was 'exiled' to the military department of the conservatoire where for a short time he 'taught soldiers to write marches'. Dissatisfied with his work, Denisov demanded that the administration transferred him to the instrumentation chair where he was soon to teach score reading and instrumentation at the theory & composition department.

In the course of more than thirty years of his job at the Conservatoire Denisov was denied a chance to teach composition. In the sixties and seventies it was explained by his 'bad reputation'; in the view of the elderly and eminent professors of the composition chair he could teach students the wrong things. But the same situation prevailed in the eighties, too. Thus, for instance, a funny case took place in 1986. The young composer Juan Gutierrez came from Spain to study composition at the Moscow Conservatoire under the famous Edison Denisov. He was greatly surprised to find out that Denisov was not teaching composition at the conservatoire since, according to the officials, he 'had no right to it'. Juan had to put forth a Herculean effort to get his way. To avoid an international scandal, the conservatoire administration allowed Denisov, as an exception, to teach composition to the Spanish student.

There arose a paradoxical situation. Though officially Denisov was not teaching composition, many musicians name him as their teacher. The studies in his instrumentation class gave the beginning composers sometimes much more than the classes in their basic speciality. To this category of Denisov's pupils belong Dmitry Smirnov, Sergei Pavlenko, Vladimir Tarnopolsky, Ivan Sokolov and Bojidar Spasov. Fearing his baneful influence the administration sent to his class students majoring in musicology rather than in composition. But those who insisted managed to get to his classes.

Dmitry Smirnov:

"At the first lesson Denisov glanced over my previous works and said that the next time I should bring an instrumentation plan of Debussy's Danseurs de Delphes. *I had a vague idea what an instrumentation plan was and, to show off my abilities, I decided to make a real 'avant-garde' score. I designed my score à la Penderecki and at the next lesson, trembling and proud, placed it on the musicstand. Denisov scanned through the score and I was shocked to hear his verdict: 'What a nonsense!'"*.

"I could not believe my ears and started to defend the merits of my orchestration, but his reply was invariable: 'Stuff and nonsense! It won't do'. He insisted that I should bring him an instrumentation plan and, fetching a pencil, he began writing the notation indicating all the parts separately. But what Denisov offered seemed to me to be uninteresting and ordinary as compared to my own sophisticated score and, disappointed, I left the classroom" (from Dmitry Smirnov's reminiscences recorded down on January 13, 1988).

At his lessons Denisov strove to inculcate in his students the logic and culture of thinking, providing them with a real school of orchestration. He never departed from his teaching method described by Smirnov above: for the first lesson his students were to bring an instrumentation plan, which was corrected and discussed, and only after that the students made a score. There were no exceptions from that rule.

Dmitry Smirnov:

"Denisov taught you to approach works by other composers not from the outside but from inside out: to show what I could do with this composition for orchestra if I were its author. I came to realise that I was being taught not only instrumentation but composition as well."

The Bulgarian Bojidar Spasov recalled some unforgettable impressions from his studies in Denisov's class. He found his classes uncommon, for there was no code of rules you had to follow. But gradually, from lesson to lesson, non-dogmatic rules and laws took shape in his students' mind consciously and willingly cultivated then by themselves. Spasov admired not only Denisov's teaching talent, but also his ability to keep within artistic limits, and his faultless taste.

Bojidar Spasov:

"I felt admiration for the composer, teacher and man who without any affectation or false democratism made me feel for the first time that I could attain something in my chosen field. Sometimes I was even not quite myself from my effort, trying hard to remember and imprint in my memory everything he was explaining in so simple words or expressed in notes. At the same time, paradoxically enough, these classes were imbued with a spirit of inner freedom and artistry not subjected to any conventional teaching rules" (from Spasov's reminiscences, 1988).

All the young composers who came into any contact with Denisov make a point of his consideration, responsiveness and concern. He was always ready to meet, advise, give scores and recordings, listen to and discuss music. One of such cases was the story of Vladimir Tarnopolsky who in the early seventies, still an unknown youth, came to Moscow from Dnepropetrovsk to show Denisov his compositions. He got qualified consultations and valuable advice upon following which he was able to attain his artistic aspirations.

Edison Denisov:

"Dear Volodya, I heartily congratulate you on your entering the conservatoire. I was sure that you would pass all the exams, though I still worried."

"The picture you have so vividly drawn in your letter reflects the actual state of affairs at the conservatoire. The level of teaching has been falling, there are no criteria, while the old generation of intellectual professors is currently replaced by persons who can hardly teach anything."

"There is no one to teach composition now, so it doesn't make much difference. I think you should enroll yourself into the class of N.N. Sidelnikov. He is of my age and he won't at least interfere with your own development, whereas some teachers just spoil the human soul. And this is dangerous" (from Denisov's letter to Tarnopolsky of August 16, 1973).

In Denisov's class in score reading and instrumentation his students became true professionals getting sound technical training.

Vladimir Tarnopolsky:

"Denisov has given me the most accurate lessons in composition in my life. He was devoid of any didactics. He just set his students on the right way. His appraisals were tactful and to the point. He merely indicated some details while his pupils were to recreate the entity. I consider Edison Denisov to be the best master in orchestration. He helped to grasp the orchestral style of a composer and tried to reconstruct the author's ideas most artistically" (from a talk on March 3, 1988).

The repertoire selected by Denisov's students for instrumentation made his classes stand apart from any others. Each student had his individual plan (except for Pyotr Tchaikovsky's *Children's Album* which was a compulsory item for all junior students). His students never had to do the same work (as was customary with other classes). The composers that figured prominently among his students' works included Debussy (Preludes), Bartók (*Mikrokosmos*), Mussorgsky (songs), Prokofiev (various piano pieces), Berg, and Schoenberg. His students recall how, beginning with Tchaikovsky and up to Schoenberg, Edison Denisov tried to teach them not only the specific features and rules of orchestration but also the secrets of the very process of sound production.

Denisov was always willing to look through the works written by his (and not only his own) students in their composition class.

Dmitry Smirnov:

"His judgements were always concise, clear-cut, often too sharp and categorical, sometimes even slighting: '... here you have been just lazy', 'such tremolos can be only found in bad incidental music to plays', 'here there is only one good page, the rest seems to have been written by another composer', 'it should be discarded'."[28]

Denisov paid great attention to the rhythmic pattern of a composition; in this respect he could not stand any monotony and primitive solutions. The instrumental texture had to be flexible, with the technical resources of each instrument used to the fullest extent. All the phrases and nuances had to be carefully delineated.

Both the composers and musicologists who have studied under Denisov view his lessons as the most valuable things learned at the conservatoire.

Bojidar Spasov:

"I owe it to Edison Vasilyevich, if to anyone else, for my decision to take up composition. I remember the day on which I ventured to show him my first endeavours. I was not even sure whether it was worthwhile for me to waste note-paper. But my urge to compose arose largely under the impact of the world discovered to myself by The Sun of the Incas, Wails *and some others of Denisov's compositions. I was dumbfounded when Edison Vasilyevich, without wasting any time on idle talk about the difficulties and responsibility involved in composition, showed me that he could help me to overcome my lack of self-confidence and go further. In this way I came to realise that each time a composer sits down to write music he should feel himself responsible for each note coming from under his pen and nobody was able to guide him."*

Denisov made the budding composers feel confident of their efforts and not to stand in awe of any indisputable authority. Any technical explanation or critical remark made by Edison Denisov was aimed to help in grasping the aesthetic value of the musical material, "with a view towards that unfading depth, simplicity and refinement emanated by his music for all those who have lost no striving for beauty" (to quote Bojidar Spasov once again).

In addition to the studies in instrumentation and composition, the students in his class used to audit a lot of music — Mozart, Debussy, the Second Viennese School, Boulez, Nono, Schnittke, Roslavets, Ligeti ... Such auditions usually took place once a week. The choice of music reflected Denisov's tastes, but occasionally it depended on the availability of scores and recordings. Before an audition Denisov used to give a short annotation on a composition they were going to hear, sometimes more invaluable than any extensive historical treatise of the art historians, and underscored the composer's characteristic techniques. The audition was followed by a general discussion. The students (including those training under the supervision of other professors) benefitted enormously from introduction to the unknown music, getting a fresh view of the familiar music (e.g., of the operas by Mozart and Debussy). The introduction to modern music filled up the gap of its virtual non-existence in the conservatoire courses.[29]

The students in Denisov's class had also several occasions to meet the outstanding musicians, among them Alfred Schnittke, Henri Dutilleux, Luigi Nono, and the flutist Aurèle Nicolet.

8. RECOGNITION

The mid-1980s brought tangible changes in Denisov's life. Unexpectedly he was included into the supreme body of the Composers Union; by a twist of fate Denisov became one of the seven secretaries of its new working agency.[30] This unusual role surprised many people, for Denisov had never before held any high-ranking posts. Besides, the Composers Union was the organization which had been fighting him all the previous thirty years of his life. His consent to occupy that post was primarily due to his sincere wish to change the numb structures of the composers' association.

Edison Denisov:

"I thought that as a leader of the Composers Union I would be more able to do something good, to help those who represented a pride of our music, whose works had never before been published, recorded or included in the official concerts. I wanted to bring to light all those remarkable compositions which, like the paintings of Kandinski, Malevich, Falk and Filonov, had been neglected for many years and ignored" (the *Sovetskaya Kultura* newspaper, February 17, 1990, p.10).

In January 1990 a new creative organization was set up in Moscow — the Association of Modern Music (AMM). Both its principles and its very name were reminiscent of a similar organization that existed in Russia in the twenties. In those years it comprised the most interesting and daring composers such as Dmitry Shostakovich, Alexander Mosolov, Nikolai Roslavets, Gavriil Popov and Nikolai Myaskovsky, who did a lot to promote new music and repel the onslaught of so- called 'proletarian musicians' against any challenging and creative works and the time-honoured traditions. The first AMM was forcibly dissolved in 1931. More than half a century later its ideas were taken up by the second AMM.

It was founded on an initiative of composers themselves as the creative alternative to the official activities of the Composers Union. The founders of this association included the most talented composers of the younger generation — Dmitry Smirnov, Victor Ekimovsky, Alexander Vustin, Yelena Firsova, Nikolai Korndorf, Vladimir Tarnopolsky, Alexander Raskatov and Yuri Kasparov. They decided that their organization should be headed by a man who all his life had been fighting against conformism, running against the stream and upholding modern music. Hence, Edison Denisov was elected President of the AMM. It was very important for the AMM members to gain the support of the world-renowned composer, with his energy, initiative, ideas and international contacts.

Edison Denisov:

"The AMM unites different composers who have nothing in common as regards the manner of their writing. Each composes in a style he likes. In my view, all similar associations should be based primarily on human empathy, mutual respect and the right to express oneself in one's own language."

The AMM is engaged in wide-ranging activities, including concerts, participation in music festivals at home and abroad, meeting with talented composers, publishing and recordings. At long last modern music came to be officially recognized. And a great credit for it goes to Edison Denisov as its most fervent exponent. The official functions (such as secretaryship at the Composers Union) spoils many persons and breaks them, but the Soviet bureaucratic machinery has failed to make Denisov compliant. He has remained honest and faithful to his artistic principles, refusing to become a conformist.

The emergence of some democratic tendencies in the Soviet society made it possible for Denisov to go on frequent trips abroad. The geography of his trips is extremely broad, embracing France, Germany, Italy, Switzerland, Finland and the USA.[31] The premieres of his works in most cases take place as previously outside his native land: *L'écume des jours* and his Symphony in Paris, his Requiem in Hamburg, his Concerto for Viola in Berlin, and his *Blue Notebook* in Great Britain. Any performance of his music wins an enthusiastic response. He often takes part in international music festivals, sitting on the jury of prestigious composition contests, among them the Guido d'Arezzo Festival in Italy (1989, 1990), the Queen Elizabeth Competition in Brussels (1991), the sacred music competition in Fribourg (1991), and the contest in Brescia (1990). In 1989 and 1991 Denisov conducted his very popular Master Classes in Switzerland (Lucerne and Bloney). For his contributions Denisov was awarded the French order for literary and artistic achievements (March, 1986).

For half a year, from September 1990 to March 1991, Denisov stayed in Paris on an invitation of the I.R.C.A.M. institute directed by Pierre Boulez. The invitations to visit Paris had been coming for many years. But no efforts on the French side would help. Only in the early 1990s (after nearly ten years of attempts) it became possible. The I.R.C.A.M. is mainly engaged in the studies of acoustic music potentialities. Denisov has always been interested in acoustic expansion of the musical space inherent in computers, as well as in various modes of interaction between live musical instruments and computers. His composition *Sur la nappe d'un étang glacé...* reveals his new creative approach to the solution of this problem.

Edison Denisov is a Russian composer of world repute. And though his music is performed mostly abroad, in recent years marked changes for the better have been taking place at home, too. In December 1985 his first official recital was held in the Moscow Philharmonic Hall. The premiere of his opera *Les quatre filles* was given in Moscow, the opera *L'écume des jours* was staged in Perm (five years later after its premiere in Paris). Here appeared some publications about his music, press reviews and his interviews (see References). In 1990 at the Moscow Conservatoire Denisov came to teach the postgraduate Yuri Kasparov, his first official pupil in composition; in 1992 he was given at last a full-fledged class, not very numerous, to teach composition.

Admittedly, the composer's recognition at home has been belated. Nevertheless, it is very important since it testifies to the fact that true music is sure to win its way and occupy eventually its worthy place among the other outstanding artistic phenomena.

Notes to Chapter 1

1.   Tomsk used to be called the Siberian Athens.
2.   In his enthusiasm Vasily Denisov, secretly from his wife, named his son after Thomas Edison, a famous American inventor.

3. In the spring of 1928 Vasily Denisov established radio communication with the expedition headed by General Umberto Nobile, travelling in a balloon, aboard the 'Italia' airship, to the North Pole, and transmitted regular weather-reports to its courageous crew.

4. Shostakovich's letters are cited in full in Appendix 1.

5. One of the authors of this book made a report on Shostakovich's Eighth Symphony in the early fifties and dared not to attack it. The next day there was an austere phone call 'from the top' (somebody duly informed the CC of the CPSU). During the same years Yuri Kholopov, being the head of a music audition circle, offered a concert programme compiled exclusively out of Stravinsky's compositions (all the programmes had to be approved 'on the top'). Banning the whole programme the authorities uttered the following apt phrase: "When he dies, we shall play his works and promote them, but while he is alive it is out of the question".

6. Everybody still held in memory the wartime plates inscribed 'A Gas-Proof Shelter'.

7. For details see: Cholopow J. Sowjetische Musik vor der 'Perestroika' und 'Perestroika' in der sowjetischen Musik. ('Sowjetische Musik im Licht der Perestroika'. Laaber, 1990. – S. 19–38).

8. From Edison Denisov's memoirs.

9. E. Denisov. Once More on the Youth Education // *Sovetskaya Muzyka*, No. 7, 1956, p. 29.

10. The report on this expedition was published in December 1954 in the *Sovetskaya Muzyka* magazine.

11. The original copy of this document is currently kept at the Composers Union of the Russian Federation.

12. While still a student, to earn some money Denisov used to make arrangements of pop music for guitar and mandolin (e.g., of Neopolitan songs).

13. The first scene was composed in 1956 and played at the graduation examination. The vocal score of the opera was completed by the spring of 1959. The full score was provided only for Scene 1 and Tsarevna's Arioso and the Lullaby from Scene 4.

14. The plot of the opera: Ivan the Soldier falls in love with the Tsar's daughter, Anna. The Tsar made a stipulation: Anna would become his wife if Ivan makes her love him within one month. Ivan bribes the foreign merchants and inside a big clock they are going to present to the tsarevna gets into her room. The opera ends with the wedding of Anna and Ivan the Soldier.

15. Denisov recalls one of his meetings with Shostakovich in those years: "I was playing my opera for Dmitry Dmitriyevich. He showered praise on it and then said: 'Your long scribbling has made you eventually a real composer'."

16. The current ideal was to use the folk song intonations, the tonal language and to follow the 'realist' traditions of Russian music.

17. Many of the analyses made during 'the period of self-education' in the form of scientific articles appeared later in various publications.

18. Stravinsky, however, was more objective in his attitude to Hindemith as a composer. Thus, before he called his music 'unnourishing', he praised some of his compositions /see: Igor Stravinsky. Dialogues. Leningrad, 1971, pp. 113–114/.

19. Denisov's article about Webern's Variations Op. 27 is a remarkable sample of musicological analysis.

20. The attempt to attend the premiere of his cantata in Paris failed, with the details to be discussed below.

21. Written in Russian, the letter is cited here in an edited version.

22. Cited is an extract from the minutes No. 3 of the session of the Secretariat of the Composers Union of February 8, 1967, which is still kept in Denisov's dossier at the personnel office of the Composers Union.

23. Khrennikov qualified the appearance of the article in *Rinàscita* as a publication in 'the bourgeois press' whereas that newspaper was released by the Italian Communist

Party. This circumstance helped Vano Muradeli, the head of the Moscow Branch of the Composers Union, to neutralize the situation, for such 'a political mistake' on the part of Khrennikov could lead to undesirable complications in international relations.

24.   As one of Denisov's students, composer Mark Minkov, reminisces: "We wanted to go to the rector Sveshnikov. But we were told that if we went to him Denisov would never be reinstated in his job. He was known to do everything to the contrary. And we got scared. But we wrote a letter asking to bring back our teacher to us" (from a talk on January 24, 1988).

25.   The *Sovetskaya Muzyka* magazine has been notorious for its anonymous reviews.

26.   This suspension has lasted to date. It is very significant that one of the best Russian musical works has not yet been published in the composer's homeland.

27.   In this way, for instance, the performance of *The Sun of the Incas*, *Silhouettes* and *Ode* was cancelled during the tour of the Bolshoi Theatre Ensemble to Austria in 1981. Another dramatic story, according to Denisov's memoirs, involved the banning of *The Sun of the Incas* to be performed in Sofia where the conductor and composer Konstantin Iliev tried to do it but the Soviet Embassy there forbade it flatly.

28.   'It should be discarded' was one of the favourite phrases used by Vissarion Shebalin, Denisov's own teacher.

29.   No doubt, Denisov inherited the teaching principles from his own tutor, Vissarion Shebalin.

30.   His designation to that post was followed by another incredible fact, unthinkable in the previous decades: the Moscow Composers Union in 1990 nominated Denisov as its candidate to a People's Deputy of Russia. His election programme included, among other things, raising the levels of musical education in Russia to be started from schools and church choirs, subsidies to the philharmonic societies and betterment of musicians' standards of living.

31.   It could hardly be compared to his rare trips to East Germany and to the Warsaw Autumn festivals in the sixties and seventies (exclusively as a member of a tourist group).

CHAPTER 2

THE COMPOSER'S INNER WORLD

A major phenomenon in music as a rule represents thereby a certain conception of the intellectual life. In the past the inner world of music took shape under the current conventional relationships between the artistic principles and the prevailing religious system (Josquin, Palestrina, Schütz, Bach, Mozart). Our century has also witnessed quite a number of cases of similar traditional predominance of religion as the basis of a composer's inner world: suffice it to mention Stravinsky, Messiaen and Webern. However, the 20th century with its acutest crisis in religious consciousness brought forth secularization and even profanation of artistic creativity as a type of intellectual activity. The individualistic approach has been gaining momentum at the expense of universal values and orientations. A lack of religiosity in a composer's inner world becomes for various reasons a standard in art. In this respect Russia occupies a special status. Several generations of Russians were growing up in an atmosphere of reprisals against religion and the church, and profanation of God's name, including those born approximately in 1930 such as Edison Denisov, Sophia Gubaidulina, Rodion Shchedrin and Alfred Schnittke. The very word 'spiritual' (as well as 'the spiritual life') since the twenties became dangerous to utter while many clergymen were openly declared to be 'enemies of the people' and exterminated. (In Russian the words 'clergy' and 'priesthood' come from the same root as 'spiritual'; the root being 'dukh' which means 'mind' and 'spirit', with the expression 'Dukh svyatoi' standing for 'Holy Ghost'.) The objective reality forced one to resort to mimicry: to preserve one's integrity, spirituality had to be shrouded in some other form. It primarily concerned art.

On the other hand, irrespective of the above, the inner world of a composer as a Russian artist reflects the peculiarities of the traditional Russian mentality. The composer's world incorporates the same typological features as the other domains of the Russian cultural life. Stressing the singularity of Russian philosophy, Alexei Losev wrote as he cited Nikolai Berdayev: "The philosophical thought in this country has always been striving to identify not an abstract, intellectual truth, but the truth as a way to live." According to Losev, Russian philosophy represents a purely inner, mystical cognition of the existing; it is inseparable from the reality. Therefore a mine of information about the unique Russian philosophy can be found in literary works by Gogol, Tolstoy and Dostoyevsky.[1] But artistic creativity, musical in particular, the more so strives to be also 'a science of life' rather than being merely 'a fine art'. Hence it is customary to expect from composers, too, to provide 'lifelike truthfulness' which can be treated, by the way, whatever you like. The approach to artistic creativity as a certain supreme type of activity (formulation of a world-view, a philosophy in imagery, secular religion) allows art to replace religion in one's inner world.

The intellectual life of a Soviet composer took shape under the prevalence of these traditions in Russian culture. A special factor of this life was the all-embracing system of dogmas and precepts which entangled a composer (as well as a writer, painter, film-maker) in the Soviet Union, especially following the adoption of the 1948 Resolution by the Central Committee of the Communist Party (see Chapter 1). In the most abstract way that dogmatic system can be characterized by the inadequate formula of 'socialist realism'. The matter was not in either socialism or realism. That was a system of bans and permits, rigidly prescribing what was allowed and what was forbidden. The famed trinity 'ideological spirit — a popular style — realism' in fact constituted a false and formal distortion of high and universally cherished concepts. The 'ideological spirit' implied exclusively the embodiment of the party slogans, and the further you departed from them, the more 'ideologically alien' you became. The 'popular style' obliged composers to write about 'the people — builders of communism' (if you depicted the people in the past, you were already going too far from the popular style), the more so, it was compulsory to use the intonations of old-time folk songs, and still better to write simply in the style of folk music. 'Realism' was treated as 'truth' as portrayed in the newspapers, decrees and on the radio; in no way it could be the real truth of life! (There was not a single composition to disclose the tragedy of the dying out villages, the more so the truth about the life in the concentration camps, or about the war and the revolution). If a composer abided by these precepts, his works were positively appraised and performed, he had good notices in the press and gained prestige with the Composers Union. As a result, his creative work became insipid. A typical case is Dmitry Kabalevsky. To retain his inner world at least relatively pure, a composer has to run against the stream. He has to be determined and daring to follow that lodestar which illuminates his inner world. He is fully aware of what his challenge involves and the banishment he will have to face. Nonetheless, he follows the first commandment of the intellectual life — progress is possible only through spiritual opposition to the environment. Such is the inner psychological mechanism of intellectual development shaping the inner world of the best Russian composers, Edison Denisov included. Spiritual glow impresses itself upon the very structure of the composer's artistic make-up and, correspondingly, stamps the spiritual image of his creations. His elation is naturally transferred on to the listener who singles out this artist in a series of more 'reliable' composers. The listener perceives artistic fervour as a divine gift to support his own soul and illuminate his own inner world.

The most essential individual traits in Denisov's inner world are visible from the interlacing and merger of concrete artistic traditions and modern trends which he is striving for and which he refutes, from a unique range of his personal ideals, sympathies and inclinations.

A major intellectual substratum of Denisov's creativity is a trend in Russian culture initiated by Peter the Great.[2] An artist feeling himself a Russian as it were comes to find himself fully merged at the same time with the forms of Western-European culture, and then his spirit hovers over the world at large. Like in Leo Tolstoy's novel *War and Peace* with its extensive fragments written in French, Denisov has produced a full-fledged opera, *L'écume des jours*, with its original libretto based on the French rather than Russian text; also six scenes in his opera *Les quatre filles* are running in French, while his Requiem has been written in several European languages. Certainly, getting used to the sounds of a foreign language is a particular detail and an outward sign, but it is no accident with Denisov; it is a manifestation of 'universal openness' of Russian culture (which was delineated by Fyodor Dostoyevsky back in his time). For Denisov such openness is one of the leading signs of creativity. His cantata *The Sun of the Incas* to the verse of the Chilean poetess Gabriela Mistral, which brought the composer wide recognition, bears out the spontaneity and freshness of non-European emotions. But on a characteristic par with *The Sun of the Incas* stand out his *Wails*, a work profoundly permeated with the Russian mentality and written to the Russian folk texts. To the same traditional branch belong *Shchaza's Complaints* by Andrei Volkonsky, a Russian composer residing in France, and still farther off in retrospection *Les Noces* by the world-renowned Stravinsky. In the context of the cultural life prevailing in Soviet Russia in the 1950s — 1960s such 'Europeanism' (persecuted as 'cosmopolitanism') was a safety valve for an artist to keep alive in the stagnant atmosphere of the official dogmata inherent in 'socialist realism'. The composer's striving to keep abreast of the cultural achievements in the world at large is not an evidence against his national Russian essence, rather, on the contrary, it fosters its free and unrestrained development.

Denisov's artistic world, the same as with most contemporary composers, abounds in contrasts. It is the scope of his individual style that raises most objections on the part of his antipodes in music. Thus, along with the traditional vocal and instrumental cycles (concerto, sonata, ensemble and symphony), it includes *Birdsong*, an unusual composition for prepared piano and magnetic tape, ranging from the enchanted elevation of his *Signes en blanc* to mass songs in *The Ship Steams Past the Harbour*. But such contrasts, as well as the patent evolution of his style, make part and parcel of its integrity inherent in the wholeness of the moral principles underlying the composer's inner world and rooted in a definite world-view, stable artistic principles which are kept intact in his persistent creative quests. This integrity gets stronger from upholding some general ideas.

In contrast to the counter-cultural trends of the left-radical type, quite widespread in the second half of the 20th century, Edison Denisov in his creative work is inspired by the idea of beauty. In his view, "music without a beautiful idea, devoid of logic, is impossible." From today's perspective it is evident that this orientation of artistic ideas is likely to have been inherited primarily from Romantic aesthetics. But it is not a repetition of the old concept, in some respects it is even contrary to it. Thus, Denisov's sense of beauty excludes 'outpouring emotionality'. Otherwise, it would be quite a different trend, something à la Rachmaninov, which is diametrically opposite to Denisov's aesthetics. The composer himself advanced the conception of new beauty in modern music: "Beauty is a major factor in art, and at the moment quite a few composers are looking for a new kind of beauty. This means not only beautiful sound, which, naturally, has nothing to do with outward prettiness, but beauty here means beautiful ideas as understood by mathematicians, or Bach and Webern." In pursuance of the composer's ideas one may as well add: "An artist is a master of beauty." While he embodies his conceptions in a work of art — in colour, sound, stone or verbal ligature — an artist not merely depicts the surrounding world but also creates a world of supreme values and the most essential of these values are artistic ones.

To quote Alexander Pushkin, "the aim of poetry is poetry." As for Denisov, he says: "The imperishable beauty of the great works of art lives in time as a reality in the highest sense of the word."

His most favourite composers are Mozart, Glinka and Schubert. Their common tendency for refined and elevated art makes the prime musical tradition to be followed by Denisov. In his view, Schubert is one of those composers without whom he "could not possibly live." His love for the author of *Müller-Lieder* is evidenced from his repeated orchestrations of Schubert's choreographic minia-tures. As an image of pure, imperishable beauty and harmony there arises a divine vision in the finale of Denisov's Violin Concerto as the celesta brings out the enchanting melody of *Morgengruss* (Morning Greeting) from Schubert's *Die Schöne Müllerin* (The Fair Maid of the Mill).

The blending of the ideals of beauty, elevation, purity and love (as the divine muse of Urania) in the process of his vital artistic activity makes Denisov, in his utterances, impart to art the properties and functions attributed in traditional religious consciousness to Christian spirituality. According to Edison Denisov, music is not only a domain of artistic, aesthetic values, it also constitutes a sphere of man's spiritual life; and not only in its general meaning (the spiritual as a field of mental activity), but also in its specific function inherent in traditional Russian aesthetics (see above). Russian art, particularly literature in its 'Golden Age', was perceived not only as an artistic matter, but had a tinge of a moral precept like religion. With the elimination of the church as the key factor in man's spiritual life, the more and more visible gaps in his moral and spiritual education are expected, according to the Russian tradition, to be filled in by the belles-lettres, theatre and music. Denisov is convinced that "music more than anything else can shape man's spiritual world." He says that today we witness "a lot of anti-spiritual music, an abundance of anti-spirituality in art. Museums (of modern art) are horrible, sometimes verging on a loss of art. But at the same time there is currently a gratifying tendency towards greater spirituality. The essence of art should be revived." Genuine music is increasingly becoming a spiritual art. "Today, with banishment of the church, spiritual values are the key aspect of art."[3] Sometimes art or some of its aspects fulfil the function of 'secular religion' feeding man's spiritual life. Denisov believes that to this category of 'spiritual music' (in this particular meaning) belong, for instance, his own Variations on a theme of Haydn (*Tod ist ein langer Schlaf*) and *Es ist genug* variations on a theme of J.S. Bach, these two compositions being kindred in spirit. Denisov's *Gladsome Light* may be regarded as a contribution to the current revival of Russian tradition-al genres of sacred music, along with several compositions by Nikolai Karetnikov, Yuri Butsko, Alemdar Karamanov, Sophia Gubaidulina, and Rodion Shchedrin.

Denisov's belief in the necessity to imbue the art of music with spirituality is closely related to the idea of light which plays a major part in the composer's aesthetics. He insists: "The concept of light is indispensable in music", "one can not exist without faith" and "one needs light in one's daily life too."[4] To turn to spirituality and light in the current context of raging 'left radicalism', slander and promiscuous humiliation and glorification of universal disintegration, degradation and breakdown means to run once again against the fashionable stream, risking to be labelled a 'retrograde' person with 'outdated' views. The artistic embodiment of positive ideals, high moral principles, light and beauty is most necessary in the times of troubles, amongst a cruel spiritual crisis which has been laid bare by Gorbachev's perestroika. The fact that art, music included, retains such moral function is an evidence of Edison Denisov's adherence to the traditional artistic concept, the Russian tradition in the first place.

Of course, we can just outline the basic moral substance of Denisov's inner world. This core has many varied and contrasting layers enveloping it. But the moral core is that light which breaks through and tinges the layers, with darkness inaccessible to it. The fact that this concept makes the moral core of the composer's inner world is borne out not only by a multitude, significance and scope of his compositions directly permeated with these ideas, such as his Violin and Viola Concertos, Symphony, Requiem, Piano Trio No. 2 and *Gladsome Light*, but also in those of his works which seem to be predominantly mournful and pessimistic such as *Wails* and *L'écume des jours*. Thus, the plot of his opera *L'écume des jours* is based on the heroine's illness and death, with a dramatic counterpoint to it in the form of absurdist universes and commonplace patches of light. But even in this opera the composer's basic moral core remains intact, the same as in his other works.

It is most important that a modern composer should keep away from any seemingly inevitable banality, not relishing banality in either ironical or satirical terms. Denisov finds it absolutely invalid to allege that our life is filthy and one has to make-believe to be superior to it. It is hypocrisy and artistic falsity. His music seems to assert quite the opposite: yes, our life is indeed full of banalities, and the general public would rather listen to some compromises with pop-art; yes, true jazz is a wonderful art and Gershwin is a remarkable composer. But art should not sink down to a level of pop-thought, it should not flirt with the public, and the sacred fire of high music is not to die out, and the artist's cause is to oppose the tendency to degradation rather than surrender to it. The artist's spiritual life is a constant struggle for true art and against any moral, intellectual and artistic compromises.

Lately Edison Denisov's style seems to be lingering in its development. Though it could hardly be viewed as a good sign, he has halted precisely at this spiritual concept of light and beauty.

Notes to Chapter 2

1. Alexei Losev. Russian Philosophy (1918). Cited from the book: A.F. Losev. *Philosophy, Mythology, Culture*. Moscow, 1991, pp. 211–214.
2. Igor Stravinsky, himself belonging to that trend in Russian culture, made an apt observation on the subject: Peter the Great "conceived to mould together the most characteristic features of the Russian civilization and the intellectual wealth of the West." Stravinsky called Peter I 'the forefather' of such personalities as Pushkin, Glinka and Tchaikovsky. See Stravinsky's article "Pushkin: Poetry and Music" (1940). Cited from the book: *Igor Stravinsky: Publicist & Interlocutor*. Moscow, 1988,

pp. 140–141.

3.   E. Denisov — Yu. Nagibin. "Variations on Familiar Themes. A Dialogue". *Literatur-naya Gazeta*, Moscow, August 2, 1989, p. 8. All the quotations have been borrowed from the authors' numerous talks with the composer, as well as from Denisov's public addresses, e.g., from his talk with the audience at his recital in the Tchaikovsky Concert Hall in Moscow, June 8, 1989.

4.   Denisov recalls how after the performance of his Requiem in Moscow three girls came up to him and said: "We thank you for light in your music. We are missing it so badly in our life."

CHAPTER 3

THE COMPOSER'S STYLE AND TECHNIQUES

1. THE SOURCES

A composer's style often reveals the tradition in which he has been reared — a definite artistic trend, school or a composer whose ideas are to be 'continued' in the works of their follower. Thus, in Scriabin's dazzling innovations you may discern the Chopinesque style of his earlier compositions. It is quite different with Denisov, like with many other avant-garde artists. The formation period of his style involved intensive searchings for his own place in an intricate mixture of modern musical trends. When he graduated from the conservatoire he was equipped not with an individual style but rather an unstable compromise between expressing his own personality and writing "comme il faut". A powerful urge for authenticity and self-expression promptly wiped off anything alien and superficial. Denisov has consciously broken with the old techniques and the alien perception of music and thereby came into his own.

A curving line of Denisov's stylistic evolution may be outlined in the following major stages of his creative career: 1. Up to 1959 — Compositions Written at the Conservatoire. The Early Period; 2. 1960–1964 — A Breakthrough to a Personal Style; 3. 1964–1977 — The Individual Style; 4. c. 1977–1980s — Stabilization.

The prime place among the sources of Denisov's style should be accorded to Shostakovich. In the deep-rooted innermost of Denisov's artistic individuality there is something akin to the composer of *The Nose*. His earlier works are marked by the same dry colourlessness, lucidity of a clear-cut melodic line, deliberate avoidance of sentimental tonal nuances, romantic 'stylish' texture and any prettiness whatsoever, and a rugged language. Like Shostakovich in his mature years, Denisov in his earlier compositions gravitates towards the neo-classical type of musical imagery and, respectively, musical formation. At that time Denisov was trying his hand at approximately the same genres and forms as Shostakovich, producing a symphony in C major in four movements, a piano trio, a string

quartet, song-cycles, an oratorio, preludes for piano, and several suites for orchestra. The ban imposed on Shostakovich's music after 1948 only encouraged his
gravitation towards it. Personal friendship with Shostakovich deepened this similarity and made it more subtle and detailed. But as Denisov's artistic individuality developed, he found himself more and more estranged from Shostakovich.

The kinship of Denisov's nature with Stravinsky is less conspicuous. In more
general terms it is evident from his antipathy to the florid post-romantic idioms
and pathetic character of emotional swelling, and from his striving for sharply
delineated patterns and structural accuracy. In more specific terms it is obvious
from his propensity for rhythmic agility based on unbalanced metrics. Abandon-
ment of tonal-triadic harmony in favour of linear polyphonic weaving of musical
fabric, as a trend in modern music initiated by Stravinsky, was also close to
Denisov. His keen awareness of potentialities inherent in solo playing of separate
instruments in an ensemble was akin to Stravinsky's, too. The impact made by
L'histoire du soldat is quite visible in many of Denisov's compositions.

Among the sources of his style notice should be made of the early influence
exerted by the artistic personality of his tutor, Shebalin. One should not be
surprised by the impact of this unspectacular composer. The very nature of
Denisov the composer carried something similar to his teacher's general tone of
statement and the carefully thought-out rationality of his musical texture, despite
all the differences between them as regards Denisov's zealous and inquisitive
mind, which made the pupil strive incessantly for something new.

Denisov's earlier compositions also reveal occasionally the influence of the
Prokofievian style which is manifest in the musical expressiveness of a characteristic gesture, a vivid imagery and polymodal intonations in major and minor
keys. It is most discernible in his earlier piano pieces, suites for orchestra and in
his Sonata for two violins.

2.   A BREAKTHROUGH TO A PERSONAL STYLE

His style, or to be more precise his 'pre-style', of the late fifties could be regarded
as a jumping board from which the young composer plunged into the unexplored
waters. Denisov's pre-style was devoid of a shade of integrity. Rather, it was a
ferment of various trends, a feverish search and attempts to disentangle himself
from the outdated fetters of conventional musical idioms. At the same time the
traits of refined lyricism intrinsic in his individuality, so perspicaciously
discerned by Shebalin earlier, came to be developed.

His oratorio *Siberian Land*, completed in January 1961, bears the stamp of the
genre of patriotic music conveying his love for the native land, its people and
history. In stylistic terms its underlying plot and genre inspired the composer to
deliver a large-scale canvas with a symphonic scope of climaxes and culmina-
tions. *Siberian Land* is Denisov's first major composition to stress the significance
of the D-major tonality. The last words of the oratorio seem to hold a promise of
a change in his style: "My sacred road, no matter how saddened I felt, was
beckoning me to other vistas full of a different anxiety."

The 'new vistas' opened before the composer within the same year. Like
many other composers of his generation, Denisov faced the notorious problem

Ex. 4   Bagatelles, *A* — No. 1, *B* — No. 7

formulated by Schoenberg 'tonal oder atonal?' The new trends in his style, however, were rooted rather in another facet of his talent. A colourful blend of aesthetic trends was marked by a line of keen thinking, chromatic intonations and subtle
expressiveness. To this type of works belongs a cycle of his piano miniatures
Bagatelles written back in 1960. In this composition you can already feel the tonal
conventions becoming too restrictive, the composer finding himself at a point
defined by Schoenberg as "An den Grenzen der Tonart" (At the Tonal Boundaries). But in this case a road beyond the tonal boundaries is different — not the
loosening of the tonal gravity (like with Schoenberg) but polystructures — poly-
modality and polytonality. The first piece in this cycle is the most revealing in this
respect (Musical Example 4 A). The polymodal, dissonant combination C (c – g)
+ G lyd. /g – a – b – c# – d/ logically brings together the sharply contradicting c^1
+ $c\#^2$ confirmed by their realignment in the second bar. As a result, one can
witness a piquant chord-formation of split tonic remaining simultaneously in
different scales.[1]
   The other bagatelles are also rich in witty details: No. 2 — after several rhythmic
surprises (such as the insertion or withdrawal of small time-values) the ending is
rendered in a tonality of a tone higher by a forte subito; No. 6 displays a kind of
fluctuating tonality, with 'polytonal' cadence of C major + E major (in C major). A
melodic line in a folk vein is combined here with a folk choral 'solo-refrain'
texture; No. 7 — a witty balalaika-type strumming leads to various humourous
effects, for instance, playing 'out of tune' (Musical Example 4 B).
   Despite the outward placidity, in such components of this style one can already
discern the actual pantonality of musical thinking, its preparedness to pass into a
new dimension. His Sonata for Flute and Piano (1960) may be regarded as a critical point of departure. Formally it is a tonal composition in the unequivocal B♭
minor. But in essence throughout the Sonata there is virtually no concentration on
any definite tonal centre. From the very beginning the polyharmonic combination

b♭ – d♭ – f (piano) and d – f – a – c♯ (flute) paradoxically closes up the enharmonic circle d♭ = c♯. What is achieved in the old tonal music through long modulations in this composition has been brought together in the first bar. The chromaticism condenses into a virtual twelve-note tonality (for instance, the eleven note-row in bars 3 and 4: d – e♭ – e – g♯ – f – c♯ – a – b♭ – g – g♭ – b). There is no space left for tonal content whatsoever. The natural development is preserved owing to departures from such density of intonation towards simpler exposition (e.g., in a subsidiary theme, beginning with bar 17). The movement 'forward' for further development is virtually impossible in the same direction.

The breakthrough is at first cautious and local, behind the solid walls of the tonal bulwarks of the neo-classical form of the Second String Quartet, written in 1961. Its three movements reveal the metabolic progression found in Denisov's techniques and style: Movement One — Allegro in F on a theme of Bartók (the quartet is dedicated to his memory); Movement Two — a transition to dodeca-phonic-serial material; Movement Three —free atonality, serialism, tonality though devoid of conclusive monotonality, and the ending in a dissonant E major.

Its first movement pays homage to Béla Bartók who helped the young Russian composer to discover many new developments in modern music. This quartet has a motto theme — a motive from Bartók's String Quartet No. 5, making that motive with its persistently recurrent notes the leading one in the quartet's principal theme. Despite a number of elements of similarity with Bartók's style, Denisov's quartet, on the whole, is devoid of any stylisation, the more so in the second and third movements he departs from the chosen stylistic model. The principal theme in the first movement is somewhat aggressively expressive. In contrast to Bartók who had oriented himself on Beethoven in the principles of form-building, this is hardly valid in Denisov's case. He strives not so much to follow the great masters, his prototypes, as to depart from them. The exaggeration of rhythmic and harmonic clashes under the stretto development of the key motive gives rise to such powerful dynamism that it wipes off the fragile tonal regulators of the classical (sonata) form and insistently calls for new form-build-ing media. The composer feels himself more relaxed in bagatelles when he draws a line at tonality. But the classical sonata-form permits no tonal uncertainty or indeterminacy, sudden changes and hard modulations. The transcendence beyond tonal boundaries, which has already occurred in Denisov's music, in turning to an extended non- verbal form of the classical tradition inevitably involves the use of other different connecting media. Having discarded the tonic-dominant foundations of sonata-form as too binding upon the flight of fan-tasy, the composer came to rely on new harmonic means inherent in polyphonic harmony. Denisov seemed to be guided by Sergei Taneyev's observation made half a century ago: "The destruction of tonality leads to disintegration of musical form... The linking power of contrapuntal forms should be especially valued in modern music the harmony of which gradually loses its tonal bonds."[2] Denisov draws on polyphony — imitation and canon, but comes to another composition method — serialism. It is not a serial technique as yet, but the method of weaving musical texture is close to it. In the second movement Denisov applies dodeca-phony in the strictest sense of the word, although not too consistently.

The second movement is written in a form of variations — both in larger (a theme and three variations) and smaller dimensions: a 'variational' approach to serialism is evident. For the theme of the variations see Musical Example 5.

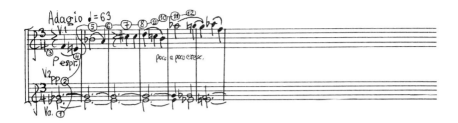

Ex. 5   String quartet No. 2, 2nd movement

Strictly speaking, it follows the twelve-note procedure only in the initial statement of the theme whereas further on the composer develops only its separate
intonations, segments of the series. The general structure of this cycle of variations is based on the principle of gradual serial intensification: The main theme —
one initial statement (bars 1–5); the 1st variation is an example of two-track
serialism (both violins) accompanied with free voices; the 2nd variation is pure
dodecaphony, a double canon (Fig. 23–25); the 3rd variation is once again an
example of one- or two-track serialism accompanied with free voices; the coda is
a single final statement of the series (bars 4–1 from the end).

The finale of the quartet combines the neo-classical idioms with serialism.
Deliberately written in contrasting tonalities, it ends in a quasi-E major.

The breakthrough into the unexplored domain was completed. The new —
twelve-note — technique revealed new facets of the composer's style. Moreover,
some of his compositions written in 1961 initiated the build-up of the style which
was all his own, i.e., the formation of what has been associated with Denisov as
an artistic phenomenon. He had arrived and made a name for himself.

As a matter of fact, 'a breakthrough to a personal style' involved a wide range
of searches in many different directions. During the period from 1961 to 1964 the
main means of renovating and releasing his own individuality was dodecaphony.
'Pantonality' to which naturally led the density of chromatic intonations (especially in his Sonata for flute) required some reliable factors of inner weaving of
musical fabric. The serial method of the Second Viennese School found itself in a
similar situation through a logical technique of functional justification of the content of melodic motives, chord verticalization, polyphonic thematic arrangement
and deliverance from chance and lack of motivation in melodic and harmonic
combinations.

Denisov's compositions *Music for Eleven Wind Instruments and Kettledrums* and his
Piano Variations, both written in 1961, are purely dodecaphonic.

The *Theme and Six Variations* (altogether, seven pieces) in a symmetrical way
correspond to his *Seven Bagatelles*, lying on the other side of the milestone in his
style, which occurred in 1961. In its style this composition is obviously akin to
Schoenberg, though in its intonations it never comes close to him. Rather, it
displays some moments of intonational similarity with the second movement of
Webern's Symphony, Op. 21 (bars 55–67), such as, for instance, the 'broken'
chords in Variation No. 3. Some idioms of Denisov's musical language have been
brought into bolder relief, among them the asymmetrical instrumental recitative

(the beginning of the theme), the rapidly flashing 'repeating dots' (Variation No. 3) and the sharply rhythmical pointillism (Variation No. 6).

The conception of his *Music for Eleven Wind Instruments and Kettledrums* is on a grander scale. Its three movements correspond to the genres of the sonata cycle — Allegro, Scherzo and the slow movement. The compositional problem of the dodecaphonic technique lies in the forms resulting from interlinking of serial note-rows. The serial successions are similar to threads from which the musical texture is woven; but what kind of pattern must be applied in it?

At first Denisov turns to the classical forms of Baroque music. The first movement in his *Music* is imbued with a forceful rhythmic current led by a general unbalanced character of the metre. The outer movements are homophonic, while the middle one is polyphonic:

Figures:	/0/————3	3————8	8————9	9————10
Sections:	Principal theme	Subsidiary theme	Principal theme	Coda
Forms:	three-part period	fugato	/ostinato/	
Harmony:	series-theme		series-theme	
/axis tones/:	P a – e	f♯ – c♯ – c – g	P a – e	
	a – g – b♭ – d	b – e – f – b♭	a – g – b♭ – d	

The prevalence of the set-form P a – e is equal to the decisive dominance of 'key tonality'.

The second movement is a traditional scherzo with a trio (fugato in Fig. 14–19). The function of the tonic chord is attributed to the last four notes from P a – e (e – e♭ – d♭ – a♭ in the brasses). The finale represents a chorale and recitative wherein the pathetic chords are akin to the passacaglia from Shostakovich's Second Piano Trio.

Another major feature is noteworthy in Denisov turning to the path of New Music. Following his oratorio *Siberian Land* which uses the full capacity of chorus and orchestra, Denisov wrote for nearly ten years exclusively chamber music, both purely instrumental and for voice accompanied by a group of instruments, or piano. The conception of some of the compositions written during that period is undoubtedly on a grand scale, such as, for instance, *The Sun of the Incas*, *Wails* and his Concerto for Flute, Oboe, Piano and Percussion. On the one hand, it was certainly a result of his intrinsic antipathy towards the sounds of the traditional symphony orchestra, to all the pathos of the neo-classical type and the very tone of a melodic line rendered by 12–16 violins playing in unison. On the other hand, he was driven by an urge for a subtle expression of his ideas and for disclosing the resources inherent in each instrument to a maximum. It was essentially a turn away from the standard cast of playing instruments and voices to its more individual forms: the bass voice and three trombones (*Canti di Catullo*), clarinet, piano and percussion (*Ode*), oboe, harp and a string trio (*Romantic Music*). This decade was devoted to an artistic investigation of vivid and impressive timbre colours, including those intrinsic in traditional instrumental ensembles (e.g., in a string trio). The 'chamber-like' character of the genres he tackled concealed pungent rhythmic patterns, an unusual abundance of tone-colours, fantasy and inventiveness in instrumental combinations.

During the period from 1961 to 1964 Denisov was merely groping for separate domains of his own soundscape. For the first time these traits of his style were all to merge in a new stylistic entity in his chamber cantata *The Sun of the Incas*. Denisov was searching his way towards the sun, step by step discarding the ordinary convention of the neo-classical manner, thematic schematicism and rigid relationships of the classical form. The refutation of such outdated techniques increasingly revealed the strongest aspects of his artistic personality. In this progression lay the essence of his style's evolution during the period from 1961 to 1964.

3. DENISOV'S STYLE

Naturally, a composer's style develops constantly. And upon finding his own voice in *The Sun of the Incas*, Denisov proceeded further on the creative path, moreover, simultaneously in several different directions. Only in the late 1970s, during the stage of 'post-avant-gardism', he came to linger somehow in what had been accomplished. But in the early 1990s there appeared some new qualities and aspects in his style.

The revelation of Denisov's individual style is a fact as much curious as it is spontaneous in its naturalness, which makes us consider modern music as a theme for discourse. What drives an artist to run against the stream, against the traditions and conventions of his environment? Today we realize that he had been right from the start, keeping abreast of the times and finding his own place and style. But in those times he looked like a madman plunging into unexplored waters. He has been consciously risking his career, breaking off with the commonly accepted views and tastes. It would be superficial to assert that his breakthrough to the New Music was due to the 'influences' of some of his contemporaries, fellow-avant-gardists. It is too insubstantial an explanation since these influences (there is no doubt about them) played primarily the role of a 'catalyst' while the inner incentives were the underlying cause. These incentives concentrate in a musical system, i.e., in the inner music whose intonation is acutely felt by the composer. The musical system in the oratorio *Siberian Land* and the Trio of 1957 only outwardly seem to be quite traditional. In actual fact, the situation of 'An den Grenzen der Tonart' is fraught with exploding the system and a composer cannot help sensing himself as a mediator granted a divine mission to take the challenge. A law of artistic nature governs the composer's steps as he approaches that 'prenatal' state. Furthermore, most different composers had already faced a similar situation, being sometimes unaware of similar experiences of other contemporaries — Webern and Schoenberg in Vienna, Scriabin, Stravinsky, Prokofiev and Roslavets in Russia, Ives in the USA and Bartók in Hungary. The new wave brought Boulez, Stockhausen, Nono and Ligeti to the scene.

No doubt, the decisive factor in a breakthrough to one's personal style is an irresistible spiritual motion, a drive to give birth to new artistic and cultural values. But to become a reality, this impulse has to be embodied in the elements of a musical system — a structure of pitches, rhythms and patterns in tune with the spirit of the times. Otherwise, it would fail to convey it. The creative principles of the 1960s could not be expressed in the patterns inherent in the times of Scriabin's *Prometheus* or Schoenberg's *Erwartung*, for these principles have evolved long ago, making up a part of a modern composer's phylogenesis. For this reason precisely the necessity to 'pass' through Bartók, Stravinsky, Schoenberg and Webern proved so irresistible when Denisov had grasped it by intuition. By having 'let it pass' through himself, a composer finds himself in a proper position to make a creative breakthrough which only then becomes possible. To be more precise, this position of jumping off, therefore, consists in a state of a musical system which has assimilated the seeds of new quality to emerge so 'suddenly' and 'unexpectedly' in the form of a new individual modern style.

These seeds are spiritual rather than structural or material, and since 'the spirit hovers wherever it likes', they are invisible in analysis of sound formations. But they are conceivable from some traits inherent in the style of the composers chosen by Denisov as catalysts for his own work. The prime place here should be given to the asymmetrical rhythms and free structures that distinguished Stravinsky, and Webern's dodecaphony together with his identification of the multi-parametered nature of music. Hence a number of new channels along which the creative innovations find their ways and which shaped Denisov's individual style. The new channels may be categorized as artistic research of the resources inherent in the elements of musical system as autonomous parameters, including some general foundations underlying the art of sound production. The examination of discovered musical artistic potentials inherent in sounds associates Denisov with other avant-garde composers, these discoveries include:

– atomization of the pitch structure (like in Webern's series divided into micro-sets in Op. 24, 21 and 28);

– emancipation of timbre, tone-colours, and sonoristics;

– emancipation of sound articulation and percussive effect;

– emancipation of sound intensity;

– emancipation of pitch lines and their elements, cultivation of spatial tonal figures based on sonoristic 'spots', layers, dimensional and 'stereophoric' forms;

– expansion of the sphere of proportions of form at the sake of 'dissonant' polyrhythmic symmetries (not traditional 'consonant' ones such as 1:1, 2:1, 4:1, 3:1, 3:2, but more complicated ones such as 5:4, 5:2, 7:4, etc.), ametrical rhythms (quasimetrical, irrational proportions) and likewise;

– emancipation of rhythm from the verse framework of the poetical word in favour of 'musical prose' with asymmetrical phrases and sentences and prose-speech 'periods'; intensification of emotional logic in life experiences with its characteristic linear 'curvature' of smooth ascents and descents; the impact of rhythms of everyday life;

– production of individualized modal structures (individual modes).

The wide-ranging spectrum of current trends in one way or another, in certain proportions and mixtures, affected Denisov's style. The distinction from other avant-garde composers was taking shape under the effect of the tradition described above, from this specific complex of stylistic premises. Of decisive importance for formation of the stylistic complex intrinsic in Denisov's music was the moral make-up of his personality (see Chapter 2).

Finally, the following inflexible traits of the composer's artistic character, his musical soul, play their regulatory role:

– prevalence of lyricism over other musical expressive media. The general overtone of Denisov's artistic world displays something akin to Webern's lyricism. In contrast to the latter, his lyricism does not dissolve in other types of sound production but rather, on the contrary, it affects them strongly, remaining relatively integral and separate from quite varied other expressive media;

– the lyricism of his music is tinged not so much with emotional forcefulness (the type of lyricism inherent in Tchaikovsky and particularly in Rachmaninov — the antipodes of Denisov's world) as with elevated contemplation. It seems to forget about the narrow utilitarian problems of daily life and worry, breaking with 'l'écume des jours', with anything artificial in our real life. The core of such lyricism is the image of absolute purity and gentleness, 'a genius of pure beauty'. Such is Denisov's subjective perception of the artists most akin to his own nature — Schubert (but not Schumann), Mozart (but not Beethoven), Glinka (but not Dargomyzhsky) and Pushkin (but not Lermontov);

– the tone of Denisov's musical utterances does not stress their subjectivity, though the lyricism presupposes the primacy of the subject of an utterance as regards a musical image. His style is more specifically distinguished for the objective integrity of the arising picture of the world;

– his music is highly emotional, characterized even by the extreme states of expressiveness (e.g., passionate rages, on the one hand, and complete prostration, on the other). At the same time, despite all the emotional extremities, it invariably retains the interrelationship of the sensory and the rational. Not infrequently a certain structure of musical expressiveness is established by the composer while his sober creative thinking is conducting a kind of 'research study' into a discovered musical domain;

– one of the key traits in his personality as a composer is the subtlety of his writing. He is very fond of transparent, lucid sounds. His melodic line in most cases is a fine iridescent thread, and the entity is made up of weaving such threads together. His subtlety is also evident in the very structure of his musical ideas, merging with the quality of its elevation;

– the individual property of Denisov's musical imagery is often identified in its pictorial nature. The musical fabric outlines for the ear certain 'forms in the air' (to use the figurative title of one of Arthur Lourie's pieces for piano, also prompted by a wish to bring music and cubist painting closer to each other). Denisov is not keen on experimentation in other arts, but introduces some influences from them into his music;

– contrary to the composer's declarations about the influence of mathematics and methods of mathematical thinking on his music, it is virtually devoid of any rational numerical, mathematical modes of thinking (though Denisov uses some elements of the serial technique, these elements are readjusted by purely auditory perception of rhythms and proportions and, as a result, produce no mathematical tonal order as it were). Moreover, the opposite factors are inherent in the artistic structure of his music — a tendency for free structure. It reveals some typological regularities underlying the Slavonic musical type, bringing Denisov closer to Mussorgsky, Stravinsky, the Czeck and Polish composers of the 20th century, but not to Messiaen, Boulez or Stockhausen;

– despite the dozens of incidental film scores and his sympathies for jazz and folk art, Denisov is alien to anything naive or artless, finding it hard to go along with the stream of pop art. His spirit with its overpowering drive for fine expressiveness denies anything elementary and sensual as too crude and primitive.

These and other traits of his artistic personality immersed in the intonational sphere of a purely musical system with its autonomous parameters (see above) bear out the specific tonal features of Denisov's style in all key fields of its manifestation — the genre system, typology of musical images-characters, rhythm and harmony, melodic and thematic arrangement, counterpoint, serialism, pointillism and sonoristics.

4.   GENRES, CHARACTERS, IMAGES

The realities of his life made Edison Denisov, as many other composers contemporary to him, face opposition of two genre worlds — artistic and applied music. The sharp gulf is often said to be widening between a sonata and rock song, a string quartet and a brass band, and so on. Perhaps in the 20th century the division of art into different genres should be based on their opposition, rather than on the traditional transcendental differentiation between the epos, lyrics and drama. The fact that the 20th century has been an age of a great breakdown of a certain three-millennia-old historical-tectonic slab finds another confirmation in an analysis of the genre system employed in modern creative works.

Despite a tangle of genre properties and tendencies in 'E-Musik' and 'U-Musik', the former ('Ernste', 'Erhabene' — earnest and elevated) is directed upwards (previously they would say 'towards God'; but Nietzsche said that God was dead...). It feeds the human spirit, being listened to for its own sake, its artistic beauty, rather than for something outside it. The phrase "L'art pour l'art", were it not so hackneyed, would suit best to express this essence of music. 'U-Musik' ('Unter- haltungs', 'Unterste' meaning 'entertainment' and 'common') fulfils the role of a mental lubricant in society for normal functioning of the social machinery to produce and reproduce the social 'body'.

Correspondingly, the division of genres inherent in Denisov's music reflects the current stage of fixating the existence of genre as the continuous creation of music (including in the long run creation as it were); it also generates musical genres which constitute what engenders (naturans) with respect to a composition and, on the other hand, what is engendered (naturata) with regard to music as spiritual creation.

As a result, in Denisov's music we see a modern cross-section of various groups of criteria for genre division (for instance, his Chamber Symphony may be viewed both as a symphony and a chamber ensemble). All the genres of 'E-Musik', one can say, 'remove' (in the Hegelian meaning) its inter-differences, having lost a difference in its immediate predestination in real life (the *Serenade* is not intended for complimentary performance given outdoors at night for a woman, the *Epitaph* is not for immortalizing one's soul on a gravestone, the *Two Pieces* resemble a 'sonata', the *Requiem* is not a mass for the dead, *Kyrie* is for theatrical performance, etc.). Everything is a 'sonata', a 'concerto', 'signs and lines', 'music', with genres representing not 'life' but just certain reflections of it.

On the other hand, we witness the enhancing role of a different highly individual approach to selection of genres. Not only the general typology of modern musical creativity depends on musical techniques which turn into a kind of genre

Ex. 6   Piano trio, 4th movement

indicators. Serialism, modality, sonoristics, new and old tonality have become major indicators of typified musical imagery, i.e., genre attributes. Certainly, typical genres with their conventional properties retain their significance in Denisov's creative output: song-cycles, a sonata for solo piano, a symphony for orchestra, and a programmatic piece. But at the same time genres-characters come to play a major part in his music. This term implies relatively definite expressive effects, or pictures-visions, or musical characters or processes (like Messiaen's 'birdsong style', a kind of sonoristic genre with him, too) used to express the recurrent emotional states in Denisov's music. In a relatively stable tonal expression they appear in the most different genres, forming a complex of certain musical types and functioning in this sense like special genres. The stereotypes of genre attributes avoided by Denisov may be regarded as an analogy of such genres, i.e., for instance, the conventional smooth rocking in a fairly slow tempo and gentle sonority (lullaby) or a number of pieces in a definite rhythm and texture of a certain formula-like type (mazurka, polonaise, boogie-woogie), or an even rapid motoric movement (toccata, etude) and the like. Denisov is little disposed to use such typical complexes, but he has spontaneously produced a whole range of similar individual character-genres. Combination of their attributes plays a role in his music similar to the use of typical genres (say, for instance, the waltz-like character with Chopin or Tchaikovsky).

'The Denisov genres' make up a ramified system, partly echoing similar 'genres' used by other contemporary composers, partly following in the characteristic genres of the past. Like the genre rhythmic-textural characteristic formulas of certain genres (a dance march), 'the Denisov genres' are also expressed in some definite combination of musical elements, the new techniques of modern music included (e.g., pointillism). Let us consider the most characteristic of his genres which in their integrity distinguish Denisov's individual composition style.

Ex. 7   *A & B*: Symphony, 1st movement

4.1. 'High Lyricism'

The composer himself attaches great importance to lyricism in his style. His genre of 'high lyricism' is marked for most expressive heartfelt lyricism rendered in gentle tones and a slow tempo, in the upper register, often in bright and captivating timbres. The dramatic impact of high lyricism is so strong that it acts to open the human heart and soul, making a person to discard all the daily vanities and soar upwards beyond the earthly existence. At this point everything is serious, light and delightful (Musical Example 6). Other samples are separate fragments from the following compositions: the Second String Quartet, 2nd movement; String Trio, bars 101–109 (shortly before a quotation from Schoenberg); Three Pieces for Cello No. 3; *Romantic Music*, the end; the Cello Concerto, the ending; the Piano Concerto, 2nd movement, the opening bars; *Signes en blanc*; the ending of the Violin Concerto; *L'écume des jours*, the love theme (see Musical Example 11 B). Denisov's 'high lyricism' stands on a par with the remarkable accomplishments of the Romantic period.

4.2. Lyrical 'Interweaving'

The characteristic 'moving' sonority, the identifying quality of the Denisov music, is a kind of 'visiting card' of his style. His 'weaving' represents the flowing of several voices appearing on a par at different times in quasi-arhythmical and ametrical rendering. As far as it possible the voices have no simultaneous statements, their dispersal resulting in 'sonority streams' acquiring various emotional nuances in dependence of the tempo, register, timbre, vertical and horizontal density of the 'weaving'. It sounds as a 'thick melody', for the constituent voices merge together without underlining the upper voice as the leading one, though formally it is designed as such (Musical Example 7 A, B). At the first bars of his Symphony several black timbre lines gradually identified, one after another, through the vague rumble are not so lyrical as severe and gloomy. But even here you feel the extremely intensified lyrical expressiveness. Lyricism is manifest in the 'weaving' quite strictly following the subjective lyrical emotional experiences, which is not subject as it were to the 'squareness' of song form but has exactly such form. The emotional experience is inwardly agitated, its waves rising in the form of a pictorial plastic rather than traditional melodic line. The emotional tension is thus conveyed more authentically than in the conventional form of a melodic line.

The lyrical emotions are most varied in their content: an emotional pressure in Musical Example 7 B, an inner apprehension at the beginning of the ballet *Confession* (bars 3–9, 11–15), a seething current, a 'boiling' and spreading mass in Agitato of the first movement in the Symphony (bars 133–243), elucidation of the mass up to its glittering (Requiem, Part 5, bars 37–45), an even temper and serenity (the beginning of the Sextet) and so on.

The introduction of heaving 'weaving' usually proceeds gradually, voice after voice. Hence any degree of similarity with fugato, up to full coincidence. In his vocal music the voices as they join in repeat one and the same words, which enhances even more its similarities with Renaissance polyphony. The instrumental texture retains the effect of rhythmical and linear thematic imitations in any degree of distinctness. On the one hand, we witness here a new form of imitative and canonical technique used in the context of free rhythms and the aperiodical metre, and on the other hand — the effect of flowing gentle lines seemingly independent of one another in their stream.

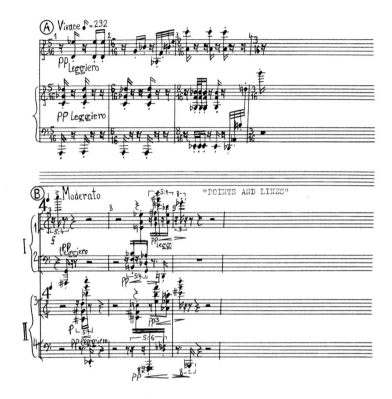

Ex. 8   *A* — Sonata for violin and piano 3rd movement, *B* — "Points and lines"

4.3. 'Shooting', 'Pricking' and Sharply Rhythmical Dots

The genre of 'shooting', i.e., quasi-unordered pointillistic simultaneous statement of accentuated staccato sounds or chords in all registers in turn, represents a kind of extremely syncopated tense 'music of action' (Musical Example 8 A). The dynamism with which the New Music entered the 20th century in the works of Prokofiev, Stravinsky and Bartók in this case flew into a new channel, achieving a higher level of musical energy. Behind the most sophisticated pointillistic texture you can easily discern its prototypes, like the finale in *The Rite of Spring* with its broken rhythms in the principal theme. 'Shooting' and 'pricking' have an extensive spectrum of nuances — from illusory splashes to powerful forcefulness (Musical Example 8 A, B).

A riot of passions raging in the finale of his Concerto for flute, oboe, piano and percussion is rendered through pointillistic 'exchange of shooting' by the participants who first engage themselves in separate 'biting remarks' and then come up to 'far stronger' expressions. In some cases the 'shooting' reaches the status of a genre devoid of the figurative meaning, this type of music becoming more conspicuous in the finales of Denisov's cycles (mention should be also made of

Ex. 9   "DSCH"

his third piece from *Three Pieces for Harpsichord and Percussion*; the finales of the Wind Quintet and the Oboe Trio, and the final piece from *Four Pieces for Flute and Piano*). But pointillistic dynamism could well suit the first movements of a cycle as well ('explosive' music of his Piano Concerto) and blend into different other contexts. The pointillistic 'shooting' sharply enhances the importance of rhythm in pauses. The 'silent durations' form their own rhythmical pattern. These are not pauses broken before reaching a climax but rather, on the contrary, sounds as rest-marks: the Piano Trio, 2nd movement (close to the end); the Clarinet Sonata; the ending of the finale in the Quartet for flute and string trio, and *Points and Lines*.

4.4. 'Dotting' and Pointillistic 'Splashes'

'Pricking' of sharp dots easily passes into pointillistic 'dotting'. For instance, such 'dotting' makes up a dotted background (like in a painting) from which suddenly emerges the silhouette of Donna Anna from Mozart's *Don Giovanni* (*Silhouettes*, 1st movement). The boundary between 'dotting' — 'splashes', on the one hand, and 'shooting', on the other, nevertheless remains. The difference is that 'shooting' presupposes an extremely tense rhythm while 'dotting' — a multilayered 'spot'. 'Shooting' delivers stabbing blows on the nerves whereas a sonoristic 'dotting' seems to stroke, albeit somewhat roughly (Musical Example 9).

'Dotting', as well as 'shooting', 'weaving', 'smooth threads' and other similar, essentially sonoristic, definitions, represent typological figurative characteristics of an artistic genre and at the same time some definite types of new harmony. In the absence of former triads and dissonance solutions there is no need for either chordal, or arpeggio-based or the conventional contrapuntal texture. The 'niche' thus formed is filled up with new types of harmonic execution. Here sonoristic polyphony produces the interwoven fabric, arpeggio-'dotting', arpeggio-sheafing, with romantic cascades of chords turning into 'pricking' and 'shooting'. But all these and similar types of execution constitute also some definite harmonic combinations but only in the field of new — dissonant and sonoristic —

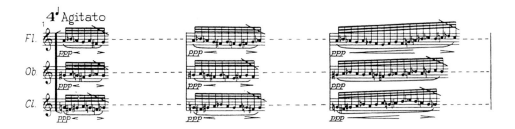

Ex. 10   Chamber symphony, 2nd movement

harmony. For instance, 'dotting' in the latter musical example is a unique, though not continuously self-identical harmony. Its structural function is similar to that of chord arpeggio in the old musical system.

4.5. 'Rustles'. 'Smooth Threads'

'Rustles', those weightlessly fleeting sonoristic passages with a great amount of sounds played in legatissimo, pianissimo, dolcissimo and allegrissimo, are still more caressing to the ear and gently and pleasantly 'stroking' (Musical Example 10). 'Rustles' often represent also a 'rolling cluster'. With sonority intensified, 'rustles' lose their illusory effect and turn into the elusively streaming smooth lines or 'smooth threads'. With slowing down the tempo and the 'threads' acquiring tonal tangibility, the latter may pass into 'lyrical weaving' the intonational similarity with which is latently inherent in the nature of 'threads'.

Gentle 'rustles' are the hallmark of Denisov's style in the 1970s and 1980s: weightless sonoristic arrays distinguish his concertos — for the cello, the flute, the piano and the violin, *Three Pieces for Harpsichord and Percussion*, Requiem, *Signes en blanc*, *L'écume des jours*, *Confession*, No. 2 (garlands of rustles), the first movement of his Symphony (in Agitato), and other compositions. 'Smooth threads' are encountered in the second movement of his Piano Trio, the first movement of the Sonata for saxophone, the song-cycles *Pain and Silence* (the first two songs), *Your Charming Image* (Part 7), *To Flore* (Part 2) and *On Snow Bonfire* (Parts 4 and 14).

4.6. Sonoristic Mixtures. Clusters

One of the latest trends in modern music is the striving for one-voice texture, usually with a virtuosic tinge in some bright and extraordinary sonoristic effects. Among Denisov's most favoured musical characters is a strictly monorhythmical mixture of several instruments, usually in a very fast tempo, with a melody having a passage-like character, while its mixture can be either precise or variational as regards the vertical confluences (Musical Example 11 A).

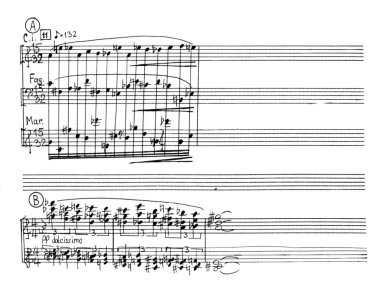

Ex. 11   *A* — Concerto for violin and orchestra, 1st movement, *B* — *L'écume des jours*,
love theme

Mixed confluences are fleeting so swiftly that the ear fails to catch them as chords as it were; they remain in one's mind as the brilliantly garish colours, the sweeping glittering threads.

Sonoristic mixtures are genetically related to the block chords widely developed by Debussy and his contemporaries. The swiftness of tempo radically changes the character of sonority, but these mixtures often occur also when the tempo is not so fast (the Piano Quintet). The principle of 'new one-voice texture' remains the same, but Denisov's specific feature is the character of selected confluences: sonority is founded on an array of sounds growing 'from down upwards' (not down from a melody) based on a major 7th interval, or the ordinary seventh chord. The tonal character is gentleness and full sonority (Musical Example 11 B).

The theme of love sounds exceptionally tender and utterly sensual. In many cases clusters also serve as a kind of sonoristic mixture. Their expressive significance is two-fold: they may represent the extreme thickening of the structure in the chord category[3], and in this case clusters sound extremely tense. But they may also arise as sonoristic thickening of a melodic line; then they become similar to sonoristic mixtures. See *Signes en blanc*, the beginning, and the Concerto for flute, 1st movement, bars 14–20.

4.7. Sonoristic Arrays

All these new types of music can be covered by the common technical term sonoristics, i.e., music of sonorities ('Klangmusik' in German). Its specifics come from the musical material in which the ear fails to distinguish separate

Ex. 12   Concerto for Flute and Orchestra, 3rd movement

pitches and intervals but perceives the tone-colour in its entirety as the emanci-
pated and enlarged timbre of a sound.

Denisov often turns to sonoristic arrays, though he does not base whole compositions on this particular tone-effect like, for instance, Ligeti (*Atmosphères*, etc.).
It is more typical for the Russian composer's style to make an occasional and
limited use of sonoristics. It is for him a certain property of music which is
effectively set off by its other properties and, in its turn, bringing them into bolder
relief.

Naturally sonoristic arrays appear more frequently in orchestral and vocal-
orchestral music. They may have the form of separate stiff sonority or, which is
more typical for Denisov, an agitated moving mass of sounds modulating in
timbre-colours, now thickening and then thinning out (Musical Example 12).

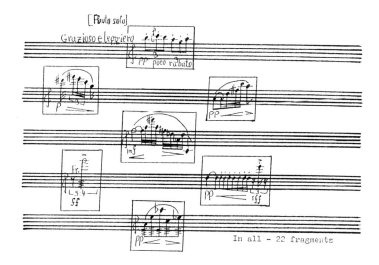

Ex. 13   *Silhouettes*, 2nd movement — Ludmila

The artistic logic of sonoristic arrays is regulated by constant expressive crescendos and diminuendos in different intersections simultaneously. Such sonoristic breathing in its essence is comparable to the expressive emotionality of a romantic melody.

4.8. Aleatory

Musical characteristics acquiring certain determinacy of an artistic genre are often closely related to the widespread types of modern compositional techniques such as sonoristics, pointillism and modality (the latter rarely used by Denisov). Following the emancipation of melody from the metrical framework of the traditional form, Denisov came to be tending to the aleatory freedom of musical texture. Out of various types of aleatory (for the composer's theoretical views see Chapter 5) he preferred 'controlled' and 'limited' aleatory. In contrast to many of his contemporaries, Denisov was not inspired by the idea of unfixed compositional structure. In a general sense the musical texture not fixed by a composer is fraught with approximation, levelling up or even excluding an opportunity for fine finishing touches to a composition. Such aleatory may even exclude the individual personality of a composer-creator who yields his role to the performer; the latter, not being an artist-creator, moreover, in a context of improvisation, is likely to fail to render high-quality material in no less perfect form.

Denisov with his principle of 'new beauty' allows no incompleteness or ambiguity in the texture or form of a composition. Yet, sometimes he does use aleatory which in his music represents a special, uninhibited world. His graceful *Silhouettes* (five pieces) are highly original in conception: out of a certain field of indeterminacies, as a result of some game, there emerge the contour portrayals of five famous musical females — Mozart's Donna Anna, Ludmila from Glinka's *Ruslan and Ludmila*, Liza from Tchaikovsky's *Queen of Spades*, Marie from Berg's *Wozzeck* and Liszt's Loreley. It is characteristic of Denisov that aleatory in this case has been used for strictly artistic purposes and not for its own sake. Aleatory here is designed to convey a quasi-chaotic state of the musical background. The portrayals of these women reveal two layers — a play on the unfixed musical texture and strict structural contours of the well-familiar melodies (Musical Example 13).

4.9. Traditional Artistic Genres

The above mentioned and similar artistic characteristic genres in Denisov's music most vividly reveal the individuality of his composition style. Their well-balanced application and highly individual tone-colours make listener perceive the composer's voice and personality in his music.

Starting our discussion with these innovations, we cannot fail to take into consideration the traditional genres as well, both classical and non-classical. These occupied a prominent place during the formative period of Denisov's style, retreating into a more modest background in the 1960s–1980s. Their role, however, is still noticeable, the renovation of the style disguising the similarity of traditional artistic genres in his music with their prototypes.

The traditional artistic genres primarily include the characteristic types of movements making up a sonata cycle, i.e., the musical types of sonata allegro, sonata adagio (or sonata andante), sonata rondo, and variations. To this category also belong the genre types of fugue, passacaglia and canon. Naturally, being expressive of typical musical content, all these types represent genres and at the same time some definite, also typical musical forms. The artistic genres also embrace some types of short instrumental and vocal pieces (toccata, chorale, romance, etc.).

4.9.1. Sonata genres are inherited by modern composers from the early music through academic education and independent verification of their value; hence a 'return' of post-avant-gardism to 'neo'-genres.

Initially Denisov assimilated the classicist type of sonata allegro through Shostakovich and Bartók. In his earlier compositions his adherence to this tradition is clearly obvious (String Quartet No.2, *Music for Eleven Wind Instruments and Kettledrums*, partly the Violin Sonata). But later on he strives to depart from the thematic types and structural principles inherent in the early music, renovating it through new rhythms and the corresponding individual patterns of dramatic development. In his concertos, sonatas and symphonies the initial allegro is regulated rather by the logic of psychological states and emotional impulses than by the realization of the classical idea of dialectical development.

The genre of sonata scherzo in Denisov's music has also been radically modified. A classical scherzo is a type of impetuous music, seemingly torn off from the earth and drawn back to it by the foot movements in a minuet-dance. In his *Music for Eleven Wind Instruments and Kettledrums* with its finale-scherzo Denisov still follows the classical prototype. But his later innovations completely transform the genre of scherzo from within. In this respect the second movement in his Piano Trio No. 2 is most revealing: its musical content is made up of incredibly tempestuous tonal lines. According to the formal definition, it coincides with the genre characteristic of 'scherzo'. But an essentially new artistic genre characteristic (see above) presented in the form of 'smooth lines' of sonorous nature prevails here over the songful nature of the classical scherzo. As a result, likewise in other artistic genres, the type of scherzo is being split into its new, individualized varieties.

The genre of sonata adagio in Denisov's music retains a tangible kinship with its classical prototype to the greatest extent. Adagio (andante) remains an inner, intimate world of human emotions. But in contrast to the classical adagio with its underlying focus on a song or aria with their verses and stanzas, Denisov conveys the key idea through a highly sensitive inner motion of the heaving sonorous weaving of voices with their gentlest 'whiffs'.

The classical final rondo lends Denisov's finales the genre type of rapid motoric movement, somewhat 'rolling' character, sometimes with 'shooting' of pointillistic tonal elements (the Violin Sonata; Concerto for flute, oboe, piano and percussion, the Oboe Trio, etc.).

Denisov virtually makes no use of minuet (and waltz as a later development), one of the favourite pieces of the classical cycle, directly associated with the daily or court life in the old times. A 20th-century composer would logically include foxtrot or blues in a sonata (like Ravel in his Violin Sonata). In contrast to Prokofiev who introduced an old genre, waltz, in the slow movement of his Sonata No. 6, Denisov simply ignores popular dances since common music is fraught with banal intrusions. Tchaikovsky could allow himself to try it, but not Denisov.

4.9.2. Fugue, Passacaglia, Canon are part and parcel of neo-classicism. Denisov inherited this infatuation from Shostakovich and at the early stage in his career paid a tribute to it in the Fugue in his Sonata for two violins. But since then he never came back to this type of music. It is hopeless to copy the concept of grand immobility of a thematic idea in the 20th century after Webern had finally broken down the trinity of pitch-rhythm-line, creating therewith a new perception of time. The ensuing new intonation of the music composed in the second half of the 20th century calls for different principles of sound organization. Therefore, the renovation of the ancient genre of fugue (like it was done by Hindemith and Shostakovich) is currently replaced by a similar splitting of this genre and turning it into something fundamentally new. It cannot be any longer defined as 'fugue', 'fugato', 'imitation' or 'canon' (though often it is close to one of them), but it still remains in close proximity to a traditional genre. Thus, at the beginning of Denisov's Piano Trio the 'weaving' of voices reveals the logic of imitation akin to the traditional fugato, nonetheless, the disconnected recurrence of intervals (pitches), rhythms and lines does not allow us to refer it to the same genre (Musical Example 14).

Similar transformations in the nature of an artistic genre are also inherent in other polyphonic types of music. (It stands to reason that the artistic genres, in contrast to the common ones, are most subject to such metamorphoses.)

Ex. 14   Piano trio, 1st movement

4.9.3. Other artistic and common genres find themselves in a similar situation. The types of genres tackled by Denisov also characterize his style, among them: concertos, motoric music (toccata, moto perpetuo, etc.), choral music (of a simple chord structure), instrumental recitative, solo-instrumental cadenza, the applied genres including dance (waltz and others) and march (both primarily in his stage music), and jazz (partly also in stage music).

As regards the artistic genres, the laws underlying their development in Denisov's music are the same as described above. It should be added that the concerto genre brings a strong influence to bear with him. The concerto principle of opposing a soloist and a group of performers, groups of soloists to one another, and solo playing against the background of rests or extended chords of the orchestra (group) is extremely widespread in his music. In contrast to quite traditional oppositions of 'solo-orchestra' in a concerto, the composer makes a wide use of the 'solo-group' opposition, as if reproducing the conventional contest in a miniature, both in his orchestral and chamber music. The concerto principle of such kind is well in line with the other features of Denisov's style, such as lucidity (rather than monumentality) of his tone, differentiated texture and a focus on micro-cells.

In addition to cadenzas typical in concert-playing, mention should be made of the still rarely encountered instrumental recitative (the Violin Sonata, 2nd movement) and a solemn (or pathetic) 'statement', which is akin to an instrumental recitative (*Fünf Geschichten von Herrn Keuner*, 1st movement). It shows the growing role assigned in the composer's style of thinking to the verbal principle, 'speaking music' and, besides, it reveals his latent kinship to Shostakovich's thinking (the same genres — instrumental recitative, cadenza, 'statement'). The genre of instrumental chorale as it is tackled by Denisov is more related to Stravinsky (*L'histoire du soldat*): see the beginning of his *Epitaph*. The chorale in the second of his *Three Pieces for Harpsichord and Percussion* is highly original: with each new sound the number of ringing tones increases by one, the growing vertical density forming an acute-angled triangle ('pictorial' hearing of Denisov's musical figures).

Despite the composer's fondness of jazz, he makes a rare use of its idioms. Natural jazz music is virtually encountered only once in his music: the plot of his opera *L'écume des jours* calls for the recorded performance of Duke Ellington. A typical basso of boogie-woogie is heard in the first story delivered in *Fünf Geschichten von Herrn Keuner* and in the finale of his sonata for saxophone. An occasional use is made of banal 'variety-stage' music whose 'modernist' treatment fails to conceal its origins (*La vie en rouge* in which banality is deliberately exaggerated; a march of policemen in the Intermezzo of *L'écume des jours*).

The general feature which distinguishes Denisov's approach to genres is a conspicuous prevalence of artistic types over the commonly popular ones and creative representation of genres over their natural reproduction. Thus, the genre nature of his music bears out the general tendency of his thought to elevate itself over the narrowly utilitarian treatment of musical imagery. His style is directed upwards and in this Denisov stands apart from the most trends of his time.

5. ON DENISOV'S ARTISTIC THINKING

As regards this major issue, we shall consider just a few general aspects associated with the concept of musical content.

For a true artist his whole life constitutes a continuous emergence of images and artistic ideas. Of course, it inevitably involves chance circumstances, commissions and money earning. But in the final analysis what really matters is the fruit of his creative thinking. The fact that while he was commissioned to write the opera *Cosi fan tutte* Mozart was asked not to touch on big social problems did not prevent him from producing a charming, most graceful and delightful theatrical performance based on a plot which would seem hardly worth of his effort. With Denisov the theme of his creative endeavours was taking shape gradually. Outwardly, his progression strikes with leaps into different directions. His undertakings are truly immense and varied: ranging from a poetical portrayal of the Incas' life, a modern version of a mass for the dead, a solo concerto in three movements, a romantic image of the young man, a parody of the Soviet songs, to recording the sounds of the Russian forests, scoring the French surrealism or the Orthodox *Gladsome Light*, and producing 'signes en blanc', 'black clouds', 'la vie en rouge' and a 'blue notebook'. Is there any theme in this motley of colours?

Yet, he has his theme. The content of musical imagery and all the sophisticated techniques inherent in modern composition are justified when a great artist is guided in his work by a search for solving a major philosophical task. In this respect the message underlying Denisov's creative work may be defined as the assertion of highly intellectual ideals in human life in the current context of the rapidly changing world. His spiritual principles are characterized neither by maximal approximation to austerity of a supreme ideal (like with Webern) nor a merger with the supreme moral and religious principles (like with Messiaen), but by his striving to embrace as fully as possible various aspects of the real life, keeping at the same time aloof from its mean and dark sides and being guided by the elevated and pure it has to offer. The creation of artistic tonal realities and objects in this spirit makes a concrete task posed before an artist. All the above mentioned zigzags in the composer's creative career can be united by this common message of his creations. The fantastic illogicalities in *L'écume des jours* reveal the 'absurdities' of our life and dissociation of the artist's high principles

In the text - "Snow-storm"

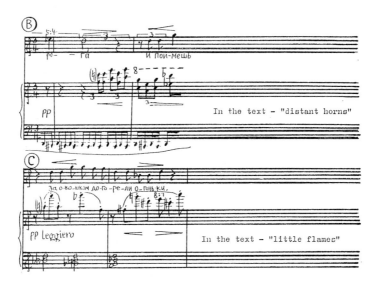

In the text - "distant horns"

In the text - "little flames"

Ex. 15   *On Snow Bonfire, A — No. 14, B — No. 4, C — No. 10*

from the 'foam' of the days, nonetheless leaving the sphere of tenderest (but not sentimental) heartfelt lyricism intact and closed in itself. Another content, but in the same vein, is intrinsic in his cantata *The Sun of the Incas*: a dazzling vividness of colours and captivating rhythms powerfully disclose the hard problems of the life in smart and hedonistically fascinating tonal images; it is the other aspect of the composer's same conception. Many of his compositions bear out some more aspects involved in it. Naturally, there is also room for making fun, perhaps, not even so insipidly and harmlessly in some cases (a satire on the official art in his show *The Ship Steams Past the Harbour*).

The content of concrete compositions is realized through their musical material, rhythm, harmony and weaving together the threads of voice-leading; also in the methods of development, form-building and an integral compositional structure. The message of the composer's art of which he is gradually becoming aware impresses itself on the results of his endeavours at each stage, beginning with a vague impetus for composition and up to the full completion of its structure. As a musical idea arises and the musical material is selected, everything gets imbued with the composer's intonation, i.e., the voice of his individuality comes to be embodied in sounds. In this way the composer's moral and aesthetic principles have their real existence in the rhythmical and melodic contours of a musical idea, the underlying harmonic forms of vertical and horizontal pitch relationships, in the methods of sound production according to the principles of various musical techniques — new tonal ('atonal'), serial, sonoristic, timbre, and pointillistic procedures.

The method of thinking in generalized musical entities — themes, motives and sonorities — prevails in Denisov's instrumental (both non-programmatic and programmatic) and vocal compositions. He does not seek, like Mussorgsky or partly Prokofiev, always to visualize a concrete object of musical expression. But concrete programmatic expressiveness is far from alien to him, particularly in music associated with the verbal text. In this case he draws on the key characters, states and separate words as the objects of representation. Thus, his song-cycle *On Snow Bonfire* contains samples of concrete expressiveness and representation (Musical Example 15 A, B and C).

His imagery is more generalized. The very title of his piece for two pianos eight hands *Points and Lines* contains an indication which may be interpreted as 'pictorial' imagery; it may also be regarded as a work of modern 'abstract' art.[4] The employment of symbolic definitions and quotations comes close to such 'abstract' imagery. The old tradition of 'lettered' themes-symbols (Josquin, Bach) was taken up by 20th-century composers (Berg, Prokofiev, Myaskovsky), developed further by Shostakovich (his monogram DSCH in a number of his compositions) and given a new impetus by the introduction of the collage technique and polystylistics. Thus, one of Denisov's compositions is frankly entitled *DSCH* and contains quotations from Shostakovich. A special role assigned to the note-letter D = Denisov came to represent D major.

Finally, another specific feature of Denisov's artistic thinking is a major part played by the methods borrowed from other arts, even most divergent from one another. One of them is speech. The relationship between music and the oratory art is an old-time tradition for the art of sounds, and rhetorics methods were used by composers living long since the times of Heinrich Schütz and Sebastian Bach, for instance, by Chopin. But Denisov and his contemporaries are drawn to speech as a companion of music because of the current disintegration of classical homophonic forms they are aware of. If a composer feels that one of the traditional *locus standi* is knocked out from under his feet, he has naturally to find support in some other means to express the movement of a musical idea. And music like speech with its introduction into exposition, story-telling (made up of several sections — 'periods') about 'developments' and a conclusion turns out to be a convenient and reliable form of thinking. For examples see the first movement of the Sonata for Solo Flute; Movement One of the Sonata for Flute and Guitar — 'Dialogue' ('conversation between two characters').

Perhaps, his contacts with another kind of art are even more characteristic of Denisov's thinking, primarily with pictorial forms of art. The composer often writes music as if he were drawing 'lines' and 'points' against a certain 'background'. It is very instructive to compare his *Peinture* for orchestra with his nonprogrammatic compositions, e.g., the Cello Concerto. *Peinture* is intended to give rise to certain associations. But his Cello Concerto in its larger portions is no less powerful than *Peinture* in arousing similar associative relationships. The beginning of the concerto is associated with several rounded figures in dark colours. The end represents a lucid sonoristic array in the genre of 'high lyricism' where through the interweaving of lines stands out a yellow-red sound in a joyous D major.

6. DENISOV'S MUSIC: HARMONY & THE PITCH-CLASS SYSTEM

When Denisov was a student he had some problems with harmony, like Prokofiev in his time. Later Prokofiev declared that he had made all academic science 'go to hell' with his *Scythian Suite*. Denisov could repeat the same about himself. But in his case we imply something different than harmony taught at school. Harmony is the art of well-coordinated sound combinations, the art of logical pitch organization. This is a new harmony. Respectively, tonality must be regarded as new tonality, too (but not what they teach at school on the basis of 1st, 4th and 5th degrees). New tonality is a system of pitch correlations with new elements (like, for instance, in Berg's *Lyric Suite* or in Piece No.3 from Messiaen's *20 Regards sur l'Enfant Jésus*). The matter involves the pitch system of musical thinking which is indispensable in music as the art of sound production. The multicoloured palette at the disposal of a modern composer's pitch system comprises several layers brightening up each layer now and then: tonality (the centralized system) with a triad as the key element; new tonality with various sound objects acting as elements of a system (a dissonant complex, a group of complexes, single sounds, etc.); a series-based system; a system of sonorities used as musical material.

The essence of his pitch system is well in keeping with the overall conception of Denisov's music. Its basic principles are founded on the predominance of two harmonic structural types — the twelve-note and new tonalities. The first involves treatment of separate sound degrees of the chromatic scale as self-contained units, the second one attaches major importance to the logically centralized pitch structures in composition.

Like all the Soviet composers of his generation, Denisov started with the traditional major-minor tonality, more gentle than that of Shostakovich and Prokofiev during the same period. But within it he already showed a tendency to the twelve-note tonality: thus at the end of the 'love' scene in his opera *Ivan the Soldier* a twelve-note 'sweet' chord is played in arpeggio. Upon embarking on the twelve-note tonality as the principal method of thinking, the composer does not part with the conventional tonality in his consciousness, though he does not use it. He just passes over onto another level of his creative mentality. Tonality (old) is still living in his innermost, invisibly present whereas it is completely removed in the reality.

The same approach prevails almost in all of his compositions of the 'avant-garde' period. As he had broken through into a new domain and found an opportunity for natural existence without any idioms inherent in the old tonality, Denisov for a long time made no use of it in his artistic music (though he readily employed it in the applied music — e.g., in his incidental scores to films). Hence

Ex. 16   *A* — Trio for oboe, cello and harpsichord, 3rd movement, *B* — the same

a specific feature of his serial, sonoristic and other 'atonal' music: it is not just atonal but rather 'anti-tonal' (to quote Stravinsky). This explains a wide use made by Denisov of new tonality. Moreover, as the time passes he is more willing to invariably bring into the foreground his 'own' tonality: Denisov may well be said to be a 'composer in D'.

There is nothing contradictory to the new tonality in Denisov focusing on various types of the twelve-note procedure. Limiting down harmony to the elementary lessons in the classical functions of T–S–D makes a great amount of musicians entertain a false idea of complete departure of modern (harmonic) techniques from 'harmony'. But if you bring into mind the innovatory techniques of the late Romantic harmony (Liszt, Mussorgsky, Rimsky-Korsakov, and Scriabin in his works written before 1910), some of these techniques anticipated the musical thinking based not on triadic combinations, but on other groups of sounds, dissonances. Therefore, a transition to the techniques of the New Music may occur in the evolutionary way, whereas the thinking in series or similar sets and groups turns out to be quite natural. This is what happened to Scriabin in his later years, Schoenberg, and Webern in his early compositions. A composer living in the second half of the 20th century comes even more naturally to the twelve-note procedures. In the case of Denisov, conventional tonality came to be replaced by the twelve-note procedures and other, more freely chosen set-forms. Serial technique provides a composer with a fully reliable and powerful method of thinking — a varied recurrence of a set. In tonal music repeated is a definite constant complex of chords and a diatonic scale while in the twelve-note tonality — a chosen dissonant set is recurred in horizontal and vertical lines. The first

Ex. 17 *A* — "Trois fragments du Nouveau testament", 2nd movement,
B — Piano quintet, 1st movement, *C* — "Wishing well",
D — Two songs on poems by I. Bunin, No. 2 — "Autumn",
E — Five studies for bassoon solo, No. 1, *F* — "The ship steams past the harbor",

Ex. 17 (continued)   *G* — "Dead leaves",
H — "Légendes des eaux souterraines", 5th movement — "Le ciel",
I — Concerto for piano and orchestra, 2nd movement, *J* — Concerto piccolo

form-building principle of repetition is unequivocally predominant in the twelve-note procedures of such type. In this sense different techniques of varied repetition within the twelve-note framework have the same function in musical composition which was previously inherent in all common (absolute in this respect) tonal techniques —classical, Baroque and Romantic.

A sample of new tonality in Denisov's music may be found in Musical Example 16 A, B. The key tone 'a' is not perceived as the principal sound of tonality but it embellishes by its predominance the sonoristic 'splashes' and 'rustles' taken as the central elements of a tonal form. The ending in 'a' imparts to a sonoristic piece the effect of completeness as if a musical idea goes back to its origins.

Similar relationships between musical material also act in any lesser dimensions. Even more simpler are the tonal-centralising effects of melodic emphasis (see Movement One in the Quartet for Flute and String Trio).

A similar approach prevails as regards concrete textural realisations of the pitch system — harmonies. It is typical for a modern style to mix the forms once divided into various types of part writing — homophony (songs, rondo, sonata) and polyphony (fugue, canon, passacaglia). In addition to mixing these traditional types, new techniques, primarily serial and sonoristic, are widely used and brought into interaction. Denisov's idea of 'new beauty' comes to involve a care for the beautiful tone of music as a whole. But this beauty should captivate the listener by its uniqueness and thereby freshness. Denisov's new harmony displays a wealth of his favourite textural forms, with the traditional category of 'chord', though not avoided, but being merely one of them. To somehow distinguish the textural forms of new harmony, imperceptibly passing into one another, let us define them in the following musical example, these definitions not claiming at all for their general theoretical application (see Musical Example 17 A–J):

A. While discussing Denisov's style we cannot assert that a chord in his music retains its traditional value of the principal harmonic category. But as one of numerous harmonic forms a chord is subjected to different treatments. Here a chord represents a monorhythmical mixture of a melodic line. Its function is purely colouristic (in some respects it is remotely reminiscent of jazz 'block-chords'). The composer strives for constant changes in the chord structure, not necessarily through a cadence.

B. Polychords are constantly used by Denisov. More often than not a polychord has two layers (in this case in the piano part, bar 2), which could be represented in the form of two monorhythmical lines, 'right and left hands'; in a kind of counterpoint these lines are opposed by a sonorous melody of the strings, with their mixture producing sort of a bow 'super instrument'.

C. Polyharmony involves not only chords but other groups of sounds, too. Here the mellow tone of a stiffened chord serves as the background for the refined patterns of scattered dots and separate finest finishing touches.

D. In the same way as the category of chord is being split into its several characteristic types, the traditional arpeggio is turned into several textural forms. Here we observe an 'array', i.e. a gradual 'collection' of notes in a set, which cannot be viewed as a certain chord because of the unequal status of its notes remaining as if in different dimensions.

E. One-voice texture abounding in leaps often represents the adjacent chord fields played in arpeggio.

F. From the distinct fields of chords played in arpeggio harmony passes over to illusory and indistinct forms. Now the contours of chords are clearly perceptible, and then harmony becomes obscure. The interchange of thickening and thinning makes such contour fabric most charming.

G. The sonorous dotted spots of the smallest sparkles make up a harmonic unit which is far from a 'chord' and akin to a cluster. But this cluster, gently glittering, resembles a play of colours. Through such cluster there often emerge intervals or their combinations: a minor 7th in the first and a hexachord in D minor in the last.

H. 'Weaving' typical of Denisov's style represents a fine harmonic and thematic elaboration. It is a kind of polyphonic harmony but in a cluster-like sonority: a single sound seems to be 'swelling' and then 'thinning', its sounding now widening (up to a third) and then being once again reduced down to a narrow dissonance. All of this is designed to convey the fine lyrical emotions.

I. Lyrical expressiveness can become still more refined through micro-chromatics. 'Lohengrin' heights (at the same note 'a') are shining in the most delicate and pungent colour nuances.

J. The operation with sonoristic colours makes the way for the tone-colours of indeterminant pitch. Such tone-effects — mostly grandiose mystical or charmingly magical — turn into the most extraordinary harmonic material.

All these or similar complexes of sounds and sonorities make up a multi-coloured picture of Denisov's harmony.

7.   RHYTHMICS

A creative approach to rhythms makes no less weighty part of the New Music than harmonic innovations. The birth of a musical idea takes place through its formation in time with its corresponding realisation in a certain rhythmical pattern. His awareness of a new rhythm emerging in the initial phrase forced Denisov to depart from traditional rhythms as too inert. Later on, a restless search for his own identity led to a fairly definite range of the rhythm types to be used by the composer for many years to come. For all its diversity, his music is characterised by a stable rhythmic style.

A point of departure in Denisov's stylistic evolution reveals its kinship with the Shostakovich rhythmics. A musical idea is cast in a song-like rhythm, though complicated by various violations of the simplest symmetries — its non-square-ness and variable measures. It is evident in his earlier compositions such as, for instance, his Symphony in C major and the Sonata for two violins. Rhythmics is thereby elevated over the formulas of simple ordinary genres, with the tone of music becoming more serious and impressive.

In his first compositions based on the twelve-note procedures Denisov's rhythmics remain approximately the same (in *Music for Eleven Wind Instruments and Kettledrums* and his Variations for piano). His enrichment of rhythm was largely influenced by Bartók and Stravinsky. In his music outlined in bars, albeit variable, the rhythmical process is often based on a group of sounds unfolding through the multiform changes in the metre, through augmentation and exclusion of the pitches or time-values and formation of derivative groups (similarly to Stravinsky's rhythms, for instance, in the finale of *The Rite of Spring*). Thus, in the

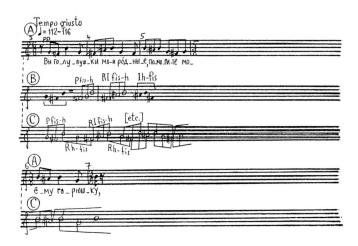

Ex. 18   "Wails", 1st movement

first movement of *Wails* the three-note groups in the vocal part are developing 'chokingly' in 'small triangles' 'clinging' to each other (with the intervals indicated in the number of semitones). See Musical Example 18:

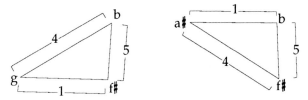

The technique of rhythmical development (directly linked with Stravinsky's *Les Noces*) turns here into a twelve-note procedure, which distinguishes Denisov from the classical dodecaphony of the Second Viennese School (compare also with Part 4 in his *Wails*). But simultaneously a certain boundary of complication is trespassed breaking away a sense of unity inherent in the metre within a measure — at first it was violated and now ignored altogether. Initially one can associate the renunciation of a measure with the solo playing of instruments in a concerto (e.g., in the second movement of the Concerto for Flute, Oboe, Piano and Percussion). But the out-measured rhythm becomes in general one of Denisov's characteristic rhythmical types (*The Sun of the Incas*, 4th movement; the Sonata for Solo Violin, wholly based on the out-measured rhythms).

The out-measured rhythm was followed by the ametrical rhythm, i.e., a free rhythm without the indicated time-patterns for notes (see the second movement of the Sonata for Saxophone, *Crescendo e diminuendo*). The interpretation of the points outlined by the composer is left up to a performer. As a matter of fact, it is already an aleatory technique. The performance would depend on a mode of rhythmics and metrics employed by a musician on different occasions, which may radically change the message of one and the same succession of pitches. Naturally, freedom of compositional texture may extend over the whole fabric, thus giving rise to aleatory rhythm as it were (in the second movement of *Silhouettes*). Aleatory music cannot be predicted before performance and its concrete rendering may be presented to the audience in varying degrees of rhythmical freedom: one performer may be capable of treating the indicated pitches metrically and, as a result, we shall hear, for instance, the predominance of the customary variable metre; another interpreter will render the material in a deliberately arhythmical vein, i.e., all the sounds will turn at his hands to be of varied and even non-proportional length, producing an irregular (irrational) rhythm.

Let us consider once more the beginning of *DSCH* (Musical Example 9). A sonoristic block is outlined accurately in rhythmical terms. However, it is futile to try to catch a 'splash' or 'dotting' as a discursively thought-out structure similar to a polyphonic one used by Shostakovich or Hindemith. The very principle of rhythm here is different. The traditional European rhythms are of additive nature: to properly hear it and perform, one has to proceed from the smallest time-value which can come within a measure of all the larger ones (herein lies the rational and discursive nature of rhythmical thinking). The sonoristic blocks (Musical Example 9) are not made up of the smallest time-values, but rather of asymmetrical macro-units. In other words, the 'smallest' value here is the full length of a block. Such rhythmics are partial, or to be more precise, it is the rhythmics of separate particles of one indivisible large entity. The shape of a block is composed of finely calculated processes underlying the formation of a macro-unit of a definite extent in time and space (horizontal and vertical arrangement), also in stereophonic 'depth' (in the third dimension of musical fabric) and the processes of definite intensity — their growth and decline in a certain parameter, the speed of the processes and so on. Here we witness a new concept of rhythm. The partial rhythm involves formation — development (i.e., various kinds of expansion and narrowing of the soundscape, thickening and thinning of musical fabric; all as a single process in the undivided temporal stream) and completion (i.e., the end of a process, its 'rounding-off' or 'running dry', or a sudden 'rupture' of the rhythmical stream).

The innovatory approach to rhythm as a process brings forth a kind of its synthesis with the traditional additive principle. The course of this 'synthetic rhythm' (the synthetic principle of rhythm) in conformity with its two-fold nature allows for arbitrary approaches to one or another 'shore', i.e., predominance of one or the other principle depending on a given artistic conception. Such fluctuations, however, are characteristic of the 'genres' which are widely used by Denisov and the corresponding forms of musical texture ('weaving', 'dotting', 'rustles', etc.).

Let us return to the above mentioned piece — Piano Trio (Musical Example 14). In the final analysis rhythmical relationships allow for a discursive adjustment of all durations, though the common denominator (time-value) is likely to come down to an infinitesimal unit. It is inaccessible to hearing and further on, at the level of the smallest time-values, it is neither possible to perceive rhythm as their addition (for this rhythm is partial and not additive). The musicians orient themselves on a general measure — the quarter note pulsating in their mind (but not in real measures). Measurement of all rhythmical patterns at the level of the

Ex. 19   Sonata for clarinet solo, 2nd movement

quarter note is an indisputable sign of additive rhythmics. However, hearing without looking into a score virtually excludes perception of the even rhythmical pulsation and, on the whole, the partial principle comes to prevail again: you hear the 'rolling', out-measured indistinctly flowing chords of 'weaving', now expanding and then narrowing, now a bit more rapid and then a bit slower, moreover, the microcells of each voice fancifully being reflected in one another, adding to it a rhythm of microthematic repetitions into the bargain.

In the finales of Denisov's cycles you come across a type of swift, sharply rhythmical music with its characteristic incessant variability of a measure. The composer seems to be trying to produce the effect of ultimate syncopated dynamics from making his music devoid of the basic time-patterns and a definite measure. Let us call this type of music 'broken rhythm' (Musical Example 19). Similar rhythms in Stravinsky's music (*The Rite of Spring* and *L'histoire du soldat*) presuppose a different conception of musical form, which is based on the asymmetrical variation of the leading motives. As for Denisov, his main principle is never to repeat the rhythmical and thematic cells.

Simple unordered rhythmical rows belong to the category of new types of rationally calculated rhythms. Thus, for instance, the song *Twilight*, a musical setting of Ivan Bunin's verse, proceeds throughout against the background of the soprano piano pedal colourfully painted in arithmetical progression (in semiquavers): 8 7 6 5 4 3 2 3 4 5 6 7 8 (nine times). The enigmatic impassioned voice is ringing out without mixing with the mellow expressiveness of other sounds, and flowing beyond them. In serial music the simple unordered rhythmical rows acquire the implication of the unordered rhythmical series (see, for instance, Part 4 of the cycle *Italian Songs*).

8.   SERIAL TECHNIQUE. 'SERIES ELABORATION'. SERIALISM

The twelve-note composition method is the destiny of 20th-century music. However, owing to the vastness of the twelve-note musical field it gives rise to most dissimilar kinds of fruit. And the Second Viennese School remains for composers precisely a school, rather than a style. Igor Stravinsky on the threshold of his conversion into the twelve-note faith thus spoke about dodecaphony (of the Viennese type): "It is like a prison. Dodecaphonic composers have to use the twelve notes. As for me, I can use five, eleven or six notes — as many as I will. I'm not obliged to use all the twelve notes. I'm doing it according to my wish preferring to remain within tonality."[5] In his article about dodecaphony Denisov got engaged in polemics with the official attacks against the New Music, calling for a differentiated approach to the twelve-note procedures used by Schoenberg, Nono, Stockhausen and other composers.[6]

Denisov's serial technique is not a certain stable totality of compositional procedures. As far as we know, none of dodecaphonic composers have ever been fully consistent in their endeavours.[7] No modern composer adheres to 'orthodox' dodecaphony, being guided by the principle of looking for new resources inherent in the twelve-note field, up to a return to the sets out of 'five, eleven and six notes' (according to Stravinsky). Denisov, as we have pointed out above, showed a tendency to the twelve-note composition method in his earliest works. In 1961 he turned from tonality to dodecaphony, though he has never discarded tonality altogether. In *The Sun of the Incas* he resolutely gave up pure dodecaphony in favour of freer serial and sonoristic procedures. His compositions dated back to the mid-1960s reveal some elements of serialism with not only one parameter (pitch) being serialised but also rhythm, articulation and dynamics. At the same time there was a tendency to washing out serialism and passing over to sonoristics and aleatory and transforming various sets into a quite narrow complex of the motto-thematic intonations. Hence a diversity and mixed character of the serial technique used by Denisov.

In his set-forms one can discern the recurrent combinations of sounds which bear out the essential features of his composition style. The key role is assigned to the semitone intonations attracting the composer's ear with their expressive refinement, which is somewhat reminiscent of Webern. A semitone is, besides, a typical interval of the twelve-note interval system — hemitonics. Denisov makes a frequent use of triads and occasionally of tetrachords.[8] His later works reveal the enhanced role of paired semitones (1.1) in varied combinations introducing one of the composer's favourite melodic phrases known as the EDS intonation.[9]

In his first dodecaphonic compositions Denisov adhered to the standard procedures similar to Schoenberg's. His great respect for the pioneers of serial music is felt in certain tinges of 'classicism' of the Schoenberg type, for instance, in the first movement of his Sonata for Violin and Piano and in some passages of *Music for Eleven Wind Instruments and Kettledrums*. In style and sonority this music is close to the traditions of Shostakovich and Stravinsky, but the character of treating a series as an entity makes it imperceptibly akin to Schoenberg and through him to the 18th century.

Denisov's conceptional composition — *The Sun of the Incas* — ushered in the period of his highly original twelve-note technique differing from Schoenberg's tenets. The opening 'Prelude' makes an exposition of 'non-classical' dodecaphony. Its main principal row is based on an unrepeated treatment of the twelve-note system. The composer selects his own method of weaving musical fabric out of the qualities inherent in the twelve-note universe and a series for each composition or part (of a cycle) or separate section of musical form. It may be also regarded as logical continuation of the serial principle underlying the individual selectivity of a musical structure: from now on, not only a series is selected for a composition but also a progression from a set-form to musical texture. Denisov started with a breakdown of a series in the development sections

Ex. 20 *The Sun of the Incas*, 1st movement

and in transitional passages. The prelude falls into three movements. In its exposition everything is strict and accurate. The incomplete statements emerge in the middle, development, section (from bar 13). The series is based on the changed order in the succession of notes (contrary to the principal tenet of 'classical' dodecaphony) and on its division into separate fragments like in sonata-form or in a fugal episode (Musical Example 20).

The after-climax in this piece (bars 38–41) offers a 'settlement' of the structural tension: the series retrogrades to the initial note 'a' in the French horn, with this sound playing thereby the role of 'tonics' in this new tonality.

The third movement of *The Sun of the Incas*, Intermezzo, is based on the first hexachord in the series a – f – e – bb – b – c♯. The figure six becomes here a kind of master key: 6 notes of a sub-series, 6 instruments, the principal metre with digressions largely around six — 7/8 and 5/8, and in the concluding cadenza six instruments play the six-note motives (bar 26). In the final 'Song About the Little Finger' the charming 'primitive' or 'childish naivety' is conveyed through special treatment of the series: notes of its segments (e – c – b, gb – ab – bb, eb – db) are repeated over and over again, turning their scales into modal ones. The series is presented in the vocal part over the whole 13 bars and distributed over 40 syllables of the text. Hence a drastic modification of its intonation structure, with the series acquiring almost a diatonic character, something akin to a folk song.

The next stage in Denisov's serial technique, which occurred in the mid-1960s, involved serialism, production of inter-parameter connections and relationships. In the final song 'Assumption' in his cycle *Italian Songs* six pitches, the first half of the series, interact with the other integral parameters (Musical Example 21). The initial two blocks conjugate 6 pitches, 6 time-values and 6 gradations in dynamics:

	P:					
Bars:	1			2		3
Pitches:	Ab	D	Eb	G	A	Bb
Durations of initial statements /in ♪ /:	4	3	5	2	1	6
Time-values /in ♪ /:	25	5	9	21	9	17
Intensity:	f	pp	pppp	mf	ppp	mp

Ex. 21   "Italian Songs", 4th movement

The initial block turns into a kind of 'theme' or 'motive' of the piece repeated with certain development (see bars 3–6):

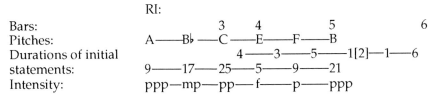

It can be easily seen that the second hexachord of time-values represents a realignment of the first hexachord. The same happens to dynamics. Their coupling is overlapped by the series of durations of initial statements. The first group of serial blocks embraces six hexachords (bars 1–12), the second — four tetrachords (bars 12–18); the further development is more complicated. The mysterious pointillistic modulations are consonant with the mystical character of the text: 'and over the fogs in the valley there arise three dead tsars'.

In Denisov's serialism some passages in his *Wails* and *Fünf Geschichten von Herrn Keuner* are particularly significant. Thus, the third part of the latter cycle based on the texts of Bertold Brecht bears the 'philosophical' ironical title 'Form and Content'. The serial composition technique involves serialisation of more than one parameter. In this case we observe serialisation of the following three parameters: (1) pitch, (2) rhythm of time-values and (3) dynamics. The fancifulness of the arising thereby pointillistic texture is in symbolic conformity with the text dwelling upon a picture wherein 'the objects were shaped in a very strange form'.

In the context of the Soviet musical life Brecht's bitingly satirical text ridiculed the endless debates unfolding in 'the advanced Marxist science of aesthetics' on the problem of conformity in form and content, which allowed the official hacks to instruct the creators. Herr Keuner made the following remark on the subject: "Caring too much about the form one loses the essence of the objects", recalling how once, when he had been working as an assistant gardener, he had to trim a laurel plant in a tub trying to make it look a perfect ball. At long last he got what he wanted, though the ball turned out to be too small. "But where is the laurel?" — exclaimed the gardener in distress.

The third part in this composition also has 'a very strange form'. The singer does not sing but recites his text accompanied by a quartet of wind instruments as the most expressive in timbre out of the seven instruments involved in this cycle. This part has the following pitch series:

bb – eb – ab – a – d – f# – c – c# – e – g – b – f

The pitch rows are conjugated by a bridge (coincidence of the last note /or notes/ of one row with the initial note /or notes/ of the other row). This piece has the following 12 pitch rows:

Bars 1–11	P bb – f	R b – e	I a – d	RI ab – eb
Bars 11–22	R eb – ab	I c# – f#	RI c – g	P d – a
Bars 22–35	I a – d	RI ab – eb	P bb – f	R b – e

The pointillistic texture is strangely asymmetrical, being devoid of recurrences in rhythmical motives. Time-values are fixed at certain pitches. Thus, the note 'bb' is invariably a quarter, the note 'eb' is a semiquaver, and 'd' — a demisemiquaver, and so on, with each pitch having its own duration. These time-values have been derived, however, from the series used in the first movement in the following way:

The ordinal number of a note in the series indicates the number of demisemiquavers in each note:

Series in Part One:	d	eb	g	e	ab	c	f	bb	b	f#	a	c#
Number of a note in the series:	1	2	3	4	5	6	7	8	9	10	11	12
Time-values:	♪	♪	♪.	♪	♪♪♪	♪.	♪.	♩	♩♪♪	♩♪♪	♩♪♪.	♩.

Correspondingly, the series in Part Three gets the following time-values:

Pitches	bb	eb	ab	a	d	f#	c	c#	e	g	b	f
Series number in Part One:	8	2	5	11	1	10	6	12	4	3	9	7
Time-values:	♩	♪	♪♪♪	♩♪♪	♪	♩♪♪	♪.	♩.	♪	♪	♪.	♩♪♪.

In the other set-forms — R, I, RI — and in any pitch position these note values are steadily retained in each of serial voices, i.e., in the succession of pitches in a given note-row. But since the notes of a single-track row are distributed among two, three or four parts of instruments, there arises a problem of intervals between the notes in an ensemble of voices. For their regulation, use is made of two tables of number notation with the note-rows written down in a chromatic order from Prima and from Inversion (retrograde forms are to be read from right to left):

P:

bb	eb	ab	a	d	f♯	c	c♯	e	g	b	f
8	2	5	11	1	10	6	12	4	3	9	7
9	4	11	8	2	3	12	1	7	5	6	10
6	7	8	9	4	5	1	2	10	11	12	3
12	10	9	6	7	11	2	4	3	8	1	5
1	3	6	12	10	8	4	7	5	9	2	11
2	5	12	1	3	9	7	10	11	6	4	8
4	11	1	2	5	6	10	3	8	12	7	9
7	8	2	4	11	12	3	5	9	1	10	6
10	9	4	7	8	1	5	11	6	2	3	12
3	6	7	10	9	2	11	8	12	4	5	1
5	12	10	3	6	4	8	9	1	7	11	2
11	1	3	5	12	7	9	6	2	10	8	4

I:

bb	f	c	b	f♯	d	ab	g	e	c♯	a	eb
8	7	6	9	10	1	5	3	4	12	1	2
9	10	12	6	3	2	11	5	7	1	8	4
6	3	1	12	5	4	8	11	10	2	9	7
12	5	2	1	11	7	9	8	3	4	6	10
1	11	4	2	8	10	6	9	5	7	12	3
2	8	7	4	9	3	12	6	11	10	1	5
4	9	10	7	6	5	1	12	8	3	2	11
7	6	3	10	12	11	2	1	9	5	4	8
10	12	5	3	1	8	4	2	6	11	7	9
3	1	11	5	2	9	7	4	12	8	10	6
5	2	8	11	4	6	10	7	1	9	3	12
11	4	9	8	7	12	3	10	2	6	5	1

The diagonal digits thus derived, when converted into the note values, provide for the rows of durations which determine the time of the alternate initial statements in the instrumental parts. With two instruments involved, we have two alternate elements (the set-form P bb – f):

duration of initial
statements: 8   4   8   6   11   9   10   5

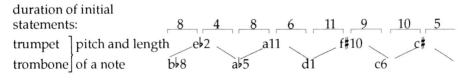

trumpet ⎤ pitch and length   eb2   a11   f♯10   c♯
trombone⎦ of a note   bb8   ab5   d1   c6

(the subscripts at the notes indicate their time-values in demisemiquavers)
Musical Example 22.

With a third instrument joining in, the notes of the set are uniformly arranged, also alternately, within trichords, with four instruments — within tetrachords. In case the length of a note and the duration of initial statements coincide (see the first note 'bb'), the next note is stated immediately like a legato. In case the

Ex. 22   *Fünf Geschichten von Herrn Keuner*, 3rd movement

duration is longer than the length, the adjacent notes are divided by a pause; if it is less, the preceding note is overlapping the subsequent note (see the coupling a–d in bars 1–2).

A complex of durations of initial statements, making up four diagonal lines, becomes a kind of 'rhythmic theme' of the piece which may also involve its retrograde statements. Differences between rhythmic themes in the prima and inversion diagonal lines, which may arise occasionally, are nevertheless perceptible by the ear. In the Prima cycle there predominate larger time-values, not shorter than a quarter (a single third is an exception) while in the Inversion cycle there are a lot of small time-values (one of them containing five semiquavers and the other — three dyads and two triads).

The rows of durations of initial statements are overlapping the pitch-class rows, and for the exception of the beginning of the exposition, do not coincide with their disposition. The diagonal rows of durations are progressing in the following way (the arrows showing the direction of diagonal rows):

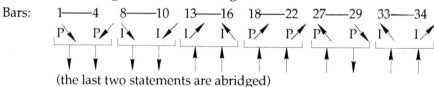

(the last two statements are abridged)

Finally, the whole dynamics of the piece are serialised. Likewise the length of a note, its intensity is ordered in Set 1

d	e♭	g	e	a♭	c	f	b♭	b	f♯	a	c♯
1	2	3	4	5	6	7	8	9	10	11	12
pppp	ppp	pp	p	p̌>	mp>	mf>	f>	f̌>	ff>	fff>	ffff>

The nuances are not mechanically accurate throughout. Of the form-building importance is a radical change in the system of the volume gradations in Bar 17. Herein end the first six statements of the pitch-class set and begins the second hexachord of serial statements. The dynamics of sounds of definite pitch is changed for the opposite, bringing forth a retrograde statement of the dynamics set. The note 'd' acquires the 12th degree of intensity, ffff, the note 'e♭' — the 11th, fff, and so on. The last note 'e' sounds forte >.

To attain the desired effect, the performers have to be absolutely precise in rhythms and dynamics. In this case the wind quartet accompanying the recitalist produces a tonal fabric which captivates by a mysterious logic of its flashing dots.

A multiform free treatment of a series as a 'common thematic source' of a composition (Denisov's principle) presupposes a multitude of procedures defined here as 'elaboration' of a series, in contrast to the 'classical' type of 'statement' propounded by the Second Viennese School. These procedures include omission or realignment of notes, their recurrence, the rooting of one note-row into another, fragmentation (the use of separate segments), interversion, multiplication (a multiple repetition of one interval or a segment), the transition into free development (not involving a complete statement of a note-row), a polysemantic approach to the arrangement of a note-row (may be regarded as any note-row), and combinatorics (when out of two note-rows of the same set-form a hexachord of the one note-row turns to be complementary to a hexachord of the other). A wealth of such serial procedures is inherent in the impossibility (for the most part) to clearly discern the statements of a series from the first to the last note even in orthodox dodecaphony. The actual results of serialisation are more important than the formal approach to complete statement of the whole series.

Denisov, being in full command of the serial technique, usually selects for his compositions a certain twelve-note set. At the beginning it is often easily discernible. But then, sometimes almost immediately, the development of a piece is guided by the principle of a 'common thematic source'. By providing for the intonational integrity, the set-form performs its formal structural function. At the same time it is already another principle differing from dodecaphony. Strictly speaking, a 'series' constitutes a note-row whose repetitions give rise to the entire musical texture. As for Denisov, in his compositions written in the 1970s–1980s a twelve-note row often represents a thematic impulse rather than a series as it were. Paraphrasing the words once uttered by Denisov about dodecaphony, we may assess his own twelve-note technique in the following way: "It will never do to bring everything together and call it 'serial technique'." It is unquestionable evidence of the impact made by the post-Webern principles of composition which are also characteristic of Boulez, Stockhausen and the modern times in general.

What is being built on the basis of a series or outside it, with Denisov, often involves the EDS complex and the above described sonoristic compositional procedures. A frequent use of these techniques brings back composition today from too exaggerated individualisation (when any new work seems to have been written by another composer) to stability of stylistic idioms employed by a given composer in which we discern his own unique voice. Perhaps, the stabilisation period in Denisov's style exhibits too many repetitions... Though, one should not take a one-sided approach to that matter, for the composer is striving, even within the range of his acquired stylistic complex, for ample diversity in many of his works.

Notes to Chapter 3

1. Akin to a polymodal splitting of G major at the beginning of Bartók's ballet *The Miraculous Mandarin*, with an ostinato of the scale g – a – b – c – d – e – f# – g# in the violins.
2. Sergei Taneyev. *Florid Counterpoint in Strict Style*. Leipzig, 1909, p. 6.
3. The last stage in the process of thickening: the octave → quint octave → triad → 7th chord → non-chord → cluster.
4. For example, Salvador Dali's *Madonna* at close range seems a dense field of big dots while from a distance you can see the image of God's Mother.
5. Cited from the book: *Igor Stravinsky: Publicist & Interlocutor*. Moscow, 1988, p. 413.
6. See the article: Edison Denisov. Dodecaphony and Some Problems in Modern Composition Techniques /*Music & Modern Times*, Issue 6, Moscow, 1969, pp. 524–525/
.
7. Perhaps it was only Webern who from his Op. 17 to his last, Op. 31, never 'returned' to anything else, but his style was also evolving until in his famous Symphony, Op. 21, he discovered a world of the New Music as it were.
8. Some of Denisov's sets are given in Appendix 3.6.
9. We single out the EDS intonation because it is not only very expressive and easily discernible but also very characteristic of the composer. Many of his compositions written since the mid-1960s are permeated with this intonation, among them: Cello Concerto; Violin Concerto, 2nd movement; the song-cycle *At the Turning Point* (the last song in this cycle ending with the three-note cluster eds); *L'écume des jours*, the beginning of Scene 1 and the final scene in which you can hear a chord repeated several times and whose lower notes make up the EDS intonation (a kind of Denisov's signature-tune).
    To all appearance, it is no accident that this intonation means Edison Denisov's monogram. It is noteworthy that these three letters present the sole possibility of expressing the composer's name in musical terms. Repeated twice, they form a three-note motive and its inversion:

Edison	Denisov
e d s	d e s
Primus	Inversus

CHAPTER 4

MUSICAL COMPOSITIONS

Edison Denisov is such a prolific composer that a survey of all his compositions would prove too bulky and lengthy. Moreover, separate aspects of some compositions have already been covered in the previous chapters. The matter of genres in his music has also been looked into in Chapter Three.

The main purpose of the present chapter is to give concise annotations of his major works and their general description. The order of their presentation is based on the genre principle.

1. STAGE MUSIC

After his early opera *Ivan the Soldier* Denisov for nearly two decades never returned to the genre of theatrical music. In 1980 he came out with three works for the musical theatre written one after another — two operas (*L'écume des jours* and *Les quatre filles*) and a ballet (*Confession*). Their common feature are romantic plots and vivid lyrical nature of their music. As for the opera *L'écume des jours* , together with the earlier written song-cycle *La vie en rouge*, it represents a separate page in Denisov's creative output. Both compositions have been based on the texts of Boris Vian, a French novelist and dramatist, whose works had made a strong impression on Edison Denisov.

1.1. EDISON DENISOV AND BORIS VIAN

Boris Vian was one of the prominent personalities of his time. Though he had lived a short life (1920–59), he tried his hand in most diverse fields: he was a prolific writer, as well as jazz trumpeter and a jazz music critic, a chansonnier of his own songs, a sculptor and a painter.

But first and foremost he was known for his literary works whose diversity of genres is truly impressive, including novels, plays, poetry, short stories, operatic librettos, critical articles on jazz, song lyrics and translations of his own and somebody else' works into English. His personal contacts with Jean-Paul Sartre, Simone Beauvoir and Eugène Ionesco had a strong influence on the trend of his literary pursuits. In his works one can discern the echoes of Sartre's existentialist philosophy and some elements from Ionesco's theatre of the absurd.

His highly original literary style has left its imprint on Denisov's music predetermining the emergence of new imagery in his creative world and the corresponding elements in his musical language.

Boris Vian's novel 'L'écume des jours'

He was writing this novel during the hard years of World War II. Completed in 1946, it became one of Vian's most popular literary works.[1] In a condensed form it reflected the sentiments of the French intellectuals in those years — their scepticism, lack of faith into life, grotesquerie, and their nostalgic yearning for beauty and poetry in their daily existence.

Its main idea may be defined as a clash between one's dreams and the reality, as man's failure to oppose a certain fatal force. Vian's world is split into two parts. On the one part, there live people with their loves, warmth and comforts. On the other part, there exist some forces alien and hostile to man, a weird city, urbanistic nightmares, motor cars and the omnipotence of money. Vian's characters are living in a certain abstract city in abstract time. They meet, fall in love and daydream as if shutting themselves off from the reality in their narrow circle. But upon facing the reality once and coming down to earth, they find themselves carried away with a maelstrom of life ('the foam of days') and, being powerless to withstand it, they perish.

This fundamentally romantic idea in the middle of the 20th century got complicated with many subsidiary trends. Thus, it was quite in the spirit of the times to introduce in the novel the images of two key personalities in French literature of the 1940s — Jean-Paul Sartre, who came to figure in Vian's novel under the ironical name of Jean-Sol Partre, and Simone de Beauvoir represented as Duchess Beauvoir. The scenes of the novel involving these two characters are tinged with grotesquery.

The novel's major dramatic features are based on the following idea: "People don't change, only things change". This idea predetermines the presence of two dramatic lines running across the whole work. One of these lines is permanent, concerning the life of human beings who, according to the author, are not subject to change but living under the changing circumstances in which they find themselves. The second line is variable. It involves the life of things and inhuman creatures. The mouse, a major character in the novel at first is playing merrily in the sunrays sharing the common state of peace and happiness. During the illness of the main heroine the mouse hurts itself with glass and walks on bamboo crutches with its feet bandaged. After Chloé dies, the mouse commits suicide. The room in which the main characters are living is also changing. A spacious and brightly lit at the beginning, it takes the spherical shape, then becomes more and more narrow and eventually the ceiling merges with the floor. The bed on which Chloé is lying, with the progression of her illness is sinking down to the floor.

The novel *L'écume des jours* is multilayered. It incorporates three plot and semantic layers whose interaction and interweaving lend to the work peculiar colouring: the first layer is lyrical; it is related to the pair of the main characters — Colin and Chloé; the second layer, associated with Jean-Sol Partre, involves the other pair of the characters — Chick and Alise; and the third layer is 'absurdist'. Some scenes in the novel are associated with a theatrical trend which got currency in Paris in the 1950s. The techniques borrowed from the theatre of the absurd are designed to stir up the reader, striking his imagination and giving rise to the most vivid and unconventional associations. Indeed, Chloé's illness is felt more acutely when it is presented to us not in its ordinary implication (T. B.) but in a most extraordinary interpretation: a water-lily is growing in one of Chloe's lungs and such illness should be treated not with medicines but flowers hostile to the water-lily, whose scent is to kill it. During the surgery operation performed on Chloé a water-lily three metres long is cut out from her lung. In this case a water-lily becomes a symbol of illness. Vian's poetic vision makes it possible to view the flower as the direct cause of human death.

This novel has a tragic denouement. All of its main characters are perishing, but the reader is not left with the feeling of irreparable loss and hopelessness. After all Vian finds something invaluable and worthwhile in this world — it is love and jazz while all the rest, in his view, is doomed to disappear as ugly things.

Edison Denisov's Opera 'L'écume des jours'

The Story of Writing the Opera and Its Libretto

The opera was completed in 1981, but it had been conceived back in the early 1970s when Denisov first read Vian's novel and was attracted by its 'lyricism and the writer's open and naked soul'. The world premiere of the opera was given in March 1986 in Paris.

The libretto was written by the composer himself in French (Denisov believes Vian's language to be very musical). In contrast to its literary source, the opera's libretto focuses largely on its lyrical aspects, losing the multilayered nature inherent in the plot of Vian's novel. The composer devoted his undivided attention to the principal lyrical line. His opera captivates the listeners primarily by its strikingly lyrical intonations.

In addition to the novel and a large amount of lyrics taken from Vian's own songs, the composer introduced in his libretto some other texts too. Thus, the final girls' chorus was set to the anonymous text from a collection of religious songs, while the tenor's prayer in Scene 13 of Act 3 was borrowed from the funeral service. The Latin texts were used in two scenes: Scene 2 in Act 1 delivers some of the masses *Credo* and *Gloria*, while Scene 13 in Act 3 contains extracts from *Agnus Dei* and *Requiem aeternam*.

A brief description of the opera's scenes is given in Appendix 3.1.

Traditions in *L'écume des jours*

In view of the French plot, the language of the opera's original source, and its genre designation (lyrical opera), it is quite natural that the basic traditional line would be traced back to France and the genre of the French lyrical opera in particular. Below we consider the specific features which make Denisov's opera akin to that tradition:

– The very plot in its main outlines is reminiscent of some 19th-century operas, e.g., Verdi's *La Traviata* which had also imbibed main characteristic traits of the French lyrical opera.[2]

– The feelings and experiences of two main characters are brought into the foreground. It is in fact a duo-opera, though it involves a lot of other characters;

– A mixed type of the opera since through scenes in it alternate with separate items;

– Alternation of lyrical scenes with those depicting daily life to create the background for development of the main action;

– Use of various operatic forms such as arias, ensembles and chorus as well as the presence of the motto theme of love, an indispensable element in a lyrical opera (see Musical Example 11 B);

– Melodic nature and the role of a melodic line in the opera.

Denisov is convinced that the key role in an opera belongs to the text and vocal intonations. It is no accident that the composer insists that the opera's text should be translated into the language of a country where it is to be produced. Emphasis on the importance of the text and orientation to its perceptibility are also rooted in the French tradition, specifically in Debussy's operatic aesthetics. The general atmosphere of his opera *Pelléas et Mélisande*, its serene lucid ending and the absence of any dramatic climaxes — all these characteristics may also be attributed to *L'écume des jours*. Even the type of the opera with its predominance of vocal principles over instrumental ones turns out to be similar (another coincidence in defining both operas as lyrical drama).

The influence of Wagner's *Tristan und Isolde* is also visible in this opera, though Denisov rejects musical drama as an operatic type. This traditional line is most conspicuous in some through scenes and particularly in purely orchestral fragments which often accompany its major developments.

Quotations & Allusions

Quotations and references play a major part in the opera. Their stylistic range is limited mainly to Duke Ellington's songs. As a matter of fact, all of them are mentioned in Vian's novel and in this respect offer musical rendering of the writer's text.

One more quotation — the motto theme of languor from opera *Tristan und Isolde* — stands apart. It appears in Scene 9, Act 2, performed by a saxophone, trumpets and trombones in a somewhat revised, as compared to Wagner's, jazz vein. Its use may be explained in two ways. On the one part, according to the plot at this moment Colin is reading for Chloé a love story with the happy end. And the appear-

Ex. 23   "L'écume des jours", act II, scene 9

ance of this motto theme in such arrangement, as the composer's bitter irony, gives rise to gnawing doubts about the truthfulness of all what is unfolding on the stage. On the other part, Colin and Chloé may be associated with Tristan and Isolde: and though the story which Colin is reading has the happy end, in reality the tragic destiny of the heroes has been predetermined (Musical Example 23).

The allusions used in the opera have two historico-stylistic reference points. The first of them is associated with the 20th century: it is jazz and songs of French chansonniers (the policemen's chorus in Act 3); the second one goes back to the early monodic music (in Scene 2, Act 1, the solo tenor is singing the prayer *Et in terra pax* in the spirit of a Gregorian chant).

The quotations and allusions fulfil three main functions in the opera: to concretise the author's ideas (the quotations are used not on their own but make part and parcel of the unfolding action); to impart a kind of local colouring to convey the British and American orientations of the French young people in the 1940s; to serve as an expressive factor in stylistic contrasts.

The Main Operatic Elements

The opera *L'écume des jours* falls into scenes and intermezzos making up two dramatic planes developing on a par. The scenes form the foreground representing the principal dramatic plane. The fourteen scenes in this opera by their prevailing mood and character may be tentatively divided into three types: the scenes of action (wherein predominate the scenic action and the intensive unfolding of the plot), the scenes of state (staying in one inner state) and the scenes of reflections (talks on philosophical subjects, expression by the characters of their views and attitudes).

The intermezzos make up the second, subsidiary dramatic plane. Closely related to the scenes, they have their own auxiliary functions, the connecting lines and associations in the imagery and themes (e.g., Intermezzos 5 and 6 are intended for the orchestra to convey the urbanistic nightmares, while Intermezzos 4 and 7 are assigned to the chorus). The role of intermezzos in the integral dramatic pattern of the opera involves the following three basic moments: development of the plot, delineation of external circumstances and creation of the inner mood. Intermezzo 8 (between Scenes 12 and 13) stands apart. Here we come across a case of interaction or, to be more precise, even switching from one dramatic plane into the other. Up to this moment all the main developments of the plot took place in the scenes. In Act 3 the denouement in respect of one of the characters (Alise) occurs not in a scene but during an intermezzo (Alise sets fire to a book shop and herself perishes in it).

The Main Dramatic Functions

Denisov's opera is a dramatically coherent entity presenting an intricate complex of various interacting dramatic principles and plot lines. The following four dramatic functions come naturally in *L'écume des jours*: exposition (Scene One in Act 1 has even Colin's 'entry' aria), the start of the plot (Scene Three in Act 1, the main characters' meeting), development (the whole of Act 2) and epilogue (the last scene of the opera).

But the above four functions are virtually indispensable in a dramatic work and in this respect have nothing new to offer. The specific features of Denisov's opera involve two other functions — denouement and culmination. Let us consider these two factors:

- a dispersed denouement extends over the whole of Act 3 owing to the multilayered nature of the plot. It is a succession of the main characters' tragic end:

Scene 12 – Chick Intermezzo 8 – Alise	denouement of the line associated with Jean-Saul Partre
Scene 13 – Chloé Scene 14 – Colin	denouement of the lyrical line
Scene 14 – the Mouse	denouement of the 'absurdist' line

– the absence of explicit culmination; of course, the opera has separate climaxes but they, first, fail to attain the level of culmination and, second, occur at the beginning of the opera and therefore are not psychologically perceived as culmination points (since nothing has happened yet). To such climaxes we may refer two scenes in the first act: Scene 2 — because of its sharp division into two parts (a waltz on the skating-rink and the death of a skater) and Scene 4 which is a lyrical climax (a kind of peaceful culmination).

There arises a paradoxical situation. On the one hand, we witness obvious intensification of the tragic element. Before our eyes throughout Act 3 all the main characters are dying. On the other hand, the absence of conspicuous dramatic culmination smoothes over that tragic quality. Our emotions remain approximately at the same level throughout the opera. Anticipation of the main characters' death in Scene 2, Act 1, is also conducive to that experience. Besides

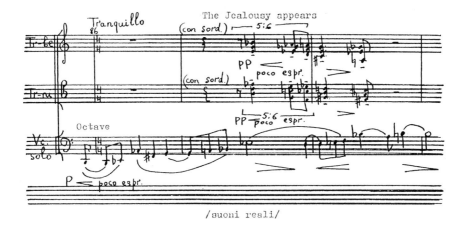

Ex. 24 "Confession", scene I

we learn about Chloé's grave illness in Scene 7, Act 2, i.e., as early as in the first half of the opera. Beginning with this scene, the main heroine is gradually dying. This gradualness does not involve any sharp emotional outbursts. Our sensations have been prepared for a tragic twist of the plot. And all the developments in Act 3 come falling on the psychologically prepared soil, not catching us unawares. Hence the sensation of even emotionality inherent in this opera.[3]

1.2. THE BALLET *CONFESSION* (1984)

Denisov based his ballet on Alfred de Musset's novel *La confession d'un enfant du siècle,* one of the most revealing literary works from the golden age of Romanticism. The main character of the novel is a young man suffering from 'the sickness of the century' whose main symptoms are disappointment, boredom and loneliness. Leading a dissolute life in the world of intrigues and love adventures and racked by passions and jealousy this young man comes to experience a genuine feeling; yet, even if fails to fully transform his sick soul.

The ballet's libretto written by Alexander Demidov delineates the fine and fragile nuances in the emotional states of its main characters. Denisov makes Octave a passionate, tender, sincerely loving and painfully sensitive man desperately looking for harmony in his feelings. The ballet came to incorporate some new characters, not to be found in Musset's novel. These are Octave's companions representing in an allegorical form the traits of his character — Pride, Hope, Jealousy, Melancholy and Conscience. Episode One: "After the curtain goes up Octave's figure gradually emerges from emptiness as if from non-existence. Approaching us slowly from the depth he seems to be entering life, having no experience of misery or disappointment yet. We watch the birth and 'formation' of his dance — a dance of man preoccupied with exploration of the surrounding world.

"Then there arise Octave's companions, the permanent companions of humanity. At first it is Pride: it seems to be teaching him 'keep straight', showing him his way, stirring ambitions, calling for disobedience and trying to impress upon him that the most important thing in life is self-confidence. Pride arouses Hope. The latter is teaching him to be guided by his noble impulses, she is impetuous in her movements, beckoning to him to follow her, but her flight is 'cut short' by Jealousy. In a broader sense it is doubt and lack of self-confidence unexpectedly aroused in his soul. It is haunting Octave and 'entangles' him as soon as he begins to cherish a beautiful hope. It deprives his dance of its divine flying quality, giving rise to suspicions and bringing him down from the heavens to earth. And then Melancholy sets in in Octave's heart, doleful and sad, enlightening and comforting him. And slowly, in solemn static motions, Conscience comes up to the youth, turning his thoughts to the eternal issues, the transitory nature of life and the importance of 'not losing oneself' in its fuss" (cited from the ballet's libretto).

The first number in the ballet is exposition of the characters of Octave and his companions. It consists of three sections: Octave alone, Companions, and Octave surrounded by his Companions. Each of the Companions has been provided with its own imagery and characteristic thematic material: Pride with its willful six-part chords, Hope with soaring sonoristic whiffs and trembling trills, Jealousy with enveloping imitations of a web of doubts, Hope with songful lyricism, and Conscience with grand bell-like sonorities. After separate exposition of each character they come all together (from bar 115). The themes are 'fighting' one another, each Companion striving to take hold of Octave and attract him to itself. The keynote of the multilayered texture is permeated by the motto theme of the main character (Musical Example 24).

The ballet has 16 scenes:
1. Octave
2. Masquerade
3. Octave and Desjenais   Act One — 'SICKNESS'
4. Octave's Monologue
5. The Tavern
6. Octave's Loneliness
7. Duet of Octave and Hope
8. Brigitte   Act Two — 'HOPE'
9. Fever
10. Bacchanalia
11. Duet of Octave and Brigitte
12. Octave's Doubts
13. Phantasmagoria
14. The Masks' Round Dance   Act Three — 'ENLIGHTENMENT'
15. Parting
16. Epilogue

The ballet has two culmination points: No. 11, a lyrical culmination, and No. 13, Phantasmagoria. According to the traditions of an integral dramatic form, several through lines are outlined, for instance, lyrical duets (Nos 2, 5 and 11), Octave's delirium (Nos 9 and 13). The ballet has also several recurrent themes: in the first place it is the motto theme of Octave (as well as his motto timbre — the cello), then the motto theme of Octave's friend, Desjenais (who appears in Scene 2), and the themes of his Companions passing throughout the ballet.

The ballet's through lines and its scenic and musical associations are visible from the following scheme:

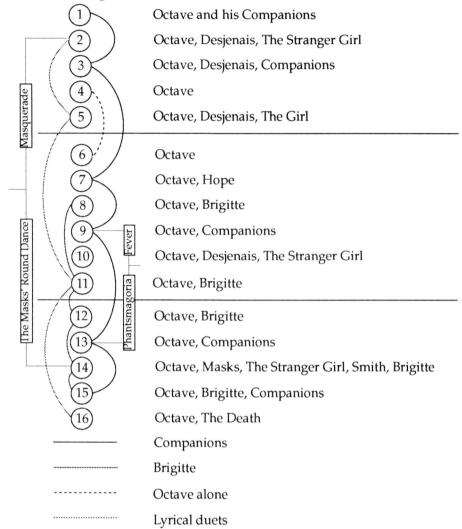

1	Octave and his Companions
2	Octave, Desjenais, The Stranger Girl
3	Octave, Desjenais, Companions
4	Octave
5	Octave, Desjenais, The Girl
6	Octave
7	Octave, Hope
8	Octave, Brigitte
9	Octave, Companions
10	Octave, Desjenais, The Stranger Girl
11	Octave, Brigitte
12	Octave, Brigitte
13	Octave, Companions
14	Octave, Masks, The Stranger Girl, Smith, Brigitte
15	Octave, Brigitte, Companions
16	Octave, The Death

—————— Companions

------------------ Brigitte

- - - - - - - - Octave alone

····················· Lyrical duets

In his ballet *Confession* Denisov was striving, in his own words, to avoid the applied dance quality and produce not a show consisting of separate numbers but a large symphonic canvas in three movements. His first ballet was staged in Tallinn in 1984 (by the ballet company of the 'Estonia' theatre, with Tiit Härm acting as director and the principal male dancer).

1.3. THE OPERA *LES QUATRE FILLES* (1986)

Out of Denisov's theatrical works his opera *Les quatre filles* is distinguished for its chamber cast of performers (four soloists — two sopranos and two mezzo-sopranos, and the occasionally appearing chorus) and its chamber-like music. The opera has six scenes; its performance is most effective in small theatres and auditoriums which would set off certain mysteriousness and irreality inherent in its plot and music.

The opera is based on Pablo Picasso's play of the same name. It has no plot in the conventional sense of the word: in the course of the whole action the girls are playing and dancing in the same garden either in the sunshine, under the rain or in the moonlight.

The opera's libretto written by the composer in French also includes some verses by the French poets René Char and Henri Michaux to lend Picasso's play some elements of tender lyricism and sensuality. Denisov believes that childhood renders the most complete and clear perception of the world and that it is in childhood that a person experiences the strongest sensations. Hence his attraction to that plot. The keynote of the opera is eternal beauty and light so characteristic of Denisov's music (for brief description of the opera see Appendix 3).

2. WORKS FOR ORCHESTRA

2.1. *PEINTURE* (1970)

This is the first large-scale orchestral composition written by Denisov after nearly a decade of his preoccupation with chamber music. The initial conception was to produce a symphony in three movements: Movement One was to be entitled 'The Red Room' after Boris Birger's painting (what is now known as *Peinture*), Movement Two — 'Small Black Fish' after a painting of Yuri Vasilyev, and Movement Three — 'Dance' after Boris Kozlov's painting. But this conception has failed to be completed in full, producing just a separate piece under the title *Peinture* devoted to the work of the Moscow-residing painter Boris Birger. In the composer's own words, in this piece he sought to translate Birger's manner of painting, his colour technique and some general principles of composition into the musical medium. The piece lacks any concrete 'plot' programme. In his annotation to this composition Denisov writes: "As in Birger's pictures, the subject is placed in the centre of the musical process, determining both the general composition and the different stages of development in which even the minor phenomena appear to be subordinate to the culmination point of the composition, which is essentially its plot."

The orchestral texture of the piece draws a close analogy between the tonal mixture in music and a palette of colours in painting: in good orchestral mixtures combination of a particular range of timbres and clear-cut intonational lines may produce a completely new tonal quality the same as in good painting a finely selected palette may produce a new colour quality. In his *Peinture* the tutti of the full orchestra (large, massive tonal spots) is combined with fine lines of solo instruments. As a result, the sounds seem to be now thickening and then thinning. Shortly before the end the strings are divided into a multitude of parts: 16 of 1st violins, 12 of 2nd violins, 10 violas, 8 cellos and 6 double-basses. And the vast movement of self-sustained sounds (with the range extending over more than four octaves) gradually disperses and disappears (Musical Example 25).

His *Peinture* concentrates the specific features of orchestral technique which characterizes Denisov's other compositions for orchestra. For instance, in his piece *Bells in the Fog* the orchestra is treated not as a mass of musical instruments but rather as a palette of multifarious timbres and instrumental colours while in his exquisite *Aquarelle* for the string orchestra the gentle timbre of the strings seems to be ramified in numerous solo lines. And it is no accident that these orchestral pieces bear the titles adjacent to the figurative imagery of painting.

2.2. CONCERTOS

Denisov turned to the concerto genre in the early 1970s and since then it has played a major part in his creative output. But long before that he viewed it as too spectacular; besides he disliked virtuoso performance. So a priori his attitude to the concerto had been negative. The composer was firmly convinced that he was never going to tackle it. Later on Denisov, however, changed his mind. All of a sudden the concerto turned out to be very dear to him and the concertante style became a very characteristic principle of his instrumental thinking. If we call to mind some of his chamber compositions written in the 1960s, we shall glimpse some signs of the concerto genre in his early works such as, for example, his *Ode* written in a vivid concertante style, and his *Romantic Music* with its undeniable features of a double concerto, which gave rise to his later double concertos.

Denisov has to his credit 12 concertos (let alone his earlier Chamber Concerto) for different solo instruments, among them the cello, piano, violin, viola, oboe, clarinet, flute, saxophone, and guitar. In many cases these concertos have been written expressly for particular performers.

The concertos written in the 1970s are the best in this genre. Varied in form, the concertante level and the principle of correlation between the solo instrument and the orchestra, all these compositions represent a kind of experimentation within this free and flexible genre.

THE CELLO CONCERTO captivates by its heartfelt lyricism. As a matter of fact, the concertante style as contest between the soloist and the orchestra is not so conspicuous in it. Denisov himself believes this concerto to be an essentially orchestral work (in the type of his *Peinture*) in which the cello is not opposed to the orchestra playing the role of the concertante protagonist, with almost equal status being accorded to the oboe d'amore, alto flute, vibraphone and electric guitar.

The instrumentation of the Cello Concerto is refined. The woodwind section presents not its basic instruments but only their varieties such as the alto flute, piccolo clarinet and double-bassoon; five saxophones came to replace French horns. The orchestra includes also the 'ringing' metallic percussion instruments, harp, celesta, and electric guitar.

A major part in the dramatic intonation of the concerto is assigned to the BACH anagram contained in its note-row. This theme acquires the greatest importance in the middle movement (bars 112–116). The note-row itself is used in the composition not as the basis of pitch organization but as its intonation axis: it is subject to sonoristic modifications and may be compressed within a cluster of quarter notes (from bar 123).

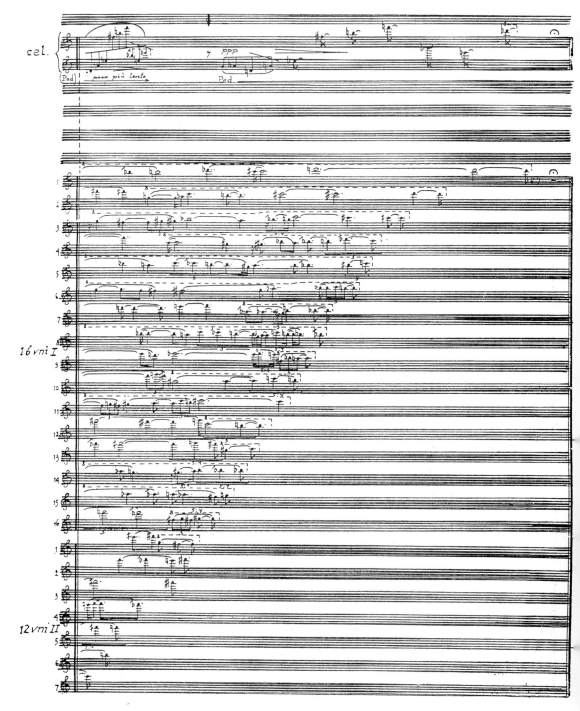

Ex. 25   "Peinture"

The form of the concerto is characteristic of Denisov's extended one-movement works. It is built as a three-part composition with transitional passages (the form of a large Adagio):

LENTO   ANIMATO   LENTO
from bar 1   from bar 85   from bar 167

The coda is crowned with the finest sonoristic colours (with separate glimpses in D major) of the soaring strings interspersed with occasional touches of the percussion instruments.

THE PIANO CONCERTO is the only one of Denisov's concertos to follow the traditional specifics of the concerto style to the fullest.

The concerto falls into three movements (according to the type fast — slow — fast). The outer movements are closely interlinked, both starting even with the same signal of trumpets. In Movement One the piano is opposed to the orchestra and used largely in the pointillistic form (with 'scattered' leaps). The orchestra employs the following three types of musical material: clusters, quasi-jazz chords by saxophones and brass instruments, and scale-like lines of the woodwind instruments, making up the moving clusters. The first movement is virtually devoid of any colours imparted by the strings.

The second movement is an intermezzo. In contrast to Movement One with its extended intervals, the whole material here seems to be compressed. The main interval is a second, with the prevalence of the strings.

The compositional ideas get their realization in the finale, with jazz elements coming to predominate in its development (Free Jazz, according to Denisov, bordering on modern music). The saxophone and trumpets are playing solo cadenzas arousing the sensation of freedom and ease. Ensemble playing appears to be prevailing. For instance, the piano and four saxophones (from Figure 21) playing together seem to represent a deliberate insertion from a work of another composer. The finale also rounds off the aleatory line (in the string section) which has been outlined in the first movement.

At the close of the finale the mounting noise and the aleatory 'chaos' are coming to outdo the soloist. The fully expanded tutti is cut short by striking a tam-tam (as in Movement One).

THE CONCERTO FOR FLUTE AND ORCHESTRA is the first concerto to be accompanied by a chamber orchestra. It was written on the request of Aurèle Nicolet. The concerto falls into four movements closely interrelated in the common dramatic idea and motival development of a twelve-note series. This development is so intensive that in the first movement, in addition to the form of sonata Allegro, there arise some signs of variations:

		sonata-form:	*variations:*
bars:	1 – 12	exposition	Theme and Variation No. 1
	13 – 16	transition	
	17 – 75	development	Variations Nos 2–4
	76 – 92	recapitulation	Variations Nos 5–6

The outer movements of the four-part cycle are very close in their music (both starting with the same phrasing of the flute). A major part in these movements is assigned to micro-intervals used for expressive purposes. The structure of the first movement is transferred at a larger scale onto the structure of the entire cycle: Movement Two involves intensive development of the flute part now distinguished by great leaps and new timbre techniques (the beating of vents); Movement Three — the solo of the flute and the strings (development of the cadenza principle); Movement Four — a radically modified recapitulation of the cycle bringing back the music and instrumentation of the first movement but with the intrusion of the material from the two intervening sections.

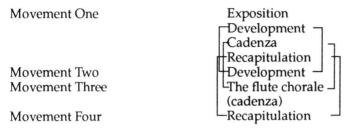

The third movement calls for special consideration. When Denisov was writing it, he got the news of Dmitry Shostakovich's death. He was so grieved that it found its manifestation in the chorale of Movement Three which is, according to Denisov, a kind of homage paid to Shostakovich (though it has no direct links with the great composer's music).

THE VIOLIN CONCERTO is one of Denisov's best. A drive to write a violin concerto had arisen long before Denisov set down to composing it. But Denisov believed that a violin concerto was a very serious genre (in view of the violin concertos of Brahms, Tchaikovsky and Berg) and you should undertake it when you had been fully prepared for it inwardly. Denisov considers his violin concerto to be one of his most successful compositions.

The concerto's two movements are of unequal status in their functions. The first movement represents in a broader context a kind of overture to the second, principal, movement. These two movements — Allegro risoluto and Adagio — are sharply contrasting in their substantive meaning and expressing two fundamentally different emotional states. Their unification is based not on the principle of confrontation between its dramatic imagery and lyrical line; the second movement directly ensues from the first one (as another part of the same soundscape), as its outcome and apprehension of the developments unfolding in Movement One.

The first movement comes as a 'shock' to the listener, with its harsh 'uncomfortable' music progressing continuously and resolutely (ff sempre). The ostinato ends only upon reaching the culmination point.

The second movement is the 'endlessly' flowing cantilena of Adagio. For many years Denisov had been entertaining the idea of writing a composition with 'a large and continuous Adagio'. He tried to do it in his first concertos. But, as the composer himself believes, he came most closely to it in the second movement of his violin concerto.

The main developments unfold shortly before the end with the emergence of a quotation from Schubert's *Morgengruss*. The principle of its incorporation is reminiscent of a similar technique in the Finale of Berg's Violin Concerto. At its initial appearance Schubert's music is cut short by the violin's protesting and restless phrases. Then the quotation begins to be modified subjugated to the basic material of the movement. It comes out in C major, but with its recurrence D major imposes itself on it (Musical Example 26).

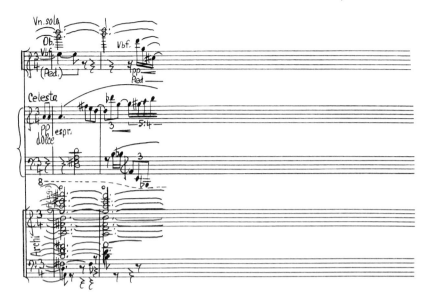

Ex. 26   Concerto for violin and orchestra, 2nd movement

Schubert's melody sheds special light on everything which has been unfolding in the concerto before its emergence. Schubert's 'morgengruss' symbolises the beginning of a new life, light, harmony and emotional peace.

The first movement is divided into three sections; these are three 'waves', each with its own culmination point and each climax being higher than the previous one. The ostinato of the solo instrument is interrupted only thrice, at the culmination points, each time in a similar way: the phrasing of the solo violin is contrasted by the sounds produced by a group of concertante instruments (marimba, cor anglais and bassoon). This group is treated as a three-voice instrument. During the second culmination this group is joined by flutes and clarinets, and in the third culmination — as well as by trumpets. Another concertante group of instruments playing in Movement One includes four French horns placed at both sides of the platform and delivering the interrupted unison performance of canons (producing a kind of stereo-effect).

Exposition	Development	Recapitulation	
Fig. 1–25	Fig. 26–37	Fig. 38–51	
1st culmination	2nd culmination	3rd culmination	
Fig. 23–25	Fig. 36–37	Fig. 48–50	

A characteristic feature of the three-part second movement is its flowing cantilena. Its sections have no clear-cut endings, smoothly taking one from another. The second feature is an extensive coda generalizing the impressive conception of the composition. The coda starts and ends with Schubert's melody.

Exposition	Development	Recapitulation	Coda
bars 1–60	bars 59–92	bars 91–152	from bar 153
	Piú mosso, agitato	Tempo I	Molto tranquillo

Within the same years, in addition to the violin concerto, Denisov produced his CONCERTO PICCOLO, a highly original composition written expressly for the saxophone player Jean-Marie Londeix and 'Les percussions de Strasbourg'. The concerto is intended for one saxophonist and four saxophones: one and the same performer plays alternately the saxophones of various ranges (soprano, alto, tenor and baritone). The soloist's virtuosic part is accompanied by a vast multicoloured set of percussion instruments producing the soundscape of extraordinary freshness and artistic expressiveness.

In his CONCERTO FOR FLUTE, OBOE AND ORCHESTRA, written for Aurèle Nicolet and Heinz Holliger, Denisov once again had his cherished dream about 'a large Adagio' come true. The whole of the concerto constitute a continuous and expressive Adagio lasting 32 minutes. The composition is based on dialogues. Hence a great amount of cadenzas, both solo and double; the orchestra falls silent while two soloists are left to themselves to get engaged in lengthy interchange of their phrases.

The concertos written in the 1980s–1990s are more stable and less diverse in their style and form, reflecting the general tendency towards stabilization in Denisov's style during that period.

In its character and the type of musical imagery THE CONCERTO FOR BASSOON, CELLO AND ORCHESTRA stands close to such of Denisov's compositions as his Requiem and Variations on a Haydn Theme. Two low-ranged solo instruments predetermined the general muffled and somewhat gloomy colouring, and the instrumentation and timbre principles of the whole composition based on the use of different registers in the concerto's dramatic pattern. The unity of registers and a contrast between the soloist and the orchestra and opposition of the solo instruments' registers — all these performance techniques are inherent in the concertante nature of this particular genre.

This one-movement composition incorporating the three principal sections represents in fact the above mentioned type of a large Adagio. The main thematic idea, after a short orchestral introduction, is stated by the bassoon. It is a melodious lyrical theme intonationally based on playing up of thirds and seconds so typical of Denisov. The second section offers its intensive dramatic development. The keynote of the composition is an extended cadenza of two solo instruments. In the third, recapitulation, section the material and character of the middle part is repeatedly restated. The decline of dramatic tension leads to a lucid coda.

THE CONCERTO FOR TWO VIOLAS in style and form is close to other concertos written during that period. It is distinguished only for its chamber-like sonority since the soloists are accompanied by the string orchestra and harpsichord. Its form is typical of Denisov's one-movement compositions:

1st section	2nd section	3rd section	Coda
exposition	development	recapitulation	
Lento	Poco agitato	Lento	
(bars 1–138)	(bars 139–212)	(bars 213–332)	(from bar 333)

a   b   a(1)
   bar 55   bar 79
   cadenzas
   of two violas in d

                                                             G major

Out of Denisov's latest concertos (including those for the oboe, for the clarinet and for the guitar) his CONCERTO FOR VIOLA AND ORCHESTRA stands apart as one of the most impressive compositions of the stabilization period. The concerto was written on the request of Yuri Bashmet. The first two movements of the four-part cycle are kindred in character, with the principal role assigned therein to the melodic principle. All the orchestral lines are exceptionally melodic. The second movement (written exclusively for the strings) delineates the solo part of the 1st violin playing in duet with the viola. The melodic line reaches its peak at the end of the movement (from bar 109) when the group of 1st violins is divided into nine self-sustained voices (Musical Example 27).

The third movement is a virtuosic Scherzo. In contrast to the two initial movements, it is deliberately devoid of any melodic line. Here prevails a different type of writing — the pointillistically broken texture. The contrast is intensified by the appearance of new timbre colours in the percussion instruments — marimba and tom-tom.

Movement Four is the principal one in the cycle. Once more, though in a different context, Denisov resorts to a Schubert melody in his variations on a theme of Schubert's Impromptu in A♭ major, Op. 142. The type of variations used in this movement was first employed by Denisov in his Variations on a Haydn Theme for the cello.[4] It was to become the basic form of the composer's variations — Variations on a Handel Theme for the piano, Variations on a Schubert Theme for the cello, and Variations on a theme of Bach's chorale *Es ist genug* for the viola. The same principle is used in the finale of his viola concerto: in the first section the theme is stated in full, then it is split acquiring collateral parts and gradually modified completely. In the middle section the theme virtually disappears to be restated once again in the recapitulation in its original form. The outline of the theme is akin to finding stability and peace of mind.

It should be noted that a number of Denisov's compositions not defined as a 'concerto' are essentially concertante in their style. Those include the above mentioned Variations on a Haydn Theme, his composition *Happy End* and his *Chamber Music* for viola, harpsichord and strings. The formal features of sonata-form in the latter composition (two sections correlated in the type of the principal and subsidiary parts; the development section, transposition of the subsidiary part) constitute a tribute to the concerto form to which this piece belongs in its essence.

Special mention should be also made of Denisov's Partita for violin and orchestra based on Bach's violin partita in D major. The solo part of the violin provides a lot of possibilities for its multi-voice treatment. The composer's train of thoughts proceeds from simple arrangement to complete modification of the material. The outlines of Bach's music are filled with new intonation and harmonic content only remotely reminiscent of the original. His variations of the Chaconne are more in the style of Brahms rather than Bach.

2.3. SYMPHONY FOR FULL ORCHESTRA (1987)

This symphony was written expressly for L'Orchestre de Paris, on a commission of its conductor Daniel Barenboim. Denisov used this chance to unfold his artistic concepts in a large-scale work in this purely musical genre. Despite its large size — the duration of the symphony takes nearly an hour, the composition is imbued with lyricism in various forms and it may well be defined as a 'Lyric Symphony'. Three of its four movements are in slow tempo:

Ex. 27   Concerto for viola and orchestra, 2nd movement

1. Lento. Agitato
2. Tranquillo
3. Agitato
4. Adagio

Devoid of any neo-classical shade in its musical content, the symphony in its general outlines resembles a classical cycle with tense dramatic pattern, restlessness and impressive contrasts in the first movement, a cantilena in Tranquillo, similar to lyricism inherent in the traditional Andante, in the second one, an easy and transparent third movement akin to a scherzo, and its final epilogue. The development section is highly original in its conception. The first movement highly complicated in its thematic message is based on a contrast of Lento and Agitato, enrolling the enormous capacities of full orchestra (with six percussionists). In the two intervening movements the opposites break up into two polar groupings. The second movement is exclusively in a slow tempo with the strings reigning supreme throughout it. In other words, it is a different orchestra 'detached' from the general team. The third movement takes up only *agitato*. It is oriented on the timbre of wind and percussion instruments; the strings soon join in but playing *pizzicato* almost to the very end, which sounds as continuation of the percussion. Only in a final cadenza there appear the extended chords *arco* (bars 6–1 from the end). So the middle movements of the symphony are complementary in timbre. The finale is retreating back to the beginning: first cantilena like in Movement Two and then *tutti* like in Movement One.

The introduction to the first movement, Lento, forms two leisurely but strong waves of crescendo. The first wave moves towards D major (bar 23) with the equally plastic diminuendo. The second wave — towards a gentle and mellow 33-voice concord of the softest in timbre instruments at the end of the introduction. Agitato abounding in idioms typical of Denisov's stable style is structured in extended sonata-form. It sounds most unusually being based on sonoristic effects. The principal theme consists of various sonoristic rustles. In contrast to those used earlier in his chamber music, sonoristic rustles in full orchestra appear in a riot of sparkling musical colours: whiffing of four flutes is recoloured into the sounds of four clarinets, upon repetition this colour is transferred into a rustle of four muted trumpets; the latter are overlapped by transparent eight-voice rustling of the violins whose trills are echoed in a cluster of six muted French horns, and so on. The composer seems to be revelling in the luxury of various colourful shades of lightly sliding sonorities. A startling contrast is presented by a subsidiary theme in the form of a strict gentle sonoristic chorale of four trombones to be continued in a number of other sonoristic developments.

The first movement is devoid of any hackneyed 'symphonic' dramatism or tragic elements, though it offers quite a few moments of full sonority arising from confrontation of multi-voice tonal layers. The hearer may take a rest in a calm flow of the second movement which starts with a one-voice melody of the violas to be followed by its imitation-polyphonic development. We witness paradoxical rapprochement between fundamentally different styles in forms of musical thinking — modern sonoristic polyphony and polyphony in the early music, e.g., in the so called motet form with its own imitation structure corresponding to each line of the text. The form used by Denisov is also similar to a series of increasingly developed fugato employing, in addition to simple imitation, a shortening of a theme, mixtures (of dissonant chords), counterpoint of layers-mixtures, etc. The cantilena of the strings results in a beautiful *pianissimo dolcissimo* with two players of flageolets set in counterpoint against the background of the overhanging multi-voice sonoristic chord.

Against the same background there breaks out the cool restless tapping of the percussion instruments producing their own canonic imitations. Their nervous tremor affects the other instruments — clarinets, bassoons, trumpets and French horns which, one after another, join in this disquieting rapping. Their initial statements should be called 'percussion melody'. Denisov makes use of the 'Morse code' like he did it in *The Sun of the Incas*, his Violin Sonata and some other compositions. It has its own rhythmical theme in the numbers of notes divided by pauses: 1 – 2 – 2 – 1 – 6 – 1 – 1 – 2. Entering into the note-row consisting of twelve pitches (a – b♭ – e – b – c – f♯ – g – f – e♭ – d – a♭ – d♭) the rappings retreat into the soundscape of the percussion instruments of indefinite pitch (Bongos, Tom-toms, Legno). The onrush of fugato waves with their percussion themes gradually involves the ever-new instrumental groups and sections of the full orchestra. The idea of dividing the orchestra into timbre specific ensembles or mini-orchestras follows in line with the second movement but in a more differentiated form and in the accelerated order:

Bars:		
	1–8	– the percussion ensemble
	9–13	– the wind ensemble, duodecimette
	12–14	– the indefinitely-pitched percussion ensemble
	15–22	– the woodwind duodecimette
	21–27	– the brass duodecimette
	24–30 (cont.)	– the percussion ensemble (in a new composition)
	30–35 (cont.)	– the mini-orchestra of percussion and stringed plucked instruments (i.e., *archi pizzicato*)
	36–41 (cont.)	– the orchestra of percussion, plucked and brass instruments
	42–51	– *tutti* (with plucked strings)

The timbre-sonoristic idea combined with superfugato in an endless ladder of initial statements differing in thematic content of voices rallies, on a superpolyphonic basis, a huge amount of sounds. The erected tower of sounds unexpectedly collapses and falls into a 'cadence-like progression'. Its quivering fragments form several splashes, air-impregnated rests: (in bars)/1 1/2 – 2 – 1 1/2 – 2 – 2 1/2, and finally the overlapping gentle soft spot of the strings' mellow timbre *arco* comes caressing the ear after the endless tension of 'broken' rhythms and ominous rappings.

The catharsis in the third movement of the Symphony makes natural spiritual renewal and release from tension brought about by the finale. Adagio of the finale is a direct opposite to Agitato of the first movement and at the same time its reflection. As Agitato of the first movement, the finale is structured according to sonata-form with the principal theme representing an extensive fugato on a melody including the hemitonic EDS. The subsidiary theme appearing from bar 22 in a sonoristic chorale is similar to the subsidiary theme of the first movement. The symbol of serenity of the principal theme is a prolonged pedal in G which in bar 17 flows in a pure triad of fine French horns. The subsidiary theme is mobile in its tonality, progressing cadentially within the quarter d–g^I.

The similarly non-dramatic and cantilena-like development is followed by reinstatement of the pedal chord in G major (bar 83). The recapitulation of the principal theme repeats its initial statement in the upside down form, developing not from down upwards but from top downwards. As for the subsidiary chord, it joins in at the impressive culmination point with the transparent shining sounds of the triad in D major delivered by four trumpets and four trombones (bar 133). The new tonal reference points are used by Denisov sparingly in his symphony but in the most conspicuous places. The first movement begins with the note 'D' and ends in D major. The finale is also tending to the same tonic; though its overall tonality is G major, the last pitch taken by Campane is also 'D'. The concluding bars of the finale are exceptionally poetical and lyrical. Following the anti-fugato — gradual dispersal and switching off of the voices, the 1st violins are leisurely soaring 'in the skies' reaching the note 'b' of the third octave and sustaining it for a long time. The reminiscences of the main images delineated in the first movement logically sum up the content of the symphony overviewed throughout from the great heights. The gentlest sounds produced by flageolets, harp, celesta and vibraphones (see Musical Example 6) crown up the symphony with a halo of beauty.

3. CHAMBER INSTRUMENTAL COMPOSITIONS

Chamber music (both instrumental and vocal) makes the most extensive part of Denisov's creative output. It is noteworthy that chamber genres came to predominate in the 1960s, during the period of intensive development of the composer's individual style. The fact that chamber compositions in those years virtually ousted all other genres revealed Denisov's bent for refined writing, for lucid and clear-cut colours and lines, easily perceptible in all the details of the musical fabric, and his tendency to bringing out the substantive richness of each voice. And afterwards (after 1970) when Denisov once again turned to symphonic genres and large-scale compositions, his approach showed their chamber-like treatment: separate groups of instruments are treated as soloists (as if several chamber ensembles at once), the parts written for separate instruments are individual in most cases and not to be repeated by other instruments, and bow instruments are used in multi-voice *divisi* performance.

In contrast to Shostakovich who had managed to produce 15 string quartets, such adherence to the standard cast of performers is absolutely untypical of Denisov's chamber style (e.g., three of his trios have been written for various combinations: a string trio, a piano trio and the last one for oboe, cello and harpsichord; the same concerns his four quintets — a wind quintet, a piano quintet, a quintet for clarinet, two violins, viola and cello, and a quintet for four saxophones and piano). His tendency to individualization manifests itself not only in his striving to base each of his compositions on a unique intonation set (series), but also in his selection of instruments. Not infrequently following outwardly the traditional cast of movements and tempo correlation, he lends his chamber cycles quite a different and singular character.

3.1. CRESCENDO E DIMINUENDO
for harpsichord and 12 strings (1965)

This piece very colourful in its sonoristic effects is based on the mirror-dynamic conception. In its first section (bars 1–13) a cluster is gradually structured from the initial note 'b♭' of the first violin; then comes the solo of harpsichord in a freer rhythm. In the process of its development the composition becomes more and more mobile. The basic compositional principle lies in destruction of the initial static movement and supplanting of musical by non-musical sounds.

The key section (from Figure 4) is crescendo executed in aleatory. The mass of sounds is gradually thickening, with 12 strings joining in succession in aleatory squares. The material of these squares is pointillistically sonoristic. The culmination is reached in Figure 15, with the harpsichord joining in with its cluster material. And in general the harpsichord in this piece has a freer structure than the strings. The decline of the culmination is gradual, with the strings switching off one after another. The solo of the harpsichord and the initial statement are repeated in a retrograde form; there unfolds the condensed mirror-like return to the beginning. The piece ends with the initial note 'b♭' of the first violin.

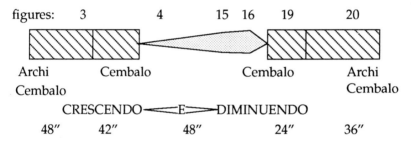

3.2. THREE PIECES FOR PIANO FOUR HANDS (1967)

These pieces were written on the request of the British duo pianists Susan Bradshaw and Richard R. Bennett. At the time Denisov was intensively mastering the serial techniques and was also fascinated by Stravinsky (the influence of *The Rite of Spring* is evident in Piece No. 3). The pieces are also based on a clear-cut structural ides: one and the same twelve-note row is treated differently in the three pieces, providing three visions of one and the same tonal material. Initially the pieces had the titles to reflect their structural principle: Melodies, Harmonies and Rhythms. Later on Denisov decided to give up the titles.

In the first piece the basic material undergoes melodic (horizontal) treatment, which is rooted in a cluster chord (bar 4) and repetition figures (giving the basic shape of Piece No. 3).

The second piece presents the harmonic (vertical) treatment of the basic material. In addition to conventional multi-voice chords, use is made of the rhythmically organized arpeggios giving rise to certain resonance (Musical Example 28).

Ex. 28   No. 2 from three pieces for piano, four hands

The third piece is mainly devoted to the rhythmical development of the material. Rhythms here constitute a projection onto the rhythmics of numerical series underlying a melody. Each note is carefully calculated while rhythmical progression is gradually complicated through opposition of regular and irregular rhythmic structures. Denisov thus comments the development of the third piece: "The sound matter now gets together into thematic blocks and then falls into its constituent elements; the rhythmic structures become gradually displaced in the soundspace making the latter multidimensional."

3.3. THREE PIECES FOR CELLO AND PIANO (1967)

In their tone-colour and technique these pieces for cello are similar to those for piano four hands. In the outer pieces the music is deeply lyrical and meditative: the tense cantilena of the cello finds response in the softest sounds delivered by pedal-playing of the piano in a high register. The refinement and elevated 'purity' of its expressiveness is akin to Webern's strict lyricism. It is set off in the middle piece by the dynamism of asymmetrical 'pricks', 'strikes' and 'shots' with their intrinsic great rhythmic energy. Major importance is attached to micro-details.

The pieces are written in a free serial technique. The main principle is based on differentiated use of intervals within the set-form: semitones occur in a melody while the remaining tones form chords (bar 3 in the first piece). The third piece is particularly poetical (Musical Example 29).

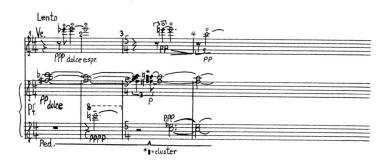

Ex. 29   No. 3 from three pieces for cello and piano

3.4. *ODE* FOR CLARINET, PIANO AND PERCUSSION (1968)

Written on the request of the clarinettist Lev Mikhailov, this piece is rather mournful in character and somewhat elevated.

The composition is based on dialectical interaction of two opposite tendencies. The first tendency is destructive. The basic series falls into its constituent elements and gets modified, which eventually leads to gradual disappearance of serial bonds, destruction of the serial logic and eventually — to the emergence of the aleatory element of chaos.

The second tendency is constructive, leading to the formation of melodic material. It is marked by continual striving for exaggerated melodic development of intonationally expressive sections of the serial note-row. This tendency culminates in the final solo of the clarinet which demonstrates the outcome of the conflict between two mutually excluding lines.

The whole of the last section (*tempo libro*) is a coda. The composer felt it necessary to change the timbre at the close of his piece: there appear tam-tam, bells, piano strings and clarinet as a low bell (Musical Example 30).

3.5. *ROMANTIC MUSIC* FOR OBOE, HARP AND STRING TRIO (1968)

This piece has been dedicated to Heinz and Ursula Holliger. Its main content is evident from its title. It is all-embracing lyricism — from serene contemplation to emotional tension. Generally speaking, *Romantic Music* is a work in the concertante style. The composer disclosed all the virtuoso resources inherent in the instruments (especially the oboe); each instrumental part is thoroughly developed and only the solo cadenzas identify the solo instruments.

The composition has three sections. The first one is an introduction making an exposition of the solo instruments; the extended solo of the oboe is followed by the solo of the harp. The development principle of the key section (from bar 1) is

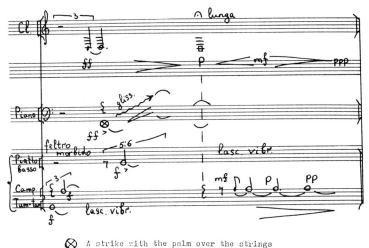

⊗ A strike with the palm over the strings

Ex. 30   Ode

wave-like. Two of the most conspicuous waves are ending in climaxes. The first climax (bars 8–12) is rather weak, it occurs almost at the beginning of the key section; it is followed by a short diminuendo. A very long crescendo leads to the second climax reaching the highest dynamic point of development (around bar 71 — the chords of the oboe, glissandi and clusters of the harp). The climax is followed by a prolonged diminuendo. The third section presents two small solo cadenzas (reminiscent of the introductory ones). The music is gradually getting quieter, with the sounds ringing off in a high register where everything dissolves.

The composition reveals the patent features of the concerto: quiet and repressed tone-colours at the beginning and at the close, a very expressive and most colourful middle section preceded by a gradual line of crescendo and followed by diminuendo.[5]

As for the dodecaphonic technique used here, the series is treated as an intonation basis of the composition which implies both the repetition of the whole note-row (according to Webern) and of its separate fragments viewed as independent units. It is the so called 'elaboration' of the series (see the last section in Chapter 3), its transformation and variation similar to the traditional treatment of musical material. A wide use is also made of serial pedalisation, i.e., free repetition of the already stated tones of the note-row in the form of resultant sounds. The initial cadenza in *Romantic Music* performs the role of serial exposition and therefore all the eight statements of the series here are complete and relatively strict. However, the first exposition of the series with the harp's initial statement is accompanied by numerous resultant repetitions, i.e., 'pedalisations' (Musical Example 31 A). Segmentation, i.e., development of separate segments of the series, comes later, see bar 1 of the bow instruments P e♭ – g, the tones 1 – 2 – 3 – 4 – 5 – 6|6 – 5 – 4 – 3 – 2 – 1; the tones 7 – 8 – 9 – 10 – 11 appear further in the parts of the harp and the oboe. After that, without caring too much about the serial order

Ex. 31 *A & B*: "Romantic music"

(which is out of the question with Webern) the 'remainders' shoot up in the harp's passage in a new serial note-row RI e – a♭ in bar 2 (Musical Example 31 B).

The content of serial complexes is the basis of harmonic and modal phenomena in dodecaphonic music. The paired cadenza is highly effective owing to a contrast between the oboe's one-voice modal complexes and the harp's sweeping multi-voice sets. In contrast to the strict restrictions of tonal forms prescribed by the masters of the Second Viennese School, this music is substantially free from any preconceived limitations, which accounts for a 'romantic' aspect of figurative perception. The textural forms of this music reveal a pictorial-graphic character of musical imagery which is so characteristic of Denisov. The oboe's voice is leading a very fine line, flowing either in cantilena, then falling into a riot of staccato sparkles, now remaining still and then suddenly pulsating. With the initial statement of the harp the graphic nature of the oboe's lines is replaced by a harmonic richness of running chords now 'firing' mini-clusters and then softening up to luxuriant 'fades-in'.

3.6. D S C H (1969)

The instrumentation of this piece includes one instrument from each group — clarinet, trombone, cello and piano, hardly compatible in their range and tonality, but this fact precisely helped the composer to solve his highly original acoustic tasks, with the piano acting as the uniting instrument.

The composition makes use of two quotations from Shostakovich's music: from his String Quartet No. 8 (the lettered theme DSCH) and from his First Symphony (bars 53–54). The quotations are substantially modified through the type of writing and the twelve-note series. It begins with the notes DSCH operating both in a micro-scope (being part of the serial succession — bar 2, the clarinet part) and in the macro-scope (playing the role of cantus firmus). The serial technique sheds a fresh light on Shostakovich's music, organizes it, placing it into another focus and making the whole work integral.

3.7. *SILHOUETTES* FOR FLUTE, TWO PIANOS AND STRINGS (1969)

While condemning polystylistics as a general rule, Denisov does make use of other composers' music now and again. *Silhouettes* is a collage composition reproducing some female musical images from operatic and vocal music which are dear to the composer's heart.

The cycle was written on the request of the Polish pianist and composer Tomasz Sikorski for his ensemble comprising a flutist, a percussionist and two pianists.

Silhouettes are based predominantly on the principle of altering the musical quotations, with the method of alteration never to be repeated. In the first part the quotation from Mozart's *Don Giovanni* is modified through a series; with the quotation broken down, out of the sonoristic-cum-pointillistic background there emerges a contour 'portrait' of Donna Anna. The second part assigned for the solo flute presents aleatory music; it is structured as improvisation of the note groups. Short phrases from Ludmila's aria (Glinka's *Ruslan and Ludmila*) are mixed in arbitrary order producing an interesting tone-effect: familiar motives appear in an uncustomary form. The part ends after all the groups have been played (see Musical Example 13). In the third part collage and the composer's own music are proceeding on a par. The flute persistently repeats a phrase from Liza's Arioso (Tchaikovsky's *Queen of Spades*) while two pianos and vibraphone provide a musical commentary to it. In the fourth part the quotation appears as an 'insertion' into Denisov's music. The scattered sounds in a fast tempo and free rhythm rendered by the two pianos resemble the noise of waves spilling out the melodious phrases of Liszt's *Die Loreley*. In the fifth part the series is complemented by the notes of Marie's song (from Berg's *Wozzeck*).

Moreover, the very modulator underlying the alteration of the collage material in this piece belongs to someone else. Denisov has made use of a series presented to him by the composer Roman Ledenyov as a New Year souvenir. So the foreign material has undergone treatment in a foreign series. To quote Denisov himself: "This composition is of little importance to me, though it is quite refined."

3.8. TRIO FOR VIOLIN, VIOLA AND CELLO (1969)

Denisov composed this piece on a commission of the young musicians of the Trio à cordes de Paris. Though the predominant tempo in this Trio is slow, Lento espressivo, its inner mood is marked for restless tension and unbalanced character fraught with an outburst of strong emotions. Its style bears the stamp of an expressionistic statement holding something akin to Schoenberg's tonality. The content of the Trio unfolds a dramatic progression of emotions in a successive flow of episodes-developments. The initial tense expectation is broken off by a fit of excitement (bar 21). Its decline unexpectedly gives rise to the image of 'divine' beauty in the gentle sounds of the lucid flageolet chords (bars 59–62). A new emotional upsurge leads to spontaneous raging full of unaccountable spasmodic apprehension (bars 85–89) and towards the culminant statement of the main motives (bars 90–91). It makes a sharper contrast with the following airy flageolet sounds (bars 102–109) soaring over the 'earthly' passions and fears (the intonations of the principal theme here recur in a modified form). The illusory tremolo of flageolet notes introduces a similar tone from Schoenberg's String Trio, Op. 45, bars 116–121.[6] In the final section 'rappings' of pointillistic pizzicato reflect the nervous rhythms of the fiery culmination, now coming in quieter tones devoid of any dramatic tension, with the intertwining phrase of the violin from the same Trio by Schoenberg, also in the appeased manner.

A nearly theatrical (or cinematographic) dramatic pattern of development does not prevent from using in this composition the logic of a musical form in the classical romantic tradition. In its form the Trio is based on the type of structuring a slow movement in the sonata cycle — an extensive rondo. The principle section framed off in a ternary form is opposed by contrasting episodes the first of which come with the bars 21–58, the second — bars 71–101, and the third (the Schoenberg quotation) — in bars 111–115. The form is complicated by a dramatic line of 'heavenly flageolets' (bars 59, 101 and 151) and the interaction of Denisov's style with two quotations of foreign music.

The style of this kind corresponds with the so called 'athematic' arrangement when a musical idea is not so much as concentrated in the key melodic theme but polyphonically distributed among various musical elements which jointly create a certain musical character. The pitch components of a composition are interrelated through the common source of pitch texture — a series. The basic note-row in this Trio ($e - g\flat - f - b - c - a\flat - g - d\flat - b\flat - a - e\flat - d$) is not presented as a melody but in parts (in various combinations) is delivered by different voices (Musical Example 32).

However, the initial melody (see below) not identical to the series is characteristically woven out of vertically repeated semitone intonations. The melody is discernible in its recurrences in the recapitulation as the substantive core of the

Ex. 32   String trio

theme (in bars 60–61 and 64–66, modified in bars 101–104, 117–120 and others). Nonetheless, the extensive development in the composition as perceived by the listener is guided more by the dramatic logic of its interacting characters than by the traditional thematic correlation.

3.9. THE WIND QUINTET (1969)

This quintet written on a commission of the Danzi-quintett of Amsterdam is a composition of a mature style. A two-part cycle, it is knitted together through a simple but vivid and convincing idea of a sharp contrast of tempo, rhythm and pace:

The first part resembles a poetical nocturne. The mellow and soft singing of the wind instruments forms an ensemble of gradually entering, one after another, instruments like in fugato, but each with its own melodic pattern. The freely and continuously changing number of ringing melodic voices — from 1 to 5 — creates an impression of 'pulsating' musical fabric with its sounds in the middle and high registers, without any low-pitched notes. The development is becoming (from bar 9) somewhat agitated. Having no motto theme in the traditional classical sense, the composer employs other means to produce the effects of a thematic composition. His key means is to express some definite characters, their shades and contrasts. The middle section surpasses the initial serene music by the agitated passages of the clarinet and the flute, though quite soon coming back to the quiet singing of the principal theme (from bar 20). The modern tone-colour of serial music easily reveals the traces of its classical prototype — the form of 'sonata adagio' (used by Beethoven, Mozart or Chopin). By the end of the first part the music breaks into emotional and tense pauses while the played fragments are getting

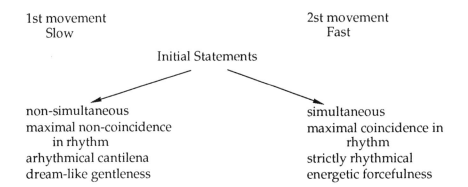

1st movement	2st movement
Slow	Fast

Initial Statements

non-simultaneous	simultaneous
maximal non-coincidence in rhythm	maximal coincidence in rhythm
arhythmical cantilena	strictly rhythmical
dream-like gentleness	energetic forcefulness

more and more shorter: 9 – 7 – 5 – 3 ..., to be finally dissolved in the flat and dark tone-colours...

The main idea of the finale presents a striking contrast. The ensemble players face a true test in their synchronous entry within the shortest possible beats into the sharp knife-like sonoristic chords. The beat-chords are dispersing and then once again unite. The finale is structured according to the type of classical rondo wherein the principal theme with sharp syncopes is set off by several more musical ideas — lightly fluttering dots and short trills cutting tense melodic lines through the dotted fabric (the key contrast, bars 44–64), pointillistic scattering of dots and 'pricks' and once again the scanning sharp beat-chords.

The wind quintet rests on the new tonal foundations. The five notes of the initial hexachord a – b♭ – e – e♭ /d/ – c♯ form the final chord C♯ – e – e♭^{1} – a^2 – b♭^{3}. The traditional classical forms meet with support from the new tonal elements.

3.10. SONATA FOR SAXOPHONE AND PIANO (1970)

The word 'saxophone' is immediately associated with jazz. Denisov's style is far from being alien to such elements of jazz as its sharp (rag) rhythms, melodic patterns reminiscent of the melodic contours of jazz improvisation. Denisov, however, is not inclined to reproduce the 'natural' jazz forms in the vein of Debussy, Ravel, Milhaud and Alfred Schnittke. The saxophone sonata dedicated to Jean-Marie Londeix is one of the most characteristic compositions in which Denisov's style comes close to jazz. Its first movement carries some features similar to jazz improvisation. The slow second movement sets off the tense rhythmic current of the outer movements by its exaggerated ametrics and arhythmics. The finale adds up a characteristic 'striding' bass to the staccato-like, quasi-jazz melodic patterns. At the same time, Denisov's style is absolutely free of any banality intrinsic in jazz which neither Ravel nor Stravinsky nor Schnittke were sometimes shunning.

The character of the music in the first movement is preset by rhythmic energy and hot pulsation of the initial theme. The 'rag' patterns of the saxophone's melody stress the accents and syncopes with their exciting effect. The staccato-like bass sounds and sharp chords of the piano add up to this effect. The constantly changed accents of time-signature deprive the music of any regular rhythm. The

Ex. 33   Sonata for saxophone and piano, 3rd movement

piano chords start uniting into persistent and increasingly louder repetitions: 1-2-6 and 4-11 beats. The saxophone sonata is a serial composition. The series selected by the composer is headed by the note-group DSCH (c♯ – a♭ – a – b♭ – g – f♯ – e – f). Within the basic note-row the DSCH formula is repeatedly discernible in subsequent statements. Therefore, the Sonata for Saxophone stands out as another composition symbolically dedicated to Dmitry Shostakovich.

After the impressive ending of the first movement Lento presents a striking contrast. It is played almost exclusively by the saxophone alone, with the piano joining in only at the end for a few chords concluding the saxophone's quasi-cadenza and paving the way for the finale. The absence of measures and constant avoidance of rhythmic regularity create the impression of absolutely free flowing of musical material. This impression is getting stronger as the saxophone plays the particularly fine melodic motives in quarter-notes. The microtones pass beyond the tones of the tempered scale as well as the asymmetrical rhythms — beyond the metric scale. Lento begins with tritonality produced by the traditionally one-voice instrument; similar sonoristic tone-colours sometimes appear further on too, at the cross-sections of the form. Despite the free flowing of the musical material, the general structure of the second movement resembles in miniature a classical Adagio: the principal theme, transition to a subsidiary theme (a bitonal tremolo), restatement of the initial principal theme and recurrence of the subsidiary one.

The principal theme of the finale is a short ground bass akin to boogie-woogie, of course, with the non-standard six-note progression (the note-row with interpolation: 1 – 2 – 12 – 3 – 4 – 5). Likewise in the first movement, here again predominates the 'iron rhythm' abounding in all kinds of syncopation and other 'misplacements'. The theme looks particularly resilient owing to the dynamic tension between strict rhythms in octinato bass and quasi-improvisatory melodic patterns in the saxophone's part.

A specific feature of the finale is the introduction of the second intonation material in addition to the basic one — the common note-row for the whole sonata. The additional material plays the role of a subsidiary theme with its intervals contrasting to the principal one. Moreover, the second material is used as a series theme the main version of which includes 12 various pitches: d – f♯ – a – c♯ — f – a♭ – b — e – g – b♭ — e♭ – c . Denisov's serial method implies treatment of the series as a theme, allowing for its breakdown, incomplete statement and repetition of its separate segments. With this allowance taken into consideration, the finale of Denisov's saxophone sonata is polyserial. Both series are correlated as principal and subsidiary ones. The second arises in counterpoint to ground bass beginning with bar 7 (Musical Example 33).

The idea of third stream making the basis of the second series prompts the method of its repetition — transposition by a fifth up (in bars 7–9–11–13). It is rooted in the transposition by a fifth up within the series proper: d + f♯ — a + c♯.

Two themes-series are quite similar to the principal and subsidiary themes in sonata-form. This relationship is intensified by the resolute polychordal theme in bars 16–20 representing the exposition of the key musical ideas. Then comes their extended development in bars 21–53 and recapitulation where the character of the principal part is imparted to the material of the subsidiary, second series (from bar 53). The loud and open statement of DSCH (in the notes 7–8–9–10) prepares the introduction of recapitulation; hence the finale of the sonata comes to incorporate the complete sonata-form. The dual nature of rhythm running through the entire sonata is becoming extremely sharp at the close of the finale, reaching ecstatic tension in the piano's final impatient beats the number of which is growing in progression 2–4–6–8–12.

The composer's skillful employment of the serial technique allowed him to produce a remarkably spirited and virtuosic piece in the concertante style.

3.11. CANON IN MEMORY OF IGOR STRAVINSKY
for flute, clarinet and harp (1971)

Denisov was one of those who contributed a musical offering to the death of the great composer, one of his musical 'forefathers'. This composition reflects the spontaneous emotional impulse which moved Denisov to pay homage to the memory of the artist: the depression that overwhelmed him, the contradictory feelings that took hold of him at the news 'which is hard to take in'; the feeling of doom in his heart protesting against the inconsolable grief; the heart sinking and everything dying down in lucid prostration.

The grief is expressed mainly in sighs (reminiscent of the first movement in his Piano Trio). In their weaving these sighs form a coupling of intonations of the EDS type filling in the semitonal field $d^1 - c♯^2$ (flute in bars 1–5). In this form the 'chromatic' succession of EDS reproduces with deeper expressiveness one of the

Ex. 34   Canon in memory of I. Stravinsky

favourite Baroque formulas — passus duriusculus; but in the twelve-note thickening it is rather 'passus durus' — fixed (though, not 'too rigid') tense progression. In the second part of the composition (from bar 19) the sighs, the finest glissandi at the end of the phrases (bar 7) are further developed through the refined microtones (the flute — bars 19–20). As superchromaticism as regards the 'diatonic' nature of the twelve-note degrees, these microtones are sounding extremely tenderly and at the same time tinged with deep lamentation.

Not only the emotional mood is associated with the name of Igor Stravinsky, but also the formal principles and some symbolic features of the composition. These are transparency and cool tonality of two fine lines delivered by the wind instruments (flute and clarinet) which are framed by the light background of the harp-lyre — the ancient symbol of art. Similar transparency distinguishes the memorial compositions written by Stravinsky himself — *Elegy for J.F.* (1964) where the vocal part is accompanied by three clarinets. Denisov's composition has the form of canon, the same as Stravinsky's another opus *In Memoriam Dylan Thomas* has the form of a mournful canon. The relative strictness of the work's canonical form bears the illusory stamp of neo-classicism. As in Stravinsky's composition, the twelve-note texture occasionally reveals diatonic fields (bar 3), particularly in the part of the harp, an instrument essentially diatonic in its harmony (bars 9–11, 18). Denisov's *Canon* has the root tone, which Stravinsky used to call 'pole'. And, of course, it is the note 'D'. It opens the composition and within the framework $d^1 - a^1 - d^2 - a^2$ there runs the melody of the harp's leading voice at the close (the last five bars).

The symbolic moments are discernible in the directions of its melodic patterns. The composition falls into two sections. The first one is marked for the persistent contrast of movement: in contrast to the harp striving upwards (bars 1–5), the clarinet is drawing downwards; and vice versa (bars 5–7 and further on). This contradiction is particularly evident in the culmination of the first section (bars

14–18). The two voices are crossing, passing through each other: Fl. Cl.

In the second section there predominates dejected resignation of the 'reconciled' voices. All three instruments are sliding down in concord producing the deep prolonged 'sighs' (bars 19–21, 22–24, 25–27). Five short weakening 'sighs' render a poetical ending of the piece (Musical Example 34).

Ex. 35   "Signes en blanc"

3.12. SIGNES EN BLANC for piano (1974)

"And there appeared a kingdom but it was hidden in whiteness". This epigraph to his piece *Signes en blanc* was taken by Denisov from a book by Marcel Schwob, a French writer of the late 19th century.

Signes en blanc is an allusion to painting (one of Paul Klee's pictures is entitled 'Signes en jaune'): fragile sonoristic spots of various measures and contours, quasi-tonal bell chords appear on a sheet of white paper. It is quiet refined music without any outward effects. The music is verging on stillness, having more rests than notes. And these pauses are imbued with sounds...[7]

The mysterious atmosphere of the piece is based on variations of one and the same static state. The music is rooted in the note 'A'; with the minimal initial intonation (a – b♭ – g♯) giving rise to the whole composition (Musical Example 35).

The first section is composed of four thematic elements: splitting of the note 'A' (line), lucid chords in high register, crystal-like pedal pealing in fast tempo (sonoristic whiffs) and the rolling semitone field (*poco espressivo*), the latter distinguished from the former elements by its longer duration.

The second section (starting in *molto leggiero*) synthesizes the thematic and harmonic elements of the first section in a more vigorous motion and on the whole represents the development. After a rest, with the note 'A' there begins the third, recapitulation, section of the piece, with its mirror-like reflection of the rolling semitone field. The coda (starting in *senza suono*) makes use of the methods for producing piano overtones. *Signes en blanc* disappear in the fading *pianissimo* modulations.

3.13. QUINTET FOR CLARINET AND STRING QUARTET (1987)

This quintet for clarinet in B♭ and the string quartet has the form of a three-part cycle: 1. Agitato, 2. Molto tranquillo and 3. Agitato. The range of its musical content is typical of the composer's established and well-balanced style of the latest period. It is based on Denisov's characteristic musical idioms and imagery. The first movement is predominantly made up of the virtuoso passages in the concertante style played by the solo clarinet against the background of the strings' monorhythmical chords or free fugato. The second movement represents a sonoristic cantilena of the quintet as a kind of multi-voiced 'superinstrument' bringing into the foreground alternately different colours of its timbre. The third movement, despite the identical definition of the manner of playing, is not essentially a restatement of the mood exposed in the first movement. In the finale there dominates the sharp and light pointillistic patterns of tonal lines. The uncertain finale is passing easily and rapidly, with its duration being almost four times less than that of the first movement.

The initial movement with its Agitato contains an allusion to Mozart's famous clarinet Quintet (KV 581) written nearly two centuries ago (1789). The patterns of the clarinet's initial passages are similar in both compositions. The first movement is shaped in a condensed sonata-form. A short subsidiary theme, bars 25–33, represents a melodious sonoristic chorale. The strings' quiet chords proceed from the complicated triad in D major, the composer's motto harmony. At the close of the impetuous development section (bars 104–116) there come pointillistic 'pricks' in anticipation of the finale. A noteworthy feature of all the movements in the Quintet is a lapse of all the instruments into silence, taking heed of the stillness of the rests, their number increasing from one movement to another.

The quiet second movement, despite the radical change in motion, is perceived as the slow music of the first movement. Close to its end there also arise reminiscences of the sonoristic chorale (bar 73) and passages (bar 75) from the first movement with the sole purpose, however, of introducing flageolet notes produced by all the strings against the background of which the clarinet amazes the listener by its four-voice ecmelic chords.

The message of the finale is unusual. The principal idea is perceived by the ear as a sonoristic cloud of sparkling needles and silvery dots through which there break out short cantilena-like motives, also in the extraordinary high-pitched vibrating sonority. Such material is ill-suited for development in the vein of classical forms. The development unfolds in the progressive compression of the sounding part in repetition: /in bars/7–4–2–1–1/4–1/4. The entire fabric of the finale is woven out of such small particles framed by pauses. And all of a sudden sonority spreads about in rapid quiet lines and disappears like an incorporeal vision. Owing to the third movement the structure of the cycle turns out to be highly original: fast — slow — a fleeting finale-coda.

3.14. THREE PIECES FOR PERCUSSION (1989)

These three pieces have been written in different time for different percussion instruments and a different number of performers. Nevertheless, they may be viewed as a kind of cycle with a clear-cut common idea. The pieces carry the following titles: No. 1 — 'Black Clouds' for solo vibraphone; No. 2 — 'Appearances and Disappearances' for two players (5 Tom-toms, Legno, 3 Piatti sospesi; 4 Bongos, Tamburo militare, Claves, 3 Triangoli); No. 3 — 'The Rays of Distant Stars in Twisted Space' for three percussionists (Campanelle, 3 Triangoli, Tam-tam 1 (medio); Vibrafono, 3 Piatti sospesi, Tam-tam 2 (profundo); Campane, 3 Gongs, Tam-tam 3 (molto profundo).

The pieces are united in the kindred spirit of their programmatic titles. All of them are in the same mood, being elevated, celestial, cosmic and symbolically mystical. The titles are mute and seem to be framed by omission dots; the words are pictorial and the cycle resembles abstract musical painting. The number of

Ex. 36   Three pieces for percussion, *A* — 1st movement — "Black clouds", *B* — 2nd
movement — "Appearances and Disappearances"

performers increases in arithmetic proportions: 1 – 2 – 3. The final piece absorbs
the timbres of the first one (vibraphone) and the second (3 cymbals and 3
triangles) thereby summing up their colours and developing them in mixing with
other colours. The gentle and indistinct contours of the initial piece are vividly set
off by the clear-cut dotted figures of the middle piece (all of which is of indefinite
pitch). And all of this dissolves in the lyrical full sonority of the finale. Therefore,
it is more advisable to perform the three pieces as a cycle, a suite, though they can
be easily performed separately.

The piece 'Black Clouds' is in full conformity with the genre called sometimes
in the midnight radio programmes 'Musik zum Träumen'. A kind of romantic
nocturne, this piece is filled not by cantilena of a 'midnight song' but with the continuously changing contours of dark vacillating figures ('clouds') with indefinite
facets (Musical Example 36 A).

The 'impressionistic' mood of the piece is consonant with its quite traditional
structure in the form of the classical Adagio. The quiet first section is followed by
more agitated character of the middle section (bars 31–88) in which the most
gentle tremolo leads to a great climax with sharp chords (bars 47–54) and rapidly
flowing passages in the genre of 'rustles' and 'streaming lines' (bars 55–84).

The treatment of the twelve-note procedure is typical of Denisov. At the beginning he builds up the note-row $f - b - a - bb - e - eb - db - c - ab - f\sharp - g - d$ with
the dominance of the EDS formula. However, this series is polysemantic and may
be treated as a complex of triads f – b – a (summed up f 4.2), bb – e – eb (respectively, bb 5.1), db – ab – g (g 1.5) and c – f♯ – d (c 2.4), with the dominance of two
sets of the 4.2 type (intervals in semitones) and 5.1. But further on the treatment
of the series differs from Schoenberg's. It serves as the source of various group-

models; though, the complete note-row recurs repeatedly. The cadenza- agitato (from bar 55) is founded not on the basic note-row but on the EDS complex and its derivative groups, being sonoristic in character. The third section in the nature of the first includes chords and passages-'rustles' from the second section. Through the 'black clouds' there break out the modified sounds of the four-voice chorale, even with the consonant-tritone basis. The last chord brings in the composer's 'signature' — the tonality in D major (with a soft dissonance in the melody).

The idea of the second piece 'Appearances and Disappearances' is disclosed in the initial three bars. There appear single dots which then, like streams out of drops, pour out the mutually interrupting dotted passages to be later dispersed once again. This sonoristic figure 'dots — passages of dots — dots' (='D – P – D') becomes the key theme of the piece, or to be more precise, its basic phrasing. Then follow multiform variations on this theme: 'P – D – P' (bars 4–6), 'D – P' (bar 7), 'D – P – D' (bars 8–10): Musical Example 36 B.

Following the dry beats of tom-toms, bongos and tamburo (bars 1–10) there appears another sonoristic 'character'. There arise and disperse the hissing and sustained sounds produced by suspended cymbals and 3 triangles and added to the drier dots and passages (bars 23–29). Occasionally the scattered dots are growing and widening (bars 35–40), but unexpectedly they disappear (bars 43–57) leaving the field of action to 'dots' and 'hissing'. With the concluding bars (58–64) both 'characters' beat a hasty retreat and disappear altogether.

The sonoristic-rhythmical characters in their nature are not consonant with any classical traditional form. The source of new forms is rooted in the dramatic logic of musical characters and the developments ensuing from their interaction. It is a kind of imaginary theatre. The listener's perception is also guided by the logic of these imaginary developments.

In the third piece, 'The Rays of Distant Stars in Twisted Space' the key role is assigned once again to the instruments of definite pitch. Its principal idea is akin to the opposition of the 'characters' in the previous piece. The cast of characters here consists also of two groups: 1. Trio of bright and resonant glockenspiels, vibraphone and bells and 2. The dark shapeless array of (three) tam-tams in the middle and low registers. Perhaps (let us also indulge in a 'cosmic' fantasy) it is this 'black hole' that distorts the space wherein the distant stars are shining...

The 'celestial trio' emanates soft and gentle music, with the colour of glockenspiels binding the leading voice of the vibraphone with the intonationally less definite bells. The hissing sounds of cymbals and gongs discover somewhere in the depth a mysterious spot of tam-tam (bar 10). The voices of the vibraphone and bells become more agitated and nervous while the dark spot is spreading out and getting nearer (bars 22–34) and eventually the dreary black drone of three tam-tams forces out all the other timbres (bars 35–41). Under the 'distorting' impact of tam-tams the vibraphone also starts trembling (bars 42–48) and its tremolo is reminiscent of the tremolo in the first piece (bar 31). With the black mass being past, we once again hear the singing of the initial trio of glockenspiels, vibraphone and bells (from bar 52). The finale unites all the instruments in their quiet fading sounds.

The three pieces in this cycle for percussion instruments have common sonority. It is 'music in treble clef'. Though in the finale tam-tams produce some low-pitched sounds, on the whole the predominance of intermediate and high registers is evident, and the music seems to be rushing upwards, into the skies.

4. CHORAL WORKS

A major portion of Denisov's choral compositions is associated with ritual subjects. Such are his Requiem, *Kyrie* for chorus and orchestra (a kind of 'finishing touch' to Mozart's *Kyrie* which remained incomplete) and *Gladsome Light* for a cappella chorus, written on Slavonic liturgical texts. The sole 'secular' composition produced by Denisov for chorus is his song-cycle *Spring Coming* on poems by Afanasy Fet.

Undoubtedly, Denisov's Requiem for soloists, chorus and orchestra is one of his best opuses.

REQUIEM (1980)[8]

Texts

The intricate and diverse literary part of the *Requiem* is made up of texts taken from different sources but united in their common message. Denisov started putting together various texts back in the late 1960s when he had first conceived the idea of writing a requiem. He was given a powerful impetus to compose it when he had come to read the verses by the German poet Francisco Tanzer whose texts made the basis of his song-cycle *Blätter* written earlier in 1978.[9]

Denisov's composition is based on Tanzer's short cycle of poems entitled 'Requiem'. The five parts of Denisov's Requiem correspond to the five parts in Tanzer's 'Requiem'. To entitle the first four parts of his work, the composer selected one phrase from the original poetical text to convey the key idea of each part: 1. 'Anflug des Lächelns', 2. 'Fundamental Variation', 3. 'Danse permanente' and 4. 'Automatic Variation'. The fifth part got the generalized title 'La croix'. In addition to Tanzer's 'Requiem', the composer drew on the Catholic liturgical texts, extracts from Holy Bible and the canonical Latin Requiem.[10]

In the outer parts of the composition Tanzer's poems alternate with the texts from other sources. Thus, the first part introduces a text from the Gospel. This introduction is made on the basis of repeating the following words:

the end of Tanzer's text: la lumière
the beginning of the insertion:
                             Je suis la lumière du monde (St. John 8:12)
the end of the insertion: la lumière de la vie
the return to Tanzer's text: la vie continue

Part 5 is divided into two large sections. The first one is distinguished by a rondo-like structure of the text with the musical setting of its refrain based on Tanzer's verse:
Tanzer — Psalm 25. Liturgy — Tanzer — Psalm 33 — Tanzer — Liturgy.

The second section of Part 5 presents Requiem as it were. Three parts of the canonical Requiem (*Requiem aeternam, Confutatis* and *Lux aeterna*) follow one another forming a kind of cycle within a cycle.[11]

Tanzer's original poetical text used by Denisov has been written in three languages — English, German and French. Combination of several languages is a characteristic feature of the poet's artistic style. In his cycle 'Requiem' Tanzer concentrates the idea of linguistic combination: here three languages are used not separately but within one stanza, in the neighbouring phrases.[12] All the other text, apart from Tanzer's, is sung by the solo tenor and soprano in French. Denisov considers this language to be the principal one in his composition.

In addition to three languages used in Tanzer's text, Denisov employs one more language — Latin to render the canonical phrases of the Requiem. The conclusion of the composition in Latin is neither accidental. Since olden times the Latin texts have been associated with expressing the spiritual and elevated images. And the final lucid rendering of the chorus *Lux aeterna* comes out in fact as some revelation, a symbol of purification and eternal life.

The Message of the Composition

The underlying idea of Denisov's Requiem is a vision of human life. Following in Tanzer's train of thought, the composer views human life as a chain of variations in which the first variation is one's birth and the final variation is the death. Different stages in human life are regarded by the poet and the composer as variations on the same idea:[13]

1st variation ('initial') — man's birth;

2nd variation ('fundamental') — substantial opposition of two fundamental principles in the world — male and female;

3rd variation ('permanent') — man's eternal searchings between two extremes in life — an all-absorbing passion and his striving to escape it and be wholly preoccupied with one's own mental life;

4th variation ('automatic') — reflection in children of their parents' images;

5th variation ('exceptional') — man's death.

In his identification of the word 'variation' in each part through different means (dynamics, harmony, texture) with some definite attribute ('fundamental', 'permanent', etc.) the composer has drawn a kind of 'variational line', stretching from the first to the fifth part, a line in which the 'exceptional variation' of the last part turns out to be a culmination one. In the first part of the composition the original expression 'first variation' is missing since Denisov has made a certain abridgement of Tanzer's poem. The absence of this key expression makes us think of the first part as a kind of 'theme' for further variations.[14]

The scheme of 'variations' offered by Tanzer and Denisov is on top of the next page.

Denisov's Requiem cannot be referred to the liturgical genre as it were. It is not a requiem in the canonical meaning. In its genre characteristics it may be defined as a short oratorio. Such analogy is well-grounded owing to the following several factors: the general outlines of a plot, which is not inherent in the requiem genre, use of arias and recitatives, i.e., typical forms of an oratorio, as well as the special function assigned to the soloists: the soprano delivers a real aria in the fifth part

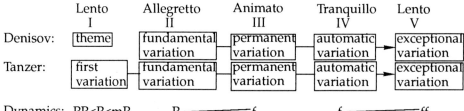

	Lento I	Allegretto II	Animato III	Tranquillo IV	Lento V
Denisov:	theme	fundamental variation	permanent variation	automatic variation	exceptional variation
Tanzer:	first variation	fundamental variation	permanent variation	automatic variation	exceptional variation

Dynamics: PP<P<mP   P————f   f————ff

while the tenor, to quote the composer himself, acts as a quasi-evangelist and it is no accident that his part is based exclusively on liturgical texts.

The Dramatic Pattern of the Cycle

Without resorting to the canonical structure of a requiem, Denisov drew on other means to make his composition integral and whole. A large-scale work naturally calls for diverse techniques to be employed to unite a cycle into an integral entity. Apart from the interrelationship of its parts through the text providing for an almost plot development of the main message, purely musical means of unification may be clearly identified in Denisov's Requiem. Let us consider the following three levels in its musical organization: the 1st level involves the explicit tendency of its four initial parts towards the finale. These parts may be regarded as an extended introduction to the final, fifth, part in which all their key images and ideas get their exhaustive manifestation.

The 2nd level may be defined as opposition of its two outer parts to the three intervening ones. The outer parts have several major moments in common:

– the first part is the largest of the initial four parts and, like the finale, it is multiform in its inner structure;[15]

– only in these two parts Tanzer's text alternates with insertions from other sources and only within these parts we hear the solos of the tenor;

– the outer parts have also the common tempo — Lento;

– the fifth part carries some elements of timbre recapitulation, with the timbre arch produced by the solo of the oboe d'amore.

The intervening sections form their own ternary cycle. The second of them (the third in the cycle) constitutes a major dramatic knot. It is multidimensional and full in its sonority, representing in fact the first culmination point in the cycle. Its framing parts (2nd and 4th) are far more chamber-like. The second is light and airy, the only part of the cycle with no chorus involved. The fourth part enrolls the capacities of chamber instruments and the chorus but never to be used together. So there arises another cycle within a cycle in which the dramatically tense middle section is framed by two chamber-like ones contrasting to it. The 3rd level comprises various kinds of thematic, tonal, intonation and timbre relationships between separate parts of the cycle. Let us identify some of them:

– timbre recurrences associated with the sounds of the organ. This instrument appears in the sections imbued with topical significance, thereby making the common thread running from the first section through the third towards the fifth one;[16]

Ex. 37   Requiem, *A* — 1st movement, tenor, *B* — 5th movement, tenor

– timbre recurrences associated with the tenor's solos accompanied in three cases by the same instruments — bells, vibraphone and organ;.

– intonation relationships between the tenor's solos (Musical Example 37 A, B);

– intonation relationships between the tenor's solos and the soprano's Aria (Musical Example 38, compare with Musical Example 37; also in the 1st part — bars 24–25, in the 3rd part — bars 41–42, in the 4th part — bars 6–7 and in the 5th — bar 133).

There are some other, less conspicuous, connecting elements between separate parts, all conductive to weaving a polyphonically ramified musical composition.

Denisov's *Requiem* touches upon major issues of human existence disclosing its deep-rooted contrasts and contradictions. The composer's monogram arising in the finale lends this work an autobiographical touch (Musical Example 39).

5. WORKS FOR VOICE

Along with chamber instrumental compositions, chamber vocal pieces make an extremely extensive part of Denisov's creative output. Throughout his artistic career he has been trying not to confine himself to purely musical forms of expression, being attracted to music associated with the poetic word. In his vocal music he is striving to convey the whole gamut of meanings and emotional colours inherent in the literary text. The sources on which he is drawing are most diverse, ranging from Catullus (*Canti di Catullo*), Bertold Brecht (*Fünf Geschichten von Herrn Keuner*), Gérard de Nerval (*Four Poems by Gérard de Nerval*), Francisco Tanzer (*Blätter*, *Wishing Well*) to Holy Bible (*Trois fragments du Nouveau Testament*).

Of course, quite a number of his vocal pieces have been written for voice and piano (beginning with his song-cycle *Merry Time* on verses by 18th-century Russian poets). But a greater portion of his vocal music has been composed for voice and instrumental ensembles: voice and the string trio (*Blätter*), voice, clarinet, viola and piano (*Pain and Silence*), voice, flute and piano (*Four Poems by Gérard de Nerval*). Denisov has also written some works for voice and orchestra, among

Ex. 38   Requiem, 5th movement, aria of soprano

Ex. 39   Requiem, 5th movement

them are *Chant d'automne* (on poems by Baudelaire), *Au plus haut des cieux* (on poems by Georges Bataille) and *Christmas Star* (for voice, flute and string orchestra; dedicated to Boris Pasternak's centenary).

Denisov's vocal opuses are extremely diverse in their style, too. Three of his vocal-instrumental compositions written in the 1960s — *The Sun of the Incas, Italian Songs* and *Wails* — are the remarkable specimens in this genre.

5.1. 'THE SUN OF THE INCAS' for soprano and ensemble on poems by Gabriela Mistral (1964)

The Sun of the Incas is one of the main opuses with which the Russian avant-garde came to assert itself in the postwar years. The artistic conception of this cantata reflected a powerful breakthrough in art irrespective of any dogmas, towards free self-expression, bright colours and fresh ideas. As a symbol, the image of the Sun is highly topical here. Though the poetess is of the Chilean origins, with the sun coming from the Incas, turning to the sun and pagan times is one of the traditions in Russian music dating back to the 19th century. A hymn to the Sun in the finale of Rimsky-Korsakov's opera *The Snow Maiden* is directly linked with 'The Sun's March' in the finale of *Scythian Suite* written by his pupil, Prokofiev.

The main message of the composition is not rooted in Mistral's text. It belongs to the composer, bringing together its various components far from homogeneous in their content and orientations. The entity is deliberately multilayered, though integral in style. The composer is not going to tackle the eternally viable elemental forces like, say, Stravinsky in his *Rite of Spring*. In raptures over colourful and impressive tonal imagery and fresh artistic perception neither is ignored the other side — a heap of damned questions facing our century. The 'sunny', brilliant, sparkling component makes it most natural when the finale with its conceptional conclusion ends in the gradually subsiding sharp and light colours of the percussion and the plucked sounds of the piano. But the verses of the second part 'Sad God' say something different — about 'the autumnal god without heat or singing' with his 'sick soul'. The 'blazing summit' over the river in the fourth part, the evening sun painting the mountains in the blood-red colours (the part is entitled 'The Red Evening'), the sad song at this hour suggest the idea: "Isn't my blood making the mountain-top glow?" Such psychological bond is unlikely to be coming from the ancient Incas. Suddenly it unveils the festering wound of the 20th century with its heavy toll of human lives exceeding that of the entire previous history of mankind, including the bloodthirsty primitive times. And the abyss is gaping in the fifth part entitled 'The Damned Word': "Following the massacre in the year... the word 'PEACE' on everybody's lips came with almost painful delight." The dots instead of the date sound as an unambiguous warning... The text of 'The Damned Word' is just recited finding its musical realization in the instrumental fantasia of the fifth part. 'Call for PEACE!' — such is the idea of the last paragraph.

The contradictions are not settled but moved aside through turning to the child's pure and naive perception. The cantata ends with the simple 'Song About the Little Finger' telling how an oyster had snapped off a little girl's finger which was then fished out by a whaler and brought down to Gibraltar. The final vocal sixth part is followed in fact by a short instrumental Postlude with soft murmuring sounds and the dying down pealings of the bell.

The general structure of the cycle:

1. PRELUDE (instrumental)
2. 'THE SAD GOD' (vocal)
3. INTERMEZZO (instrumental)
4. 'THE RED EVENING' (vocal)
5. 'THE DAMNED WORD'   (a) narration
                         (b) an instrumental piece
6. 'THE SONG ABOUT THE LITTLE FINGER' (vocal;
   with recitalists
   Postlude (instrumental)

The novelty of the musical language is due to the use of the serial technique and sonoristic effects. The serial principle is treated, as usual with Denisov, in an uncommon way.[17] Thus, in the second piece the set is often stated in separate fragments (e.g., differentiation and sequence of the first pentachord of notes in bar 7, similarly to an episode in a fugue). In the sixth piece the note-row is subjected to radical modification through various kinds of repetitions of its separate segments (in order to get, on the serial basis, an artless 'childish' melody). There are some parts written on the basis of semi-series in the form of hexachords (1–2–3–4–5–6 or 7–8–9–10–11–12). The fifth piece has no serial order as a whole, having only some remote relationship with the series, with the intonation contrasts predominating. As a result, the composition acquires the developing character as regards its intonations: 'moving away from the series — coming back to it'. Each piece has its own principle of treating 'the intonation basis' of the composition. The 'catastrophe' of the series in the fifth piece leads not merely to restoration of its expressiveness but to a radical change of the musical structure.

The first piece, PRELUDE, is structured, according to its genre definition, as a three-part prelude (12 + 14 + 15). The key elements of the musical expression are broad melodic strokes (clarinet and oboe in bars 1–5), light secco of the percussion (bars 6-7) and contrapuntal background figures of recurrent sounds-dots the light flashes of which are gradually thickening (bars 8–12).

The second piece, 'THE SAD GOD', brings into relief new colours. The predominance of the wind instruments in the previous piece is followed by a vocal cantilena against the background of decorative patterns rendered by the percussion instruments of definite pitch — two pianos and the vibraphone. Four couplets are grouped in pairs. The first pair is in transparent landscape character. The second pair, couplets 3–4, is coloured in a 'painful' glissando of the vibraphone (from bar 22); the text tells about a sick god whose heart if filled 'only with the noise of an autumnal lane'. At the moment of a prayer the voice passes into a recitative (anticipating the parts of recitalists in the cycle's finale).

The third piece, INTERMEZZO, is designed for six instruments: two woodwind (oboe and clarinet), two brass (trumpet and French horn) and two stringed instruments (violin and cello). The 'repeating dots' make the sole musical material of

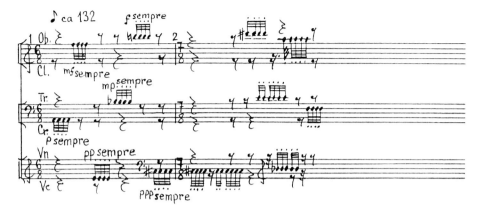

Ex. 40 "The Sun of the Incas", 3rd movement

the piece and seem to bring into the foreground the element of rhythm. The figures made up of differing number of dots are asymmetrical. The streams of dots, e.g., 4–2–5–11–2–9, are easily caught up by other instruments forming imitations, canons and strettos. The phenomena from two different dimensions — pitch and timbre — are linked together through a hexachord (see page ...). Six timbres form various combinations through the observance or non-observance of kinship between instrumental colours. Thus, Intermezzo opens with a hexachordal timbre retrograde statement. The bars 1–2 first make an exposition of two triads of contrasting timbres 'brass — woodwind — string' (it occurs twice; thenote-row being 1–2–3–4–5–6), and then, in the form of counter-exposition, the sounds recur strictly in a retrograde order 6–5–4–3–2–1 (Musical Example 40):

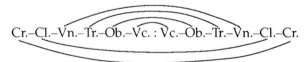

Cr.–Cl.–Vn.–Tr.–Ob.–Vc. : Vc.–Ob.–Tr.–Vn.–Cl.–Cr.

The form of the piece: Introduction (bars 1–8) and Triple Canon (bars 9–26). The six-voice stretta (in a demisemiquaver) concludes this piece in a cadential manner.

The fourth piece, 'THE RED EVENING', like the third piece being consonant with the first (both acting as preludes to the following vocal sections), corresponds with the second piece. The initial melodic lines are similar, the form of diptych clearly discernible in both cases. In the first three-line stanza, 'The Evening Hour', the initial vocal part and the flute's cadenza unite in a translucent duet. In the second stanza ('The Sad Song') both bow instruments join in, playing independently of the vocalist's duet with the flute and of each other. The free rhythms and texture are combined with a fairly strict pitch structure. 'The Red Evening' forms a pair with the preceding Intermezzo. Here the series is also composed of 6 notes. But in this case it takes the second half of the note-row, i.e., the notes 7–8–9–10–11–12. Thus, the initial phrase unfolds the hexachord a – c – f – b♭ – e – f♯. The aleatory squares of all the three instruments in the second stanza are also serialized. The 'fall' of the serial order at the close of this piece is crowned with a cadenza.[18]

Ex. 41   "The Sun of the Incas", 4th movement

The fifth piece, 'THE DAMNED WORD', presents an instrumental version. As a prelude to the final song, this piece is also free in its structure. Though, the freedom here is of different nature. Varying groups are borrowed from the series in an arbitrary order nullifying its significance as it were (it happens only once in the cycle before 'collecting' the series in the finale). Thus, in the first chord-beat d – eb – bb – a we perceive the first tetrachord the continuation of which is heard in the beats of the other piano (there are notes e and ab); but further on the serial order is missing. Beginning with bar 3 there comes into the foreground the uneven 'sprawling' dynamics. Many voices simultaneously perform different short motives, all in different dynamics and discord: some in crescendo, others asymmetrically in diminuendo, and still others in fixed dynamics. The resultant tone seems to be vibrating and scattered. It is running short and in the next episode gives way to the quiet and sharp splashes of short passages which seem to be incoherent and lost.

Finally, as in the third piece, there intrude 'crying' rhythmical canons made up of fixed pitched fast dots (from bar 19). In his subtitle to this piece the composer gave the cue of its programmatic character. Indeed, first, the swiftly overlapping chords-beats at the beginning ring out as a terrible catastrophe, a 'massacre'.[19] Second, the following inhalations and exhalations of the wind instruments represent the words on everybody's lips uttered 'with almost painful delight'. Third, the broken quiet tone, sometimes with the shortest shrieks, may be associated with mankind's 'loss of memory' (also cited from the text to the fifth piece 'The Damned Word'). And lastly, fourth, the ostinato-canonical repetitions in the 'mass-scale' tutti are likely then to be viewed as the instrumental rendering of the words 'Call for PEACE in defiance of any storms'. The pianists' final multi-octave 'D' in fff is the composer's signature tune.

The sixth piece is 'THE SONG ABOUT THE LITTLE FINGER'. The biggest contrast in the cantata is the beginning of the finale. Following the fiery instrumental tutti, the gentle motive of the song sounds placid and indifferent to everything (Musical Example 41). But its artlessness is deceptive, for it fails to completely erase from one's mind the horrible picture drawn in the fifth piece. The conception of *The Sun of the Incas* comes to a close with arousing such split feelings.

Twelve-tone music is often criticized for its too complicated language and the impossibility to catch the serial artful designs. 'The Song About the Little Finger' gives an example to the contrary. The transparency of its texture and its easily perceived melody are dramatically similar to the final 'simple chorale' in J.S. Bach's cantata. The song has four couplets (their beginnings in bars 1, 13, 30 and 47) out of which the second one is contrasting as the middle of ternary form. Besides, owing to the additional refrain at the end of the second and fourth couplets (with the intrusion of the 'refrain' of three recitalists) the couplets get paired anew: 1 + 2 (with refrain) and 3 + 4 (with refrain). The form of diptych is patently following up the structural idea of the other vocal sections of the composition.

The complex and multilayered content of the cantata has found its realization in a multidimensional coherent form.

5.2. 'ITALIAN SONGS' for soprano, violin, flute, French horn and harpsichord on poems of Alexander Blok (1964)

Italian Songs were written immediately after the cantata *The Sun of the Incas* and in many respects develop its compositional principles, though being distinguished for greater emotional asceticism.[20] The preceding *Sun of the Incas* and the following *Wails* frame up this work which may be viewed as a kind of lyrical intermezzo.

The whole text is based on *Italian Poems* by Alexander Blok (1909). As an epigraph to his verses, the poet took the Latin inscription over the clock in the Santa Maria Novella church in Florence:

Sic finit occulte sic multos decipit aetas
Sic venit ad finem quidquid in orbe manet
Heu heu praeteritum non est revocabile tempus
Heu propius tacito mors venit ipsa pede.

The epigraph used by Blok, defining the content message of his poems, as well as the general layout of the verse cycle have been retained by Denisov in his composition. It is devoted to Time, philosophical reflections on the correlation between human being and art. The four parts of the cycle — 'Ravenna', 'Florence', 'Venice' and 'Assumption' (about the fresco painting by Fra Filippo Lippi in Spoleto) represent different forms of Time. In his annotation to *Italian Songs*, Denisov writes: "The imperishable beauty of the great works of art lives on in its own temporal dimensions becoming a supreme reality while pictures of modern civilization are perceived as shadows arising and disappearing leaving no trace whatsoever. The living turns into the dead whereas the dead lives on."

In its tone-colour the composition is akin to Webern. The instrumentation is reduced to a minimum. The composer's striving for timbre purity and watercolour finesse of sounds is manifest in his choice of the instruments (one from each section): the flute (one of the 'eternal' instruments, in Denisov's view), the French horn, the violin and the harpsichord. In the third piece the soprano is accompanied by the harpsichord alone. It is a kind of timbre relief before the finale.

The polyphonic texture of the composition predetermined the relationships between the voice and the instruments. All the five musicians are of equal status: there is no accompaniment, the voices being brought into intensive counterpoint

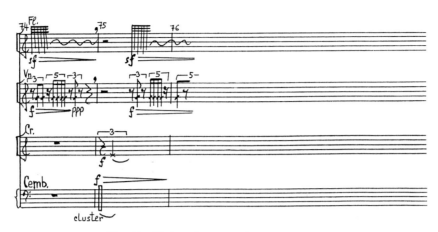

Ex. 42 "Italian Songs", 4th movement

and mutually complementing one another. A few elements of the 'romance for accompanied voice' are observable only in the second piece. In the finale the human voice comes to be completely on a par with the other instruments (as an instrument designed to intone the text). The text is subdivided into separate syllables with rests in between. In the course of the development section the vocal phrases become gradually concise, reaching their utmost compression in bar 55 (see Musical Example 21).

In the coda (from bar 72) the sounds disappear: all the performers are playing but nothing is heard. The musicians produce the hardly discernible percussion effects: the noise of the flute's valves, the striking by the bow's end on the violin's soundboard, playing the violin by the fingers without the bow, pressing the lowest notes by the palm on the harpsichord, then the keys by the fingers of both hands with the registers switched off, and striking by a metallic baton on the socket-pipe of the French horn with the sound dying down freely. It is no music any longer, but its symbol: the music which we fail to hear but just see. Such technique is of profound artistic validity since it symbolizes the death (Musical Example 42).

Italian Songs are in sonata-form. The principal, first, movement incorporates the elements of the following three movements: the genre nature of the second, the tense intellectual lyricism of the third and the resigned dolefulness of the final Adagio.

The composition follows the strict serial procedure. In the first part there arises the motto rhythm of 'tapping' (bar 27, the violin) which recurs in the coda of the finale. In the second part the general serial organization of the whole comes to exhibit certain 'Italian' elements — e.g., pseudo-tonal ending (as if the tonics and the dominant in D major) and some diatonic phrases (bars 17–18 in the vocal part).

In the fourth part use is made of the serial technique. The pitch series comprises the first six notes of the basic note-row of the composition. However, this series is virtually tetrachordal since its two last notes become the beginning of the following statement of the serial row. The last statement of the series — in bar 69 — presents a retrograde movement which symmetrically closes up the serial structure

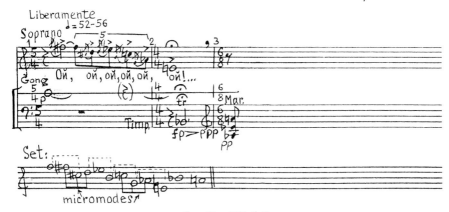

Ex. 43   "Wails"

at the same pitch before the sonoristic coda. The rhythms and dynamics are also serialized.

The series of rhythms and dynamics are strictly stated only at the beginning, then they are split up, mixed, leading to free combination of the elements. Shortly before the coda the whole dynamics are reduced to various shadings of piano: mp, p, pp, ppp and pppp.

5.3.   WAILS for soprano, piano and percussion on folk Russian texts (1966)

The vocal-instrumental cycle *Wails* stands apart in Denisov's creative output for its synthesis of the national Russian tendencies inherent in his early opuses (the opera *Ivan the Soldier* and his Sonata for two violins) and his 'avant-garde' searchings in the early 1960s.

Wails provide a musical rendering of the folk funeral rites[21]: 1. A questioning dirge, 2. An announcement dirge, 3. A dirge to accompany the carrying-in of the coffin, 4. A dirge to accompany the carrying-out of the coffin, 5. Lamentations during the funeral procession to the cemetery, 6. A dirge to accompany the lowering of the coffin into the grave. In its musical structure the cycle is undoubtedly reminiscent of Stravinsky's *Les Noces*. Denisov produced a tragic composition disclosing the psychological aspects of the folk funeral ceremony and the depth of the human drama. The work has no direct quotations and stylization, but the entire vocal part is deep-rooted in the Russian folklore and the most singular of its genres — songs of grief.

Denisov has been the first to combine the phenomena which seemed incompatible: a folk rite and the serial technique without violating the nature of the musical material. The series itself is not just the structural basis of the composition. Presented at the beginning of *Wails*, it is fraught with great intonation potentials: its basic notes (without grace notes) make play with thirds and even a triad. It is divided into elements to be repeated, played up and varied, like micromodes (the series contains a micromode which is presented twice; Musical Example 43,

Ex. 44 "Wails", 6th movement

compare with Musical Example 18). As a result, the serial technique treated in this way virtually comes close to modality while the predominating principle of serial organization involves continuous variations of sub-series and melodic patterns close to it.

The sixth part has the most clear-cut serial structure. The reduction of instrumental resources to a minimum (only the vocalist and Claves) allows to concentrate on the development of the series as much as possible. The serial note-rows follow in strict succession almost without repeating the notes and connected by 'bridges' out of two notes (only in one case by a single note):

$$\text{Pe} \overset{2}{\frown} \text{Ia} \overset{2}{\frown} \text{Pe} \overset{2}{\frown} \text{Ia} \overset{2}{\frown} \text{Pe} \overset{2}{\frown} \text{Ia} \; \vdots \; \text{(broken)}$$

$$\text{If} \overset{2}{\frown} \text{Pc} \overset{2}{\frown} \text{If} \overset{2}{\frown} \; \vdots \; \text{Id}\flat \overset{2}{\frown} \text{Pg}\sharp \overset{2}{\frown} \text{Id}\flat$$

Simultaneously with the pitch series in the sixth section use is made of the rhythm series: 1 2 7 11 10 3 8 4 5 6 9 12. It is distributed among the parts of the soprano and Claves. It becomes most evident before the coda when the broken rhythm series in the vocal part is followed up and finished by Claves (Musical Example 44).

The development of vocal intonations in *Wails* is primarily governed by emotional expressiveness — now the impressive repetitions, lamentations, then tragic shrieks, ecmelic 'sobs' and along with it — somewhat abstract intonation of dodecaphonic intervals. At different moments of the action various intonation specifics come to be exaggerated. Thus, tragic despair entails intensified cantilena in the culmination point of the fourth section (between Figures 11 and 12) or 'weakened, burnt out grief' (to quote Alfred Schnittke) in the sixth section.

Wails are marked for highly original instrumentation: the soprano is accompanied by three groups of percussion and piano, the latter treated also as a percussion instrument (the pianist plays predominantly on the keyboard strings and produces various percussion effects). The parts of the percussion and the piano create an eerie sonoristic background of the composition. In their interweaving with the singer's voice they catch up and continue her narration. The vocal part itself is most unconventional and extremely complicated. In addition to the customary vocal techniques, use is made of singing with the closed mouth, whispers and glissando. The voice sometimes resembles the sounding of other instruments, turning into just another line of the multi-voice score.

The dramatic characteristics of the instruments, as usual with Denisov, are carefully thought out. In the 1st section used are xylophone, marimba, kettledrums and charleston. Only with the climax there appear new timbres anticipating the following sections — the gloomy pealings of the bell and the callous tappings of Claves. In the 2nd section, the other percussion instruments (namely, bongos and a triangle) and the piano are playing. In the 3rd section, the soprano is accompanied exclusively by the cool timbre of the vibraphone. The most developed instrumental texture is in the 4th and 5th sections. The remote funeral knell, so remarkably delineated by Denisov, is very impressive (the end of the 4th section, 5th section). In the finale (before the coda), the soprano is accompanied by Claves, a dry-timbred instrument of indefinite pitch. Its sounds are likely to be associated with the clatter of nails driven into the coffin's lid. ("A dirge to accompany the lowering of the coffin into the grave").

In the mysterious, irreal, stillness of the coda full of enigmatic rustles (from Figure 8) 'the dumb voice' so merges with the environment that is could hardly be distinguished from the sounds produced by the percussion instruments.

5.4.   LA VIE EN ROUGE for voice and ensemble on poems by Boris Vian (1973)

The song-cycle *La vie en rouge* in seven parts is based on Boris Vian's poems written over the years. Their subjects are confined to two opposed spheres of imagery — philosophical lyricism and sarcastic grotesque. Biting sarcasm and gloomy grotesque reflected the anguish and pessimism prevailing in the life of France during the wartime and postwar years (hence 'la vie en rouge'). Three parts of the cycle are related to this layer of imagery: 'La vraie rigolade' (No. 2) represents a kind of 'feast during the plague' which is consonant with the absurdist aspects of Vian's literary style (see pages ...); 'La java des bombes atomiques' (No. 3) gives a mocking narrative about 'mon oncle' fameux bricoleur foisent des bombes atomiques' (here for the purpose of grotesque, the composer resorts to a quotation from *La Marseillaise*)[22]; 'Le prisonnier' (No. 5) is a tragic story about a soldier who betrayed his friends. On the other pole of imagery are the distressing reflections on one's values in life. Having passed through a painful process of searchings and options, the poet finds the reply to the question "Pourquoi que je vis?" — "Parce qu'est joli."

In his song-cycle, Denisov places the accent on one of the two opposing layers of imagery, namely on the lyrical line (as in his opera *L'écume des jours*). Hence the general character of the composition — a philosophical lyrical monologue, and the arrangement of its parts, with the last two parts appearing to be an outcome of the development of this lyrical line:

Ex. 45 "Autumn", 1st movement

Parts of the cycle

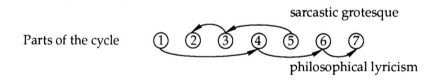

sarcastic grotesque

philosophical lyricism

The integrity of the composition is attained through the following moments:

– a striking contrast of two spheres of imagery, on the one hand, and the framing of the cycle in philosophical lyricism, on the other;

– distribution of functions between the lines of imagery: the philosophical lyrical line constitutes the image-bearing constant roots of the cycle whereas the sarcastic-grotesque line is arranged on the 'growth' principle, with the tragic and open emotional factors gradually intensified towards the end.

For the first time in his song-cycles Denisov employs jazz as a layer of musical imagery, making allusions to the songs of French chansonniers (before that he resorted to the jazz style in his sonata for saxophone). The use of jazz elements in this cycle is directly linked with Boris Vian who was a jazz trumpeter and chansonnier. Therefore it is quite natural to make use of this type of musical imagery with its characteristic rhythms, chords, articulation and instrumentation which considerably enrich the composer's expressive media and enhance the impact of music in most diverse ways (see Songs 1, 2 and 3).

5.5.   AUTUMN for 13 solo voices on poems by Velimir Khlebnikov (1968)

Autumn belongs to the genre of vocal ensembles. Its thirteen vocal parts are most developed and self-sustained.

In its structure this serial composition is based on thirds rooted in the harmonic intervals of the note-row (see Appendix 3.6) and lending the serial structure its singular tone-colour. The glimpses of consonant and softly dissonant chords of thirds are often 'enveloped' in linear motion in the other voices (1st part, bar 2).

The composer draws on the principle of the so called vertical dodecaphony: in a multi-voice statement there simultaneously progress the tones of one set-form which then passes into another set-form (Musical Example 45).

The choral techniques include such procedures as the splitting of the text's words into separate syllables in different vocal parts and the division of the vocal groups according to the three songs of this cycle: in the first piece — sopranos and altos, in the second — tenors and basses (there appear couplings and rhythmic unisons); the third piece involves all the vocal parts, though the sounding remains translucent, primarily in PPP dynamics.

The ensemble and harmonic techniques inherent in the song-cycle *Autumn* were further developed in the vocal ensembles composed in the late 1980s — *Trois fragments du Nouveau Testament* and *Légendes des eaux souterraines*.

5.6.   THE SONG-CYCLES OF THE 1980s for voice and piano

After *Two Songs on Poems by Ivan Bunin* written in 1970 Denisov for nearly ten years never turned to the duet for voice and piano. But beginning with 1979 and for four years running he produced several musical settings for voice and piano of poems by Alexander Pushkin, Yevgeny Baratynsky, Osip Mandelstam, Alexander Blok, Vladimir Solovyov and Attila Josef.

The song-cycles written in the 1980s are most revealing in their similarity with the pre-avant-gardist techniques. Retaining the typical characteristic of his style Denisov in some of his song-cycles comes close to the stylistic trends reminiscent of Shostakovich's musical media. There are even some similarities in their modal structure. For instance, in the fifth song of his cycle *On Snow Bonfire* one section is written in the so called 'Shostakovich mode' — in the minor key with all the low degrees (Musical Example 46 A).

The song-cycles on poems by Yevgeny Baratynsky, Alexander Pushkin and Alexander Blok — the Russian poets kindred in spirit — make up a kind of triptych. According to Edison Denisov, musical settings of their poetry call for natural vocal intonations. Therefore these three song-cycles are close both in their intonation structure and the compositional techniques.

The song-cycle *Your Charming Image* includes many well-familiar verses associated in the Russian mind with the definite stylistic complex inherent in the old

Ex. 46 *A* — "On snow bonfire", No. 5; *B* — "Your charming image", No. 6 — Loneliness"

Russian culture dating back to the traditions formed during the reign of Peter the Great. Some of these texts have been earlier used by other composers.

Pushkin's style has much in common with the composer's inner world, which makes a fresh rendering of the poet's verses and their musical setting in the modern style quite natural. Hence the characteristic musical content and specifics of this song-cycle. Sometimes the musical interpretation of Pushkin's verses gives rise to a melody which could have been written by a 19th-century composer. Take, for example, the sixth song 'Loneliness'. The initial melody is quite diatonic and its continuation is well in keeping with the traditional tonality. However, the fine lines of free counterpoint in the accompaniment with its ametric rhythms make up the freely-flowing texture so characteristic of Denisov. The patterns of these two lines are far from traditional counterpoint and have nothing in common with the diatonic functional harmony (Musical Example 46 B). The song ends in a major non-chord not predetermined by the tonal development in the traditional sense but freely selected for the musical rendering of the last words in the text.

All the above is also valid of the song-cycle *On Snow Bonfire* to poems by Alexander Blok. It is a large-scale work containing 24 songs and lasting for almost an hour. Snow — night — death make up its imagery and the general mood. A graphic musical line is running throughout the cycle conveying the 'snow' images (No. 2 — 'The Snow Journey', No. 6 — 'On Snow Bonfire', No. 9 — 'Snow Flowers', No. 23 — 'And Snow Once More'). Correspondingly, the cycle is sealed together with the intonation, thematic and tonal recurrences (the dominant tonalities in the cycle being G major and D major). In the last song ('The Last Journey') the persistently repeated rhythmic pattern is reminiscent of the musical rendering of the final song in Schubert's song-cycle *Winterreise* (Winter Journey) which also consists of 24 settings. The image of Schubert's lonely hurdy-gurdy man is consonant with the Denisov-Blok imagery — 'the monotonous drone and peal'.

6. SPECIAL GENRES

INSTRUMENTAL THEATRE

6.1. BLUE NOTEBOOK for soprano, recitalist, violin, cello, two pianos and three groups of bells (1984)

This highly original cycle in 10 parts is based on the texts of two Russian poets — Alexander Vvedensky and Daniil Kharms who back in the 1920s, long before Eugène Ionesco and Samuel Beckett, pioneered the absurdist method in literature. The style of the absurd characterizes the texts selected by Denisov for his composition. He took as an epigraph to his work the following lines of Daniil Kharms:

...The locomotive pipe was exhaling the steam,
or so called smoke.
And the smart bird flying into this smoke
emerged from it chewed over and crumpled...

The ambiguous and indefinite psychological underpinnings of absurdism predetermine the multi-layered nature of musical content in *Blue Notebook*. Its outer layer seems to be caustic humour whose power is rooted in making fun of the senselessness of words, actions and situations. The 'Introduction' (No. 1) does not contain a single word, so it is a musical 'introduction'. In No. 2, 'The Red-Haired Man', the recitalist in counterpoint with the vocalist (whose words have little in common with the recitalist's text) is delivering Daniil Kharms' following lines:

There lived a red-haired man who had neither eyes nor ears.
He had no hair either, so he was presumed to be a red-haired man.

He could not speak for he had no mouth.
He had no nose. He had neither hands nor feet whatsoever.
He had no stomach, no back,
and neither spine, nor any intestines.
He had nothing whatsoever! So it is incomprehensible whom we are speaking about.
So it would be better never to mention him again.
In the second half of the song the recitalist never utters a word.

Similar absurdities are encountered in the texts 'Dream' (No. 4), 'Package' (No. 5) and 'The Cashier Girl' (No. 7). Perhaps, the drive for tackling the absurd, as with the authors of the text, is explained by the endless 'stupidities of the day' inherent in the Soviet way of life: read the newspapers and listen to some official bureaucrats and, to purify your soul, you would be willing to estrange yourself from the absurdities and present them as a certain abstract object in art.

Another, more deep-going, layer of the content is expressed by musical and scenic means. Though there arise some purely comic moments ('Package' is accompanied by striking the bell hammer on the strings of prepared piano II), the absurdist texts get a completely different colouring within the general musical context. These are Denisov's favourite sonoristic 'pricks' and 'dotting' (No. 1), the murmuring sonoristic 'streams' and 'buzzing' (No. 2), the gentle background gliding on the piano strings (No. 4), etc. The typical idioms of the composer's style are combined with theatrical elements. Denisov provided the detailed instructions on the illumination and motion on the stage.[23]

Finally, there is one more pivotal layer of *Blue Notebook*. It is discernible in the mysterious images of the text, directly unrelated with one another, but making up some definite substantive backbone of the composition. In No. 2 it is the words 'In the sepulchral corridor the toneless sea is wailing'; in No. 3 — 'No roof and no bottom in this common universe'; in No. 6 — 'Demons are hovering like flies', 'And the universal God is standing in the heavenly graveyard'; in No. 10 — 'I don't like that I'm mortal', 'I'm terrified that I cannot move'. And the last words: "We are going to sit together, oh wind, on this small stone of death". Divided by the fanciful contexts and immersed in the daily routine froth, these images outline the theme of d e a t h.

It is not a requiem, however, but a surrealistic and absurdist allegory of some plots associated with it — the grave, the burial grounds, the universe, God, death, the heavens and the transitory nature of the earthly existence, the more so in the form of the deeply hidden underlying cause. The 'blind' bonds with the sacred genre find their manifestation in the cast of performers and instrumentation. The use of Campane brings up associations with the church temple. Glass chimes and Tubes metalliques made out of randomly handing accidental objects (glasses, parts of the chandeliers, bottles, rusty metallic tubes, and the like) are not specially tuned and approximate the prepared piano, representing the deformed bells. The recitalist's part has nothing in common with the priest's reading of the Gospel in the passion music, though it is a patent analogy to it.

In *Blue Notebook* there come into collision lyricism and irony, philosophy and anecdotes. The world of Alexander Vvedensky's imagery is intricate and mysterious, with the poet striving to get to the inner sense of natural phenomena. As for the world of Daniil Kharms, it is grotesque and black humour; the daily details make it look like the reality, nonetheless, this is an absurd world. So these two worlds constitute two poles apart, two facets of human life. By the end of the composition these worlds are coming close to each other. Kharms becomes more and more serious, with the elements of his humour, no matter how black it is, disappearing. The young man in No. 9 surprises the guard with his question: "How can I get to the skies?" Before the very eyes of the dumbfounded watchman the young man disappears — and along with him there vanishes the entire absurd world.

6.2. THE SHIP STEAMS PAST THE HARBOUR
for sound orchestra (1966)

This piece from the category of 'humour in music' demonstrates how the elements of instrumental theatre were interpreted in the manner of the Soviet mass-scale shows in the 1920s. The genre of this composition can hardly be defined in the unequivocal terms; coming close to a happening, it presents a highly original musical-theatrical act: the performers include six percussionists dressed in the shirts of different colours (with the rolled up sleeves and unfastened collars), a bayan-accordion player who occasionally appears on the stage in his red-calico shirt, and 12 young Pioneer boys dressed in their festive uniform, playing the drums and doing some definite motions (marching, lining up along the stage and drawing up pyramids with their bodies). Trying to reproduce the atmosphere of the mass-scale shows the composer had to add up the theatrical-scenic layer to his musical expressive media.

The sound orchestra, in addition to traditional percussion instruments, includes also the washing boards, anvils, the frying-pans, and the old and out-of-tuned piano.

The piece is based on the musical material of Soviet songs, which were widely popular in the 1920s–1930s, arising against the background of the sound accompaniment and the performers' characteristic motions. The 'form' here consists in a special succession of quotations from the songs culminating in the song 'Oh, it is so fine to live in the Soviet land!' The composer's conception clearly reveals his intention to touch upon, in a collage form, some acute social motives in the style of flashy catchwords inherent in certain contemporary cartoons.

The line making the title of the composition is taken from the popular sailor's dance song 'Yablochko'.

ELECTRONIC MUSIC AND MUSIQUE CONCRÈTE
6.3.   BIRDSONG for prepared piano
and magnetic tape (1969)

It is also a kind of 'romantic music' like the piece under this title written a year before. The magnetic tape carries the recorded sounds of the woodland to fill the concert auditorium with the birds' voices, their twittering, cooing and chirping. Denisov's composition seems to capture the wonderful fragrant picture and

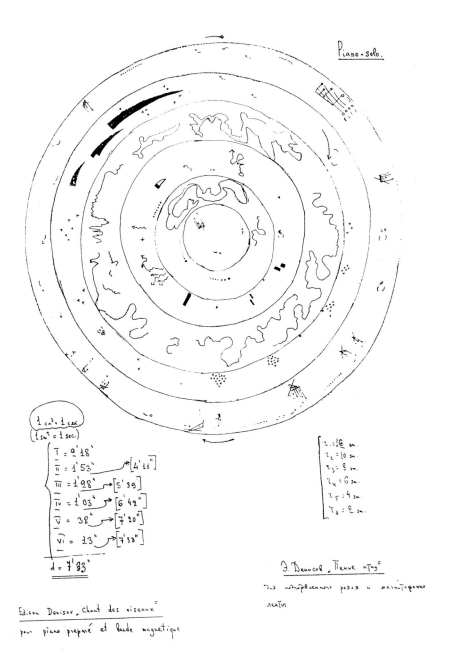

Fig.   'Birdsong' for prepared piano and magnetic tape (composer's autograph score)

render in sounds the miraculous aroma of the forest, a blessed source of pure and free life. The reproduction of natural sounds allows us to refer *Birdsong* to the category of concrete music. The natural sounds, however, were partially transformed in an electronic studio.

The instrumental part, which could be delivered instead of the piano by the other instruments as well, e.g., the harpsichord, guitar or a flute, is noted down not in the form of a stable score but in a graphical form by means of various symbols and figures (therefore *Birdsong* may be also regarded as a sample of musical graphic work). The performer has to improvise on the preset groundwork within the relatively definite sequence of six graphic fragments outlined in the form of annual rings of a tree with the inner layer encircled by five more rings (see the Figure).

The shapes and sizes of the figures excite the fantasy of the performer-improviser, also indicating the varying methods of sound production according to the way in which the piano has been prepared and it differs at each performance. Each ring depicts figures with their definite interaction in different sections. Thus, the first, outer, ring clearly corresponds with the last, small inner one. It implies a shortened recapitulation, with the length of the ring being in strict proportion with the duration of the fragment. The second ring is somewhat akin to the fourth one, the third ring partly recurs in the fifth. In this way the form of the entity makes approximately the following scheme: A $\underline{B\ C}$ $\underline{b^1\ c^1}$ a.

According to the composer's indication, each ring corresponds to a definite segment of the magnetic tape (1 cm^2 = 1 sec.). The duration of each ring gradually decreases: 1 — 2'18", 2 — 1'53", 3 — 1'28", 4 — 1'03", 5 — 38" and 6 — 13".

The performance proceeds as follows: the pianist begins playing simultaneously with the tape and first he handles the symbols of the outer ring, choosing any place to enter on his own will and thereby determining for himself the radius of transition to the inner rings. Inside the ring he moves clockwise. The corresponding six sections of the tape are synchronized with the figures depicted on each ring. Thus, for instance, the single sounds, arpeggios and clusters of the outer ring are combined with the sounds of the woodland and birds' high voices. During the performance of the second ring we hear voices of other birds with more fanciful contours of sounds. The interpretation of the sixth ring also calls for recapitulation in the part of the tape, with the recurred murmuring of the woods and the woodpecker's chirping. (Incidentally, in the fourth ring taking approximately 80 percent of the piece's entire duration one can discern a peculiar solo of frogs.)

The main artistic problem arising in the piece *Birdsong* is a rich field of interaction between the natural sounds and the conventionally artistic tone of a musical instrument. With a gap lying between the birds' voices or the murmuring of the forest, on the one part, and the tone of the piano, on the other, these seem to be mutually exclusive and incompatible. Neither would it be relevant to perform Beethoven's *Pastoral Symphony* or even the Introduction to Stravinsky's *Rite of Spring* somewhere at the edge of a forest. Nonetheless, owing to the tape recording and electronic transformation of the sounds of the woodland, tone modifications on the prepared piano, playing the piano strings and all other sonoristic effects, the natural sounds and those of the instrument come close to each other, begin to interact and sometimes even merge in relatively homogeneous sounds. Free rhythmics of modern music make it possible to reach harmony between the rhythms of singers from the wood thickets and passages played by modern musicians trained in improvisation. A pianist is inspired by an opportunity to form in the process of music-making a harmonious ensemble with the natural sounds, to imitate in a fugato or even stretto style, the streams and trills of the forest inhabitants, i.e., in the literal and not in the figurative sense to blend whole-heartedly with the nature, with the voices of birds, these 'attendants of the extra-material spheres', to quote Olivier Messiaen. As for the listeners, the next morning after the concert they feel as if they had been walking in the forest the day before and enjoyed its thoroughly.

6.4.   SUR LA NAPPE D'UN ÉTANG GLACÉ...
for nine instruments and magnetic tape (1991)

As a result of his research work at I.R.C.A.M. (where Denisov studied the most sophisticated electronic and acoustic devices) he produced this score for three groups of conventional instruments and magnetic tape recorded by using the I.R.C.A.M. equipment. Coming into close contact with modern French music, the composer retains his own style intact, merely adapting its idioms to the new acoustic material he uses. The romantic programmatic title of this piece, 'Sur la nappe d'un étang glacé...' (the first line from René Char's poem), reminiscent of *Signes en blanc*, is not to confine the composer to rendering the concrete developments of the plot, but serves to outline the poetical nature of its musical content.

As regards its genre, *Sur la nappe d'un étang glacé...* comes close to Denisov's numerous concertos. The role of the 'soloist' in this case is assigned to magnetic tape with its recording of various electronic sounds while its concertante style is manifested in its timbre contrast with the ensemble of conventional instruments. The concerto style finds another manifestation in some specifics of the composition's structure, for example, in the transmission of the musical material from the instruments to the tape and vice versa. At the same time this concertante style is of special kind. The term 'soloist' quite truthfully defines the traditional function of a participant in the 'contest' opposed to the extensive group of instruments of the 'orchestra', which is inherent in the concerto genre. But this term in this particular case is inaccurate for two reasons. First, the magnetic tape carries not a single acoustic object but several different objects. Second, in the concert auditorium these objects are not located in one place but surround the listener from different sides — from the stage, from behind the musicians of the 'orchestra', from the left and from the rear.[24]

Sixteen loudspeakers are installed in the following order:

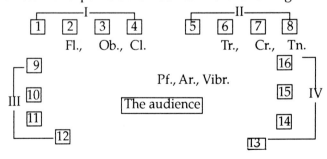

Ex. 47   *A* — "Sur la nappe d'un étang glacé...", *B* — the same

The magnetic tape carries the recorded sounds of diverse character: the tones emerging layer after layer similarly to the conventional sounds of musical instruments; the pealing of the bells (cloches) of different pitch diapason and acoustic configurations; and background noise (bruit). To the purely sonoristic effects there also adjoin the clapper of crotales and the sonoristic vertical tone-clusters. The wavelike glissando lines symbolize the wind (vent). These and similar acoustic objects-characters form their own dramatic line of development. These objects are exposed like themes of a multi-thematic polyphonic composition and undergo development by way of quasi-stretto overlappings, modifications, thinning and thickening, 'swelling' up to fanciful geometrical figures and even migration in the space of the concert hall. And all this is proceeding in interaction with the other participant in the contest — the instrumental nonet.

Sur la nappe d'un étang glacé... is not a serial composition. The main technique of arranging the parts of this piece is based on sonoristic effects. Denisov makes fresh advances in his customary operation of different sonoristic forms and characteristics. The novelty consists in the rich interrelationships of tonal and electronic sonoristics, in their mutual attraction and repulsion. The sonoristic techniques applied to this nonet of tonal instruments involve the same types which are widely used by Denisov in his other compositions, such as sonoristics of lines (e.g., six-part fugato played in unison, bars 1–4), sonoristics of mono-rhythmic mixtures and counterpoint of mixed layers, counter-blocks (bars 13–16, 23–25), sonoristics of imperceptibly streaming lines-whiffs and their counterpoint of the sonorously thickened melody (bars 29–35) and scattering of dots (bars 39–40, 43, 46). But electronics are sonorous in their very essence. At the first emergence of sounds recorded on the tape the tones in bar 4 imitate the thematic line of the initial fugato of the wind instruments through its continuation in the statement of the seventh voice (a – b♭ – a♭ – g; Musical Example 47 A, B).

The transfer of the thematic line from tonal instruments to electronic devices and vice versa is one of the key artistic problems in this composition. The fugato of the wind in bars 19–24 is sonoristic in its nature, for 'vent' has no sounds of definite pitch. But the form of the lines of the wind is clearly similar to thematic stretta. They can be viewed as a gradual entrance of voices, like at the initial bars, but only the pattern of the line is not stepwise, tonal, but presents a continuous glissando.

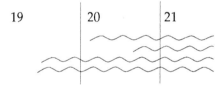

19   20   21

In other words, the chromatic type of intervals has given rise to the ecmelic one (ecmelics meaning the use of intervals of indefinite or sliding pitch). In this way the line of acoustic qualities passing from a simple melody in definite pitch to diverse sonoristic effects achieved by means of conventional tones is now being prolonged owing to the transition into the acoustic domain of electronic generators with their own tones of definite pitch, then to sonoristic confluences and further on to a wide range of sounds of indefinite pitch — to the 'vent', 'bells', crotales and, finally, just bruit. Those forms which are the most adequate to sonorous sounds, i.e., 'blocks', 'rectangles', 'triangles', etc. in the electronic part are directly notated in the shape of various geometrical figures. For example, in bar 32

the loudspeakers 9–12 have the following shape of a triangle:

The nonet of tonal instruments and electronics are also interacting in the forms of spatial music. It is particularly evident in the principal score version from a semicircular location of 16 sources of discordant sounds around the audience (see above). Two groups of loudspeakers (1–4 and 5–8) make one line along the stage from left to right. And when the sonoristic material is imitated in stretto from the first loudspeaker to the eighth (bar 86), the listener feels the physical motion of sounds on the stage from left to right (1 → 2 → 3 → 4 → 5 → 6 → 7 → 8). In case the imitation proceeds from the ninth loudspeaker to the twelfth and from the sixteenth to the thirteenth loudspeaker, the sounds flow simultaneously from the left and from the right of the audience in direction from the stage to the rear of the auditorium (bar 98). As a result, the imaginary traditional motions of sound up and down are complemented by the real spatial motion of recorded sounds across the auditorium around the listeners. But Denisov makes a relatively limited use of the quality of spatial music in his piece. It does not become its dominant idea as compared, for instance, to Xenakis's *Terrêtektorh*.

Denisov bases his composition on the sonoristic material in the spatial motion of electronic structures. Despite the remoteness of sonoristic chords from traditional melodic themes, they may well be combined with the categories of thematic arrangement, opening up a wide range of possibilities for delineating the contrasting characters and dramatic development. Thus, in the initial section of the piece there predominates the melodic line of the shortened intervals of the E D S type which is set off either in 'dotting' passages or the softest 'rustles', but mainly in a contrast of images on the magnetic tape. Further on, from bar 28 there dominates another character developed from the 'rustle' of the piano and harp in bar 13. 'Rustles', 'dotting' and 'bells' of different shadings make up an extensive episode extending up to the recurrence of the initial theme in bar 52.

It is sonoristic, rather than melodic, thematic arrangement that becomes eventually the key form-building principle in composing an extended piece. If an extensive section of a composition exhibits two contrasting characters, it fully coincides, in dramatic patterns, with the exposition of sonata-form: the principal theme appears in bars 1–27 while the subsidiary theme is delivered in bars 28–51. The recurrence of the material from the principal theme later on is a typical beginning of the development section. Since it is devoid of special tonal and thematic means of development, this section may be more tentatively defined as 'peripeteia', i.e., a series of events subordinate to the dramatic pattern of successive episodes. First it is the development of the principal theme leading to a climax in bars 66–72. Then comes another series of scenes — 'bruit' (from bar 72), 'bells' (from bar 78), 'vent' (from bar 87) and so on. The general culmination occurs in bars 118–122, reaching the highest climax in the composition. From Tranquillo then recurs in a radically modified form the succession of two main themes stated in the exposition (from bars 123 and 168), which fully conforms to the function of sonata recapitulation. The piece ends with the serene fading of the bell sounds in low register in the fourth group of loudspeakers. Of course, it is not a classical sonata form. Its regularities are reproduced not in the tonal and structural principles but in the dramatic pattern based on the logical development of successive episodes, i.e., as a secondary form similar to the secondary form in a cycle of variations.

The uniting role of the logic inherent in the dramatic pattern of sonata-form enhances the convincing development of sonoristic material and sonoristic thematic arrangement. As regards the style of this piece, it shows that the composer in his challenging sonoristic-spatial conception has been drawing on some structural principles inherent in the classical tradition.

7. ORCHESTRATIONS

Arrangement of works by other composers for an orchestra is a special art of scoring orchestral music. Many composers showed great skill in this art, e.g., Rimsky-Korsakov, Tchaikovsky, Shostakovich, Stravinsky, Ravel, Schoenberg, and Webern. His job at the Moscow Conservatoire where Denisov has been teaching instrumentation is unlikely to be too stimulating, but it has kept him busy all the time with arranging works written by other composers for an orchestra. Most probably, orchestration for Denisov has always been a means to come into closer contact with the art of the composers who are akin to his own style or dear to his heart, such as Schubert, Mussorgsky, Mosolov, and Debussy. To quote the composer himself, "Now and again I have an urge to turn to music which I love and which accompanies me all my life."[25] The artistic problems arising in orchestration are due to the field of interaction between the styles of the original composer and the arranger, between the two extremes in the latter's approach: 'stylization' (when the original composer's individuality completely subjugates the personality of a composer engaged in orchestration) and 'symbiosis' (the arranger's individuality is clearly discernible in the original texture, like in Webern's instrumentation of Bach's Ricercare). In his orchestrations, Denisov avoids these two extremes, striving for the golden mean, trying to carefully retain the composition's style as he complements its texture with certain necessary additions done in the authentic style, and occasionally introduces some features and details which are unlikely to have been used by the author of the original but which are in line with his own tastes and tone-colours.

Schubert's Compositions

All the orchestrations of Schubert's works were made during the 1980s. These include six cycles of Schubert's waltzes for chamber and symphony orchestras: Op. 9a and 9b (1981–84), Op. 91a (1983), Op. 18a (1983–86), Op. 67 (1983), Op. 127 (1984), and *Ave Maria* (1982). These delightful dance miniatures recreate the spirit of 'Shubertiades' when this genius 'Bertl' (as Schubert was known among his friends) who disliked dancing used to sit at the piano for hours on end improvising dances, waltzes in particular. In his instrumentation of Schubert's waltzes Denisov emphasizes the refinement and gracefulness of his music, the atmosphere of genuine merriment and carelessness verging on thoughtlessness inherent in his waltzes. Keeping up within this style Denisov somewhat diversifies it. Some passages fascinate by the cosy, home-like character, but in some other places you may be taken aback with the unexpected sounds of a band playing in the city gardens (a bass drum and cymbals in No. 5 from Op. 67) delivered not without a shade of humour and soft irony. Or, there may arise the mellow tone of celesta in Denisov's characteristic style (the same opus, No. 14). The instrumentation of Schubert's waltzes somewhat changes the genre characteristics of this music; composed originally as purely pianistic pieces, these waltzes become now part of the repertoire intended for small orchestras. The miniatures may be also performed for an 'encore' at a concert of modern music.

As a matter of fact, Schubert's *Ave Maria* as a result of Denisov's arrangement turned from a vocal into an instrumental piece. The vocal part of the song's three couplets was assigned to the instruments providing for a gradual increase in sonority: I — solo cello — 2 French horns — solo cello; II — duet of 1st and 2nd violins — 2 oboes — duet of 1st and 2nd violins; III — violins and violas in three octaves — violins in one octave. Denisov's orchestration accentuates the purity of Schubert's Weltanschauung which finds its manifestation in his hail of the Virgin Mary. Schubert is said to believe that his hymn "affects everybody arousing a wish to go into praying".

Mussorgsky's Song-Cycles

Denisov has made orchestrations of Mussorgsky's three song-cycles — *The Nursery* (1976), *Sunless* (1981) and *Songs and Dances of Death* (1983). Perhaps, it is the most problematic group of his orchestrations. Denisov treats Mussorgsky's initial material as a preliminary draft of an orchestral version. Since Mussorgsky was far ahead of his contemporaries in his music, there is a possibility for natural proximity of orchestral colours with the 20th-century soundscape and for employment of techniques corresponding to the orchestral palette used by Debussy or Mahler.

His earlier orchestration, of *The Nursery*, already reveals, for instance, a challenging reinterpretation of Mussorgsky's chord A– c♯ – d♯ in bars 32–34 into a passage of semibreve chords in glissando combined with the flageolet scales of double-basses and cellos. Though very discretely, but the composer brings in the timbres of the vibraphone and celesta, the instruments unavailable in Mussorgsky's time. The timbre combinations of celesta, chimebells, harp and xylophone (in the song 'Sailor Cat') are a subtle reminiscence of 20th-century music, Denisov's own music included.

Denisov interprets the texture of the song-cycle *Sunless* as being impressionistic in many respects, particularly in its two last songs. The specific features of Mussorgsky's harmony and texture make Denisov to resort in this case to detailed scoring in his orchestration. As for the song-cycle *Songs and Dances of Death*, Denisov was striving to bring to light 'the depth and finesse of the musical expression', 'psychological complexity' and colouristic aspects inherent in Mussorgsky's music (to quote Denisov). This music calls for symphonic dramatism rather than for a chamber-like atmosphere. With a view to performing the whole cycle by one singer, Denisov had to change some tonalities of the original composition. At the request of the singer Yevgeny Nesterenko he equalised the range of the vocal part in the cycle's songs.[26]

Mosolov's Compositions

In the twenties Alexander Mosolov was one of the most radical innovators and a prominent figure in the Association of Modern Music. The topicality of the content and Mosolov's daring musical language are fully consonant with musical compositions written in the 1970s and 1980s. Though in this case too Denisov places his skill in orchestration at the service of a different style, nevertheless, this style belongs to 20th-century New Music on a par with his own style.

Four Newspaper Announcements were written by Mosolov on the authentic texts selected from the newspaper *Izvestia* with a challenging intention to produce music based on the absolutely non-musical, sometimes even illiterate, words. Thus, in the second song the singer has to render the following text: "The dog has run away! It is a bitch, the British setter, white with dark-brown spots!..." Mosolov's musical witticisms allow Denisov to use a wide range of clear-cut lines and sharp effects. In the song (No. 3), 'Citizen Zaika', the name meaning 'stammerer', for instance, the ostinato flow of purely diatonic chords with seconds in the strings is combined with the strand of complementary chromatic chords delivered by the wind instruments. In the first song of Mosolov's other cycle *Three Children Scenes* the chords of a wind ensemble colourfully illustrate the text's words "Meow! Meow!" The vividness and expressiveness of orchestral colours make this instrumentation version of Mosolov's song more effective for performance than their piano original.

Other Orchestrations

Chopin's Etude cis-moll, Op. 10 No. 4, is a witty attempt to treat a virtuosic piece in the concerto style, as a kind of 'Concerto Study for Piano and Orchestra'. The orchestration is highly original. It excludes oboes, bassoons and French horns, but instead in addition to three trumpets and three trombones four saxophones (!) are brought into action and also the bass-guitar and drums (at the beginning of the middle section their semiquavers are engaged in a concerto-like contest with the piano's semiquavers). However, all these are just fine details of the score never coming in contradiction with Chopin's style.

The latest major orchestration made by Denisov is the arrangement of the klavierauszug of the recently discovered opera in three acts *Rodrigue et Chimène* by Claude Debussy after Corneille's drama *Le Cid*, which was composed shortly before *Pelléas et Mélisande*.

Notes to Chapter 4

1. The novel *L'écume des jours* has been translated into German under the title *Chloé* and into English under the name *Froth on the Daydream* (in Great Britain) and *Mood Indigo* (in the USA). Its Russian translation was published in Moscow in 1983.
2. It is noteworthy that Vian himself associated the plot of his novel with Alexandre Dumas' *La Dame aux camélias*: at her wedding Chloé appears with a big white camellia in her hair.
3. Among other specific features we should point out anticipation of a tragic end of the opera (Scene 13) in Scene 2, Act 1. This scene makes a projection of the denouement — the death, funeral and praying at the burial service. But in Scene 2 it is the funeral of an anonymous skater, whereas in Scene 13 it involves Chloé. Anticipation of the dramatic function is evident here: a shock experienced by the listener in Scene 2 makes him to expect something similar to occur afterwards.
4. These variations have been written on a theme of Haydn's canon *Tod ist ein langer Schlaf*. One of the types of variation used in this piece is based not on the development

of the theme but on the principle of its structure. The principle of canon comes to predominate in this composition. And though Haydn's theme appears only in its outer movements, canons of various types (not necessarily based on the thematic material) arise throughout the entire work.

5. A curious experiment was conducted in Paris in 1984 by the teachers of a general-education school: children of the age from 10 to 12 were invited to an audition of Denisov's compositions, *Romantic Music* included. The first time the children listened to the music without making any comments; during the second audition they were asked to express their impressions and depict them in pictures. The children's spontaneous ideas, not edited by anybody, were sent to Denisov in a letter. Some of them are given in Appendix 3.5.

6. In the last three notes of the quotation $a^2 - b^3 - b\flat^1$ the composer discerned his own monogram "De[ni]s[ov]"

7. The composer believes that the piece *Signes en blanc* should be played to best advantage in a small darkened room.

8. Denisov composed the Requiem within a short span of time on a commission of the Hamburg Radio. At the session of the Chamber & Symphonic Music Section of the Moscow Branch of the USSR Composers Union, held on April 22, 1981, this composition was acknowledged to be one of the best accomplishments of Soviet music in recent years. Alfred Schnittke who took the floor during the discussion qualified it as a milestone in Denisov's creative work for its air-like naturalness and simplicity.

9. In 1986 Denisov wrote one more composition on Tanzer's poems — his song *Wishing Well*.

10. Used are three parts of the canonical Requiem: Requiem aeternam, Confutatis (in French) and Lux aeterna; also Psalms 33 and 25 and the Sermon on the Mount from the Gospel according to St. John (8:12).

11. It is a noteworthy fact that Requiem aeternam and Lux aeterna make the outer parts of the canonical Requiem. Such textual framing corroborates the idea of a cycle within a cycle.

12. For instance, one word or one phrase is presented in three languages running: birth — geboren — né or light — licht — la lumière. In some cases a deliberate use is made of the phonic proximity of words similar in their meaning in different languages, e.g., good — gut — god — Gott or cri — cry.
    Denisov has found highly original techniques for the musical setting of such complex text by drawing on the resources of chorus and soloists. For example, one and the same text is rendered on a par in two languages, as in the second part:
    soprano: frères et soeurs
            die Unterscheidung
    tenor: boys and girls
    Another technique used by Denisov is to begin the vocal part in one language and finish it in another, as in the first part (bars 46–50, the soprano part):
    les yeux qui s'ouvrent — Anflug des Lächelns — smile.
    In the key parts of the form the chorus ends in tutti, e.g., Part 3, bar. 11 — 'Anziehungskraft' and Part 5, bars 45–47 — 'exceptional variation'.

13. In a generalized way Denisov defines the content of each part as follows: 1 — Birth, 2 — Childhood, 3 — Love, 4 — Family, 5 — Death.

14. Naturally the point here is not in a theme and variations in the musical terms.

15. For analysis of the forms inherent in the Requiem's separate parts see Appendix 3.4.

16. For the first time the organ appears in the 1st part at bar 45 with the word 'light'.

17. The set-forms of this work are given in Appendix 3.6 and in Musical Example 20.

18. The word 'cadenza' means a 'fall'.

19. The vibrating dots of the kettledrums and the cello (bar 2) bouncing off during a rest from the roaring chord involuntarily bring to mind the March to the Scaffold in Berlioz' Fantastic Symphony.

20. According to Denisov, he wanted to write a composition devoid of any colouristic effects and embellishments.
21. The texts were borrowed from the collection *Lamentations* (Leningrad, 1960).
22. At the words 'Je suis bien convaincu d'avoir servi la France'.
23. The composer's annotation on his composition is given in full in Appendix 3.3.
24. The composition has two versions of transmitting the electronic part of the score. The principal version, which is fixed down in the score, provides for 16 channels with different content. The simplified second version makes provisions for the transmission of the electronic part from the ordinary four-channel tape recorder in view of great technical difficulties involved in the 16-channel transmission.
25. Quoted from the article 'Music Which I Love', *Melodia* magazine, No. 4, 1984, p. 60.
26. In this version *Songs and Dances of Death* have been recorded by the Melodia company on a disc.
     Denisov's views on the orchestration of Mussorgsky's song-cycles are cited in full in Chapter 5.

1. Zagreb, May 1969: Makoto Shinohara, Ursula and Heinz Holliger, Alfons Kontarsky and Klaus Huber

2. With Luigi Nono in a Moscow electronic studio in the mid-1960s

4. With Pierre Boulez, Moscow, 1967

3. With Gennady Rozhdestvensky, Moscow 1988

5. With Ursula Koubler-Vian (1980s)

6. With Pierre Boulez, Moscow, 1990 (Photograph: Viktor Bazhenov)

7. Scene from *Confession* (Theatre Estonia), 1984

8. Scene from *Confession* (Theatre Estonia), 1984 (Photograph: Vladimir Krasnoperov)

9. Scene from *l'Ecume des jours* (Perm Theatre of Opera and Ballet), Moscow, 1989

10. Scene from *l'Ecume des jours* (Opéra de Paris), 1986 (Photograph: Michel Jzabo)

11. At home (Photograph: Monroe Warshaw)

12. With Yuri Kholopov and Alfred Schnittke, Moscow, 1984

CHAPTER 5

DENISOV ON MUSIC: LITERARY WRITINGS & PUBLIC STATEMENTS

The pulsation of musical ideas often prompts a modern composer to share his reflections on music. Of exceptional importance for understanding the art of sounds are, for instance, the six volumes of Stockhausen's *Texts*, books and articles written by Boulez, Nono, Ligeti and Messiaen. Though the creation of even the most innovative music can proceed without logical apprehension and formulation of the appropriate new concepts and terms, nevertheless the vision of a striking difference between forms of modern music and the failure to understand it on the part of most musicologists evoke a wish in composers to get engaged in their description and theoretical substantiation.

Denisov does not confine himself exclusively to the world of sounds but he is striving to comprehend the development of music, to grasp and formulate the new phenomena and new concepts indispensable for a modern musician. It is particularly important for the Russian musical studies which for many years have been virtually denied a chance to even touch upon any modern trends in music. But some of the composer's musicological ideas may prove to be of general theoretical importance in the research study of major concepts.

In the current musical studies there predominate the following three adjacent themes: the matters of modern musical life, the composers of the 20th century and of the earlier period, and the theory of modern composition.

Denisov's first publications deal with the seemingly 'obligatory' subject — folk music. But the composer was sincerely interested in it. He was firmly convinced in his idea expressed in his article 'Once More on the Youth Education' (*Sovetskaya Muzyka*, No. 7, 1956, p. 32) that a composer should at least once go to the country-side to collect songs.[1]

In the 1960s the subjects of Denisov's publications changed, concerning primarily the greatest composers of the century and the theory and composition techniques of modern music. Denisov the composer and musicologist proved to be a competent researcher in musical theory. The composers he was writing about in his articles, apart from such chance personalities as Alexander Goedike, included for the most part the creators of the New Music, his own guiding stars: Debussy, Bartók, Webern, Schoenberg, Messiaen, and Boulez. As for the Russian masters, they included Stravinsky, Prokofiev and Shostakovich. Denisov's views on the past and modern musical phenomena sometimes vividly reveal his own artistic individuality. Of course, his utterances covering a large span of time and not systematised at all by their author contain many subjective, sometimes too categorical, judgements; some of them are patently unfair, reflecting the composer's own artistic aspirations and searchings (the authors of this book are far from sharing the viewpoints expressed by Denisov in all their totality). And why not? After all, subjective attitudes are intrinsic in many bright personalities. All goes smoothly only in the textbooks on the history of music.

Below we cite some of Denisov's statements.

1. ON COMPOSERS AND MUSIC

1.1.

MODEST MUSSORGSKY. "None of the 19th-century composers was so far-sighted as Mussorgsky. He perceived what the others came to grasp many years after his death". The discrepancy between Mussorgsky's musical language and the conventions of his time gave rise to a firm legend about his 'errors' and bad technical skills. But "Mussorgsky never made a single mistake". "N.Rimsky-Korsakov and D.Shostakovich failed to grasp in full extent the complex and rich world of M.Mussorgsky's orchestral approach, and for this reason the original score of *Boris Godunov* has remained so far the unsurpassed orchestral version of the opera". "In contrast to the songs composed by P.Tchaikovsky, A.Borodin and N.Rimsky-Korsakov, the piano part in M.Mussorgsky's songs is often perceived as the piano score of the unrealised orchestral composition".[2]

SERGEI PROKOFIEV. In the course of his creative evolution Denisov's attitude to Prokofiev has been changing for the worse. In his early article 'Sonata-Form in S.Prokofiev's Works' (1972) he wrote: "Prokofiev could hardly be called a symphonic composer in the meaning we apply this concept to Beethoven or Mahler". In his general negative approach to neo-classicism Denisov, however, makes a subtle differentiation of the neo-classical principles: "Prokofiev's neo-classicism has no 'restoration' meaning as in Hindemith, becoming merely a possibility for manifesting his creative individuality (or his definite musical sympathies)."[3]

The study of Prokofiev's orchestration style has found its reflection in the chapter 'Percussion Instruments in S.Prokofiev's Music' in Denisov's book on the role of percussion instruments in a modern orchestra. Drawing on his observations and analysis Denisov comes to the following conclusion in his summing up of the composer's style: "Prokofiev uses percussion instruments, as a rule, either for rhythmic or dynamic purposes and never draws on the colouristic resources inherent in these instruments".[4] Later on Denisov regarding Prokofiev as 'a wonderful musician', nevertheless criticises him as a composer ("He was bad in his orchestration techniques"), including his most popular compositions such as the ballet *Romeo and Juliet* (in his view, Prokofiev's ballet forms are made up 'exclusively of angles'). As for Prokofiev's symphonies, in his opinion, the best are his Symphonies Nos 2 and 3.

NIKOLAI ROSLAVETS. Edison Denisov is one of the discoverers of Roslavets's music. In contrast to the "eminent" Soviet music scholars whom it took a long time to shake off the inert approach to the dogmas prevailing during the period from the 1920s to 1950s with their complete denial of Soviet musical accomplishments in the twenties, the composer's inquisitive searchings brought to light several innovative musicians working during the first fifteen years following the October revolution, Nikolai Roslavets included. Denisov compares him to such major painters as Vasily Kandinski and Kazimierz Malevich. In the 1920s both Shostakovich and Prokofiev were following a different trend devoid of any melodism (in Denisov's view), while Roslavets produced "melodic music". Nikolai Roslavets (as well as his contemporary Alexander Mosolov), as Denisov believes, is more interesting than Shostakovich and Prokofiev in their compositions written in the 1920s. Denisov rates Roslavets's Violin Concerto as one of his best pieces ("a very good composition distinguished for bright and talented music").[5]

DMITRY SHOSTAKOVICH. Denisov's attitude to Shostakovich has also gradually changed, as in the case with Prokofiev. Here is an extract from his statements in the 1980s: "In my student years I was greatly influenced by Shostakovich. Now (in the 1980s) I'm currently going through the period of rejecting his music. I can still bear hearing few of his compositions. His Symphony No. 4 is one of his best opuses in this genre. Shostakovich used to say that he would have gladly reduced the number of his symphonies. He was ashamed of his Symphonies Nos 2, 3, 11 and 12. His *Execution of Stepan Razin* is reminiscent of Sviridov's music and this is very bad. I fail to understand anything in his song-cycle on poems by Michelangelo; I hear notes but the music is missing. His weak point is the intonation structure. The strong point in his music is the art of shaping an extended piece and climaxes".

In his literary writings Denisov shows Shostakovich as a great master of orchestration. According to Denisov, "Shostakovich was thinking in orchestration terms already at the initial stage of writing his compositions", "all his musical ideas emerged in his mind in the ready-made timbres. In many cases the expressiveness of a timbre is of far greater importance for him than any other components (intonation, rhythms, dynamics, etc.)". At this point the composer of a new generation draws attention to what makes Shostakovich akin to himself — a sense of tone-colours. Shostakovich's orchestration is accurately coordinated with a form. "Shostakovich's music is dispersed", "the musical information of his symphonic works is arranged within definite spans of duration". "The listener's attention is consciously switched off from detailed perception of separate moments". "Shostakovich's music affects primarily by the dramatic tension of the entire piece". In his appraisal of the opera *The Nose*, which exerted a strong influence on Denisov in his early compositions, he dwells in detail on sonoristic polyphony in the scene of Ivan Yakovlevich's rushing about the embankment (Scene 2) pointing to the actual discordance in the fifteen-voice string fugato. The linear harmony in Shostakovich's early style is attributed to a certain degree of Hindemith's influence: "polyphonic coordination of simultaneously flowing lines is often purely conditional, and 'the rules of voice-leading' are virtually not observed"; in his later compositions the linear harmony retreats into the episodes of transitional and connecting importance. Combination of such linear harmony with sonoristic effects in Shostakovich's early compositions is patently akin to some "avant-garde" techniques, some elements of his pointillistic texture are somewhat reminiscent of Webern. "The whole world is presented as broken into separate fragments of sounds and becomes surrealistic". "The conventional logic becomes irreal while all strange things are perceived as customary and natural". On the other part, Denisov associates the sources and development of Shostakovich's instrumentation techniques with Mahler: "The basic principles of instrumentation inherent in Shostakovich's mature compositions could be traced back to Mahler's orchestration". As for Shostakovich's Symphony No. 14, Denisov views it as "a kind of 'Song of the Earth' in Shostakovich's creative output".[6]

In Denisov's own words, Shostakovich was "a man whom I owe a lot in my life and whom I loved though I did not always like what he was doing both as a human person and a composer".

IGOR STRAVINSKY.   This composer exerted a profound influence on Denisov in the use of asymmetric rhythms, free and individualised approach to musical form-building on the basis of the traditionally European principles of composition, and in imbibing the intonations of the Russian peasant songs. In his introductory article to the publication of the score of *The Firebird* (1964) Denisov expressed his views about its creator. Citing Stravinsky's own statements, Denisov pays prime attention to his attitude to Glinka: "in grateful acknowledgement" he stresses Stravinsky's "reverential admiration" for the founder of the Russian composition school. Denisov shares his attitude to Glinka. "Stravinsky's outstanding talent enabled him to approach the Russian folk song in a fresh, unprecedented light": the same could be said about the composer of *Wails*. In contrast to the widespread opinion, Denisov considers Stravinsky's creative output to be integral; "Stravinsky's individuality is too complex and extraordinary even for our time". His drive "to embrace and use not only every possible genre but also every possible style" is reminiscent of Picasso's creative aspirations.

Stravinsky's earlier compositions — *Petrushka, The Rite of Spring* and *The Firebird* — are particularly close to Denisov. In his book *Percussion Instruments in a Modern Orchestra* he makes a monographic study of these three early ballets by Stravinsky and his *L'histoire du soldat, Renard* and *Les Noces*. As for neo-classicism showing a composer's retrograde mentality, Denisov denies it even in Stravinsky: "I don't like his *Perséphone*, concertos, songs on Shakespeare's verse, for it is dead music. The greatest composition of the neo-classical period is his *Symphony of Psalms*. Stravinsky's later compositions are just hollow framework".

Below we cite some of Denisov's short statements about other Russian composers.

PYOTR TCHAIKOVSKY.   "The best ballet music are these three ballets by Tchaikovsky. His *Nutcracker* is distinguished for its remarkable musical dramatic pattern".

SERGEI RACHMANINOV.   "The only piece I like in his music is the song *Lilacs*".

ANDREI VOLKONSKY.   "He is one the most prominent figures in the Russian musical art". His compositions "marked an epoch in Soviet music". "Volkonsky refused to obey the claims imposed upon him as a Soviet composer". "Andrei was the most gifted among the four of us.[7] He was the first to open the door behind which we had been groping for modernity in art".

SOPHIA GUBAIDULINA. "She lives in her own world which is alien to me". The percussion instruments in her *Five Studies* for harp, double bass and percussion sound "in a fresh and subtle way". "Schnittke and Gubaidulina produce no semi-finished works".

ALFRED SCHNITTKE. "His manner of writing differs from mine. He is a remarkable master". "I like his Second Violin Sonata and *Madrigals*. But I don't like many of his compositions, e.g., his Piano Quintet".

1.2.

MOZART — GLINKA — SCHUBERT.   Denisov feels reverence and admiration for these three composers: "Mozart, Glinka and Schubert are closer to my heart than any other music". Once asked which music, classical or his own, he used to listen to when he remained alone, Denisov replied: "It is never my own music, at such moments I enjoy Mozart". "As for the Russian composers, I like Glinka best of all. His *Valse fantaisie* is a superb score. His song "I Remember That Wondrous Moment" is the only one worthy of Pushkin". "Schubert's Symphony in C major is better than any of Beethoven's symphonies. And the best piece in it is Scherzo".

BÉLA BARTÓK.   "One of the 20th century classics". In Denisov's view, his best compositions are *Music for Strings, Percussion and Celesta*, Sonata for two pianos and percussion, and all of his six string quartets. His String Quartet No. 2 already displays 'the unification of horizontal and vertical elements' (but it is particularly in evidence in his next two quartets). "Bartók was striving for the maximal unity of musical texture, for drawing all its elements from one thematic source".[8] Therefore Denisov defines such theme as 'theme-series', which is exemplified in the first movement of his String Quartet No. 4.

PIERRE BOULEZ.   One of the modern composers highly valued by Denisov, though "his music is sometimes too dispassionate and refined". His art is in writing purely "French music, in the Messiaenian style". "I like best of all his *Improvisation sur Mallarmé I*". In his *Structures* for two pianos Boulez solved a two-fold task: "First, to tear himself away from any previous trends so that to avoid any stylistic allusions; second, to unify the entire development". In his *Marteau sans Maître* the composer wanted "to impart an extra-European element to the European mentality".

CLAUDE DEBUSSY.   "His opera *Pelléas et Mélisande* is one of the best compositions in the history of music". "I fully agree with his following statement: 'It is more beneficial for a composer to watch the sunrise than to hear Beethoven's Pastoral Symphony'". "In his works Debussy was far more radical and innovative than many other masters of the 20th-century music". "The striving for non-fixed form and its birth on the spur of the moment is the characteristic feature of Debussy's music". "Debussy's music is structurally precise. Only those who have little knowledge of his music can talk about the 'indistinctness' of his musical forms". "Debussy is the greatest French composer of all times and the most promising one. His music calls for the utmost concentration".

PAUL HINDEMITH.   "His music is completely alien to me". "In Shebalin's class the most severe criticism was expressed in the following words: 'Well, here you've started writing in the Hindemith style'". "I have the impression that Hindemith had never in his life seen either sunrise or sunset. He must have written all his music behind the closed doors to exclude the birdsong or the wind blowing". "It is an impasse, no promise, lifeless nonsense".

ARNOLD SCHOENBERG.   "A traditionalist composer. His orchestrations are in the Wagnerian style, with a lot inherited from *Tristan*". "I like best of all Schoenberg's atonal compositions such as *Erwartung* (Expectation), *Die Glückliche Hand* (The Blessed Hand) and *Five Orchestral Pieces*". As for his opera *Von Heute auf Morgen* (From One Day to the Next), Denisov says: "We are constantly aware of some contradiction between a light plot and too serious, sometimes heavy, music. His humour is always somewhat gloomy and heavy".[9] On the opera *Moses und Aron*: "You feel throughout that Schoenberg has made a thorough study of all of Beethoven's compositions, following Beethoven to the letter". "*Five Orchestral Pieces*, Op. 16 is one of his best opuses".

ANTON WEBERN.   Denisov's attitude to this Viennese composer is similar to his views on Mozart and Schubert. During his dodecaphonic period Webern "discovered a world of striking beauty and harmony, devoid of anything alogical and accidental". "One of the secrets inherent in his charming music is the logic of beauty". He is logically "moving forward, discovering ever new laws of beauty". "Even if Webern's music is 'abstract', it abstracts itself from anything dirty and cruel in human life, but it is wide open for everything kind and pure in man".[10]

Below are Denisov's concise statements about other Western composers.

BEETHOVEN.   "His musical material is not very spectacular, but its treatment is superb (with Schubert it is sometimes the reverse). Beethoven makes the utmost out of each motive, bringing each separate motive to a climax". "In his Symphony No. 9 the first three movements are very good, the best is the slow movement; and awful music in the finale".

BRITTEN.   "These are not operas but just theatrical shows with music; indeed, vocal music has to be vocal".

CAGE.   "I reject such music; the musical matter is indispensable but it is missing in Cage's music".

IVES.   "He is a bright composer". "He has some first-rate compositions to his credit, but along with them some complete failures and awful music. His modelling of the world is not to be borrowed".

LIGETI.   "His *Adventures* is a theatrical piece. Three soloists — the alto, the baritone and the tenor — are speaking the imaginary language; three soloists make a love triangle".

LUTOSLAWSKI.   "I'm very fond of this remarkable composer, especially his Cello Concerto, *Mi Parti* and *Novelette* for orchestra".

MAHLER.   "He strongly influenced me. I love his quiet music, songs in particular; it is marvellous music".

MESSIAEN.   "I love Messiaen not for his birds: his *Oiseaux* are the least attractive to me". "One of the greatest composers. His music emanates light".

NONO.   "In his music you often feel a contradiction between his lyrical gift and civic spirit".

PENDERECKI.   "He is very talented, but he has borrowed everything from Xenakis. His *Devils of Loudun* is a cursive writing, just applied music".

Ex. 48 *A. — C.* Brown: Joy Spring, *B* — Denisov: Concerto for piano and orchestra, 3rd movement, *C* — "Les quatre filles", scene 5

STOCKHAUSEN.   "His is a remarkable talent! But most likely, it is not purely musical". "At the moment I don't like his music". "His best composition is *Gruppen*".

RICHARD STRAUSS.   "Debussy once said: 'Out of two Richards I prefer Wagner and out of two Strausses — Johann'; I fully agree with this".

XENAKIS.   "This is a composer of a very high level".

FOLK MUSIC.   Long before his discovery of Bartók's ideas Edison Denisov had traversed a similar road. To quote his own words, "My direct contacts with folklore in the early years have exerted great influence on me". Denisov came to share Bartók's conception according to which "folk music is not a field for exploitation but, quite the reverse, a living source for a composer to draw from now and again, which helps him to gain the truly new creative strength". The same approach was characteristic of Glinka, Denisov's favourite Russian composer.

JAZZ AND ROCK MUSIC.   "I'm very fond of jazz. It is genuine art. Louis Armstrong and Miles Davis are true great musicians. Miles Davis is my favourite musician, his harmonic thinking is as refined as Debussy's". "Top-level jazz makes use of all the means of modern music. The only difference is in the material and the principles of employment. As for the techniques, these are the same collage and twelve-note procedure". "We should not fall into snobbery and only because of the widespread opinion that folk music and jazz are allegedly primitive types of art to block their natural penetration into serious music".[11]

Probably, the impact of jazz texture and melodics on Denisov's style is greater than it may seem at first sight. The road traversed by the postwar avant-garde during two of its periods — 'onset' and 'softening' — concerned Denisov too. The stage in the development of his style which we qualified as 'stabilization' (see Chapter 3) corresponds to 'the second avant-garde' and involves a frequent use of two textural types patently close to jazz. One of them pertains to compact chords of four notes (sometimes it may be six, three or eight notes). The other type is made up of melodic patterns-passages (often descending) which are so characteristic of Denisov's texture. Compare these two types with the typical jazz texture (Musical Example 48 A,B,C).

"I'm keenly interested in modern rock music. Captivated by its uninhibited and bright styles; sometimes you may come across high poetry too. My favourite group is Pink Floyd whose serious music I can listen to every day".

ELECTRONIC MUSIC.   "Electronic music is music produced by an electronic generator with the resultant sounds being recorded on tape; concrete music is assembled from normal music and everyday sounds".[12] "Electronic music proper is limited since it is 'musical canning'". "Few talented people have been involved with electronic music. It has great potentials, but the listener may get easily deceived. I like it better when live performance is combined with tape: interaction of the living and the dead (as with Gubaidulina: 'Vivente — non vivente")'.

2.   SOME GENERAL STATEMENTS ABOUT MUSIC

ART. ARTISTS AND THEIR WORKS.   "Any true art should be spiritual. The function of any art is to convert people into some faith, and the art possesses great power of affecting the human souls". "A true artist is a master first and foremost, and the process of composition is an involved process of arranging the raw and elusive material, that incoherent array of sounds, which obeys the artist under very strict control and great guiding and organizing volition. A composer is erecting a musical building and his architecture has to be perfect, for any miscalculation (or a weak point in the structure) inevitably leads to a premature death of the composition. The reason of durability of the great creations by Guillaume de Machaut, Claudio Monteverdi, Heinrich Schütz and Johann Sebastian Bach is not only in the information they carry but also in the infinitely perfect beauty of their structure". "A true musical composition is always a discovery and, therefore, it is quite natural that it is perceived as a happening. The element of mystery is invariably present in a true creative process".[13]

CLASSICAL MUSIC AND MODERN FASHION.   "Classical pieces are the most invaluable ones in music, for they have already settled. Modern music has a long way to go. Pop music is intended for momentary perception; classical music requires repeated hearing. Currently we witness many fans of bad music. People have lost the criterion of value".

TECHNIQUES. INTONATION.   "You need techniques to be free. Supreme freedom comes with immaculate techniques. The ideal is natural technique (as in Mozart and Glinka). The key point in a technique is not a procedure but its adequacy to the form. Today we have a lot of new spectacular media. It should take time to assimilate them and not speculate on them". "I always write without the piano. All good composers have always produced the full scores of their works; only bad composers have been making orchestrations of their piano scores". A modern composer, in Denisov's view, "should synthesize his techniques. He should choose techniques according to how well they suit his purposes". "There shouldn't be anything accidental in music. Each instrument should play its own part so that it could not be replaced by another instrument".

"The intonation should be tenacious and characteristic but not senseless. Intonation calls for special attention to avoid anything accidental. The task facing a composer is to find his own intonations. The material gives birth to form, with simultaneous striving for beauty and naturalness".

THE NATIONAL AND INTERNATIONAL.   "Modern composers have departed from the idea of national music and become internationalist in their spirit. The attempts are made, for instance, to synthesize the Oriental art with ours. But it is a hard task. The traditions of a Javanese gamelan are visible in the works by Messiaen and Boulez. I regard such combinations as alien to the European spirit, somewhat unnatural. But in case a true synthesis has been accomplished, that is good".

THE CREATIVE PROCESS.   When asked "How do you compose?", Denisov replied: "When I have a chance to run away from everything, I work from morning till late at night — for 12, 14 hours a day; I never make any rough drafts". "Whenever I listen to my music, I take it hard, for it is part of myself". "The process of composition sets into action various layers of human consciousness simultaneously, with the role of the subconscious increasing to a great extent. Sometimes the subconscious dictates the solutions so rapidly and accurately that a composer turns nearly into an automatic machine recording down what seems to him to be form-building without his will and mind. You feel as if your hand is being guided by some strange power which dictates its terms to you".[14]

MUSIC & PAINTING.   The composer with the mathematical education was once asked whether mathematics helped or hindered him in his creative career. Denisov's reply was unequivocal: "It helps". However, it is not mathematics but painting that exerts its profound influence on Denisov's work. He says that his teachers of music were painters. "The laws of music and painting are identical". "Any painting involves the layout of a definite number of elements in two-dimensional space. The painter faces the problem of form — coordination of separate elements, their logical arrangement in space, the creation of rhythm within a composition, and removal of anything accidental and violating its unity and integrity. A composer has to tackle essentially similar elements". "The closest analogies arise between non-figurative (or semi-figurative) painting and music. The constituent elements in a picture are not subject here to a thematic plot while their expressive resources are manifested in colour and form". As they gave up thematic arrangement and figurativeness, both composers and painters drew on the idea of deducing all the elements of a form from the common thematic source, i.e. the idea of serialism. And Denisov discovers the serial principle of composition in painting, especially in the pictures of Paul Klee and Piet Mondrian: Klee's "Fugue in Red" (1921), "Static and Dynamic Gradations" (1923) and "Blooming Garden", or Mondrian's "Compositions" (1917–1928) and "Victory Boogie-Woogie". Iannis Xenakis turned "the musical architecture of his *Metastasis* into the actually erected Philips pavilion at the Brussels Fair in 1958"; hence modern sound paintings are compositions which may be performed as musical pieces or just viewed as pictures (e.g., *December 1952* by the American composer Earle Brown).[15]

3.   SOME PROBLEMS OF MUSICAL COMPOSITION

MELODY.   Edison Denisov, a composer of the 'avant-garde' new music, is guided by his conceptions extolling melody. "The 20th century has revealed a decline in melodiousness, even in Shostakovich and Prokofiev. The principled rejection of melody is inherent in avant-gardism. The 20th-century composers have discovered that timbre carries the same information as melody, and even greater. At the same time modern composers have been tending to new melodic lines, showing a great wish to write melodic music". In his article "On Some Types of Melody in Modern Music" Denisov vigorously upholds melodic music meaning its songfulness, cantilena. His ideas amount to the following: "The type of melodiousness which was inherent in the 19th-century musical thinking passed into genres known as 'light'". But "lately pop music also has been gene-rally tending to breaking down melody and replacing it by the elementary into-nation formulas (usually repeated over and over again)".

"You may also come across melodic lines modelling those typical of the preced-ing times. It is particularly evident in composers tending to neo-classicism, such as Max Reger, Darius Milhaud, Arthur Honegger, Sergei Prokofiev and Dmitry Shostakovich", but it is most characteristic of Paul Hindemith. "The melodic patterns of many 20th-century composers modelling the classical forms of writing are deliberately ugly and inflexible". As the examples of such melodic themes Denisov mentions some passages from Hindemith's Symphony *Mathis der Maler*, Henry Cowell's Symphony No. 15 and Křenek's Symphony *Pallas Athene*. Denisov points to the inner contradictions of the same type in the themes using all 12 semitones (Hindemith's *Cardillac*, Schoenberg's String Quartet No. 4 and Shostakovich's String Quartet No. 12). He believes the principle of notes' non-recurrence in a melody to be 'artificial'. "Dodecaphonic melody combined with a flexible and changeable melodic line sounds far more organic". He cites the example: Pierre Boulez's *Improvisation sur Mallarmé I* whose melody is based on the harmonic set of the "– notes $d^1 – ab^1 – c$" gradually revealed through leap-like intervals. In his appraisal of new melodic types in the compositions of Boulez and Luigi Mono Denisov emphasizes the bright individuality of each composer, the one displaying the traditional French melody while the other — purely Italian melodies.

In respect to the problems of melody Denisov expounds one of the laws in the 20th-century New Music: "At each moment some element assumes the function of Hauptstimme — the composer directs our attention either to intonation, then harmony, now rhythm or timbre".[16] Denisov considers intonation to be the core of the science of modern melody. His criticism of neo-classicism as a method of musical thinking and his keenness on 'intonation' elucidate the aesthetic views of Denisov the artist: he discards the now inert and formally indifferent idioms of old music and draws with all his artistic soul on the source of spontaneous musical expressiveness — 'intonation'. He rejects any static convention, striving to immerse himself in the very process of formation: "A musical composition is a living organism and the intonation density is the basis which makes this organism viable". Nowadays the sphere of intonation has expanded greatly, coming to embrace intervals previously believed to the 'non-melodic'; 'melodies' made up of sounds of indefinite pitch (in Messiaen's works we hear birdsong and 'melodies' of tam-tams, Alpine chimebells, and gongs); quarter-tones and other special types of tempered intervals (splitting of a semitone makes a melody 'particularly gentle and intimate'); colour, timbre as an element of intonation, etc. Therefore modern music has no "crisis of melody". "For a time being we have forgotten what boundless resources are inherent in melodism and have been carried away with a constructivist approach to intonation". (It is likely to be regarded as an attack on Schoenberg's dogmatically understood dodecaphonic serialism. The author's Russian nature rejects this attire upon himself as something alien, eventually as a tedious duty and discards it, turning to freedom and spontaneity. He seems to follow Stockhausen: "From Webern to Debussy".)

In his article "On Some Types of Melody in Modern Music" Denisov discloses one of his innermost secrecies of his own creative thinking. He shows on musical examples the expressive multiformity of intonation 'in different presentation'. Let us take the descending minor second b♭ – a. Depending on actual intervals, rhythm, harmony and counterpoint and, of course, timbre there arise multifarious substantive shadings of musical expression (Musical Example 49 A–H). For instance, in Musical Example 49 B the quarter-tones enhance the expressiveness of the intonation b♭ – a lending it 'greater intimacy and depth'. In Musical Example 49 C the extension of the range imparts "Mahler's expressiveness" to it. In Musical Example 49 G "the intonation is broken by a rest, register and timbre; its expressiveness is almost fully removed". In Musical Example 49 H "the intonation overlaps itself in several versions forming a moving cluster". It is easily observable that throughout, particularly in the last case, Denisov analyses his own music treating it in the light of new melodic lines.[17]

INSTRUMENTATION.   Timbre and tone-colours have come to play the leading role in an ensemble of elements inherent in the New Music. "I don't like bad orchestration, for it has become obsolete". The new idea of an orchestral score is its multidimensionality. It is evident in the scores of Mozart, Mahler and Ives. "It often involves three, four or five self-contained layers; with different orchestras overlapping one another (as in Ives)".

SERIALISM. DODECAPHONY.   Edison Denisov was the first in the USSR to produce a serious research paper on serialism and dodecaphony — in December 1962 — January 1963. Today it would be hard to imagine what severe criticism was levelled at the very word 'dodecaphony' in the 1950s–1960s in this country. Some wisecrack even misspelled it as "dodecacophony" and for a long time it was thus scornfully nicknamed.

Grigory Shneyerson in his vulgar book *Of Living and Dead Music* (1960) expressed the official attitude to dodecaphony explaining the widespread

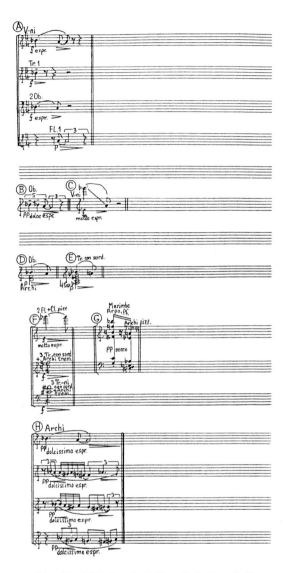

Ex. 49 Melody, *A, B, C, D, E, F, G, H*

employment of this technique in the West "by its relatively easy accessibility to each competent and fairly diligent musician (not necessarily an intellectually gifted one)".[18]

Denisov describes the prototypes of twelve-note procedure, the emergence of dodecaphony in the spirit of 'free atonality' on the basis of polyphony, the structure and use of a series, and various stylistic interpretations of the serial technique (Schoenberg, Klebe, Stravinsky, Berg, Liebermann, Mayuzumi, Dallapiccola, Babajanian). In the author's opinion, the prerequisites of dodecaphony include the equal status of all the twelve pitches, removal of a clear tonal basis, chromaticism of thematic arrangement (Liszt), non-functionality of harmony, complication of vertical lines, the complementary principle, the linear development of musical texture, unification of horizontal and vertical elements, and a number of other evolutionary phenomena. "Dodecaphony has not been 'invented' or 'imposed' by anybody on art". As for the serial technique, Denisov interprets it in a broader sense: "First and foremost, a series is the key intonation basis combining horizontal and vertical elements and bringing them together to a common thematic source". The musical texture becomes thematic throughout: "The concept of series may serve as an expanded substitution for the concept of mode".[19] Or, to be more precise, serialism constitutes an alloy-synthesis of modal and thematic arrangement. For in the past thematic arrangement was also a rhythmically individualized representation of the fundamental formulas of mode and harmony. During the Romantic period the process of individualizing these two formulas brought forth legalization of harmonic (interval) material selected for any individual composition, with the series being its extreme case. But it gives rise to a possible reverse train of thought: the extension of serialist categories over harmonic and thematic arrangement in modern tonal music. This is what Denisov is doing when he extends the category of "series" over the non-serial harmonic and thematic phenomena. In his article "Béla Bartók's String Quartets" he writes: "As a matter of fact, Bartók's later technique may be regarded as serial, for the musical texture arises as a derivative of the inner resources of a theme-series making the basis of this composition. The entire texture of the Fourth Quartet is consistently deduced from the initial theme-series".[20] This is certainly an exaggeration but it reveals the deep-going bonds between the 20th-century series and the tonality and thematic arrangement used in the 18th and 19th centuries. In a generalized way the functional concept of series as it is treated by Denisov also shows his characteristic gravitation towards greater structural freedom, which brings him close to the traditions of Russian music.

So, the series makes the musical texture thematic throughout. A theme is a logical concept, an idea that implies a subject of further 'discourse' (Stravinsky) and continuous development. Denisov defines the difference between a theme and a melody in the following forms: a melody has "a certain completeness of a musical idea whereas a theme represents primarily a complex of intonations capable of further unfolding. The structural shape of a theme is not of so great importance".[21] "A series often arises in the composer's mind already in a definite melodic pattern as the principal theme of a composition in the broadest sense of the word" for instance, in Petrarca's Sonnet 217 from Schoenberg's Op. 24.[22]

The more recent theoreticians of twelve-tone music (particularly in the USA — Milton Babbitt, George Perle, et al.) made a detailed study of the principles of the serial structure and series elaboration (relationships between the segments of a series, kinship between serial note-rows, adequate pitches for series segments, permutations, derivative series, etc.). Denisov also touches upon the treatment of a series not going into details about his own methods (see Chapter 3). Nonetheless, he describes some of his techniques: the splitting of a series and use of its separate segments as the self-contained thematic formations, and the splitting of a series into two independent chords. Denisov just outlines his serial technique in a general, technically non-concrete formula of 'common thematic source' from which the composer draws the material for the entire texture of his compositions. The way how he does it remains open to discussion. Let us keep in mind, however, that Denisov's article about dodecaphony reflects his ideas of 1962 when he was just beginning to write twelve-note music.

As Denisov understands it, dodecaphony and serialism do not exclude tonality, either old or, the more so, new. He refers to Berg's Violin Concerto where the series itself presupposes the use of tonality in G minor. He also points to the polytonal treatment of the musical material in Rolf Liebermann's Piano Sonata. In his analysis of Webern's Variations, Op. 27, Denisov finds 'tonalities', 'serial modulation' and even a 'tonal' layout in this 'atonal' composition. It stands to reason that Denisov means new tonality and not 'the old good' C major or D minor.[23]

In his comparison of the two types of thinking Denisov comes to the generalized conclusion: "The pitch logic of a series may be viewed as a higher type of tonal logic incorporating the traditional tonal logic as a particular case".[24]

ALEATORY. THE STABLE AND THE MOBILE.   The composition structure with the unfixed musical texture is one of the striking phenomena in modern music. In his article "Stable and Mobile Elements of Musical Form and Their Interaction" Denisov discloses its historical roots (the musical texture in basso continuo, the improvized cadenza in a classical concerto). In the 20th century the correlation between the determinant (stable, rigidly fixed) and free (mobile, indeterminant) elements becomes a major composition problem. Denisov gives a general classification of the structural types in dependence of the role played by the stable and mobile elements in a composition. According to his classification there are the following three basic types:

1. The form as a whole is stable but its separate structures are mobile. The fields of indeterminacy may thereby be given either in alternation with stable structures or in a parallel confluence of both elements, e.g., Pierre Boulez's *Improvisation sur Mallarmé I* and *II* and the 4th movement in Denisov's own *The Sun of the Incas*;

2. The structures are stable but their sequence provides for multiformity (rather than fixation) of realizations, e.g., Karlheinz Stockhausen's *Klavierstuck XI* and Boulez's Third Sonata;

3. The form and the structure are both mobile: Stockhausen's *Zyklus* may be taken as an example. The musical graphic scripture proved to be the most vivid manifestation of a form's mobility. 'Open' forms provide for an infinite multitude of interpretations.[25]

An impetus to mobility was given by the too rigid structuralism of serial music (with its serialization of not only pitches but of other parameters too — rhythm, articulation and dynamics). The experimentation conducted by John Cage is proceeding in a different direction "clearing the way for chaos and absurdities" because of the arbitrary selection of the musical material. But according to Denisov, "music has always been and still is an art, i.e., it involves a certain degree of organization and coherence of musical thinking".[26] He cites Boulez's words to the effect that "lack of discipline is not freedom". Denisov admits the modulation of a form from stable into a mobile one or vice versa, also in a retrograde statement (obviously, his piece *Grescendo e diminuendo* is based on this principle).

POLYSTYLISTICS.   In 1984 Denisov stated: "The so called polystylistic trends have always been alien to me. I regard it as eclecticism. And as before I still view eclecticism as a drawback in a work of art. Nevertheless, I have resorted to quotations in a few of my compositions". Among the latter he lists his String Trio, *DSCH* and *Silhouettes*. According to Denisov, his rare collage-type compositions serve only to demonstrate that his style is devoid of any polystylistics.

MINIMALISM.   "My attitude to minimalism is negative. It bears the marks of artistic conformism, being expressive of some fatigue. Minimalism arises from a wish to find facile paths in art. Some Americans are engaged in it, e.g., Steve Reich and Philip Glass. It is quite uninteresting".

The brief outline of Denisov's system of views in this chapter reveals the artist's subjective self-awareness. It is an integral part of his musicological studies. Of course, Denisov is primarily a composer. But the importance of his contributions to the science of music makes us consider him to be a major musicologist as well. In his concluding lines in the Introduction to Denisov's book *Modern Music and Some Problems Arising in the Evolution of Compositional Techniques* the eminent musicologist Mikhail Tarakanov quite justifiably wrote that this collection of articles "makes a useful and substantial contribution to our musical science" containing "invaluable information". The value of Denisov's major musicological studies is primarily due to the fact that his ideas proved to be the most innovative at the time of their publication for the Soviet musical science. He took the challenge in writing about the modern musical phenomena and the composers whose names were forbidden to mention.

The views of Denisov the musicologist reveal his character traits of a human person and an artist. His main trait is openness to all the new trends, natural response to the newly discovered artistic domains and his striving to share immediately the musical values he has come to learn with other people. And the last but not the least, Denisov is endowed with that musical gift which makes his musicological treatises highly informative.

Notes to Chapter 5

1. In his article published in 1954 in co-authorship with Alexander Pirumov, Denisov cited a remarkable song from the Kursk Region, "Chimes Are Pealing in the Town", in the whole-tone mode.
2. Cited from the article: "Music Which I Love", *Melodia* magazine, No. 4, 1984, p. 60.
3. Cited from Denisov's collection of articles "Modern Music and Some Problems Arising in the Evolution of Compositional Techniques". Moscow, 1986, pp. 31, 46.
4. Cited from Denisov's book *Percussion Instruments in a Modern Orchestra*. Moscow, 1982, p. 153.
5. The credit for the discovery of the Russian musical avant-garde dating back to the beginning of this century goes to the German musicologist Detlef Gojowy.
6. Cited from Denisov's collection of articles "Modern Music and Some Problems Arising in the Evolution of Compositional Techniques". Moscow, 1986, pp. 46, 48, 59–65, 74–76; also from the book *Percussion Instruments in a Modern Orchestra*. Moscow, 1982, pp. 161, 168.
7. The other three included Denisov, Schnittke and Gubaidulina (the authors' note).
8. Cited from Denisov's collection of articles "Modern Music and Some Problems Arising in the Evolution of Compositional Techniques". Moscow 1986, pp. 22, 24, 27.
9. Ibidem, p. 166.
10. Ibidem, pp. 168, 206.
11. Ibidem, pp. 164, 163.
12. Ibidem, p. 151.
13. Ibidem, p. 154.
14. Ibidem, pp. 13, 14.

15. Ibidem, pp. 157–159.
16. Ibidem, pp. 137–141.
    "Hauptstimme" (the graphic symbol H) is the notation sign of the leading melody used by Schoenberg and his school.
17. Cited from Denisov's collection of articles "Modern Music and Some Problems Arising in the Evolution of Compositional Techniques". Moscow, 1986, pp.148–149.
18. This and other similar phrases are cited by Denisov in his article "Dodecaphony and Some Problems in Modern Composition Techniques" published in the collection *Music & Modern Times*, Issue 6. Moscow, 1969, pp. 478–525.
19. Ibidem, p. 490.
20. Cited from Denisov's collection of articles "Modern Music and Some Problems Arising in the Evolution of Compositional Techniques". Moscow, 1986, p. 27.
21. Ibidem.
22. Cited from the article "Dodecaphony and Some Problems of Modern Composition Techniques", p. 491.
23. Cited from the collection "Modern Music and Some Problems Arising in the Evolution of Compositional Techniques", pp. 174, 175, 199.
    According to some witty remark, "to look for old tonality in dodecaphony is like to try splitting the atom with the help of an ordinary hammer".
24. Ibidem, p. 199.
25. Ibidem, pp. 119–133.
26. Ibidem, p. 132.

AFTERWORD

Each artistic phenomenon accumulates at least some key problems of its times. From this viewpoint Denisov's art represents one more variation of "the Russian question". Once Vladimir Smolensky, a poet of the Russian diaspora, wrote:

There is no room for art
When the life is so cold and horrible.

As it turns out, there is always room for art. Indeed, our century has witnessed the terrifying developments: the destruction of the great Russian empire forcibly deprived of its invigorating and fascinating idea. (The current 'parade of sovereignties' and the breakdown of the country remind of the situation in which Russia found itself in the 12th–13th centuries; who is going to act as a new Mongol?) The Russians are not exiled from Russia any longer. But they are leaving at their own will. Some of them are looking for reunification with the West, which is inherent in the Russian culture; to this category belongs Denisov who after his stay in Paris and his work with the I.R.C.A.M. came to live in Moscow again. Others are leaving this country of unlimited troubles for good.

The great thinkers of the past — Dostoyevsky, Vladimir Solovyov, Pavel Florensky and Nikolai Berdayev — saw the solution of 'the Russian question' in Orthodox religiosity. Florensky wrote about a special 'spiritual beauty' viewing beauty as a criterion of leading a proper new life in one's spirit, i.e., in religiosity. But the modern realities within the last three quarters of a century have been far from such ideas. The art, on the whole, is also far from them. A kind of vacuum of dominant ideas has been created in modern Russian music no longer guided by "the only true" precepts of 'socialist realism'. In the atmosphere of relative artistic freedom the noticeable part came to be played by the eclectic 'polystylistics' fixating the non-identity of an individual and running down to banality which attracts by its easy accessibility. In this context one of the underlying ideas in Denisov's art — new musical beauty — accurately reflects the good features inherent in the present-day Russian spiritual life. However, the approach to beauty in this case differs from that of in the Russian religious philosophy. Rather, it makes Denisov akin to one of the traditions of Romantic music — Schubert, Glinka and, paradoxically as it may seem, Webern. During the stage of a cruel crisis it is not necessarily at all that art should convey the situation of disintegration. An artist may choose to stand in opposition to the adverse effects of the environment.

The art of Denisov's composition, despite its reliance on the past traditions, belongs to the innovative line in modern creativity. His 'avant-gardism' was not a tribute to the current vogue, and in the post-avant-garde 1980s he did not turn to the currently fashionable 'neo' and 'retro'. As compared to the most radical avant-gardists such as, for instance, Stockhausen and Boulez, Denisov's innovations prove to be quite moderate. Boris Schwartz in his extensive treatise on Soviet music pointed out that in Denisov's *The Sun of the Incas* you could perceive the echoes of the Russian spirit. The unconscious orientation to the Russian musical community makes the composer's innovations singular and determines their measure. In his thinking he draws on the twelve hemitonal musical system wherein the parameters of timbre, pitch and duration lying within the common acoustic field and, correspondingly, harmonic and rhythmic colours appear to follow one and the same line. Among the hemitonic models the key place belongs to the most concentrated structure 1.1 (in semitones), most frequently encountered in the form of the EDS formula. But at the same time in his compositions Denisov is not striving for the strictest rational regulation of the structure making it free to a certain extent. At a new turn of the spiral historical evolution the structure of avant-garde music comes unexpectedly to be associated with Mussorgsky. Thus, having abandoned the strict fixed order in the turnover of the twelve non-recurrent pitches, the composer does not impose upon his composition any other strict principle (as it does, for instance, Boulez does it) for the sake of spontaneous emotional expressiveness, particularly in conveying the meaning of the word and mood of the text in vocal music.

Today Edison Denisov is already regarded as a classic of modern Russian music. Indeed, he is the only one out of the composers currently living in Russia who has set a creative trend if not his own school. Nowadays he has become a source of tradition in his own right. When asked what composition he himself believes to be his best, the creator usually replies that he has not yet written it. A true artist is always heading along and the listeners are entitled to expect from him what he cannot foresee himself.

APPENDIX 1

LETTERS FROM DMITRY SHOSTAKOVICH TO EDISON DENISOV

All letters from Dmitry Shostakovich to Edison Denisov were first published by Detlef Gojowy in *Musick des Ostens* No. 10 (Kassel•Basel•London. 1986) in German. In our publication we have omitted some everyday details and repetitions.

LETTERS FROM DMITRY SHOSTAKOVICH TO EDISON DENISOV

June 28, 1948. Moscow

   Comrade Denisov (I'm sorry I don't know your first name and your father's name), I acknowledge the receipt of your letter. I've read it with great interest. I would like to argue with you on some points but I do it badly on paper. I hope we'll meet some time in the future and have a talk. I'm very glad that you love music and show keen interest in this art which is so dear to me and without which I can't imagine my life. I wish you all success in your work and personal life.
   Shaking your hand firmly,

D.Shostakovich

December 23, 1949. Moscow

   Dear Comrade Denisov! If my memory does not fail me, your name is Edik. I've received your letter with your critical remarks about my music. I thank you very much. You've touched upon serious questions. But I'm not a great master at writing letters. Perhaps, we'll have a chance to meet and have a talk. Probably we'll reach understanding or maybe we are going to dispute. In any case, it would be beneficial. I wish you all success and a Happy New Year.

Shaking your hand firmly,

D.Shostakovich

February 28, 1950. Moscow

Dear Edik, I've received your letter. I'm glad that you are so bent on music and aspire to become a musician. But before you take such a serious decision (entering the Conservatoire) I would ask you to send me your compositions. In case you have only a single copy of your works, by all means make a copy and send it to me. I don't consider myself entitled to determine whether you are endowed with composition gifts or not and, therefore, I'm going to consult with some people more experienced in this matter. And then I'll write to you if it is worth while for you to enter the Conservatoire and become a composer. So the question is settled, send me your compositions.
Shaking your hand,

D.Shostakovich

P.S. Please send me some details such as: how old you are, your full name and whether you can play the piano.

D.S.

March 22, 1950. Moscow

Dear Edik, your compositions have astonished me. If you don't have the elementary musical education, it is just a wonder how you could be so proficient in your composition which looks fairly professional to me. At any rate, I would ask you again to advise me on the following questions: 1. What musical education have you got? (the knowledge of musical theory, solfeggio, harmony, instrumentation, etc.); 2. Do you play the piano well? 3. How old are you? 4. Your full name.

Many things in your compositions I liked very much. I believe that you are endowed with a great gift for composition. And it would be a great sin to bury your talent. Of course, to become a composer, you have a lot to learn. And I mean not only the metier itself, but many other things as well. A true composer should be able not only to pick up a melody and the accompaniment and provide a good orchestration. Every competent musician is likely to be capable of it. But composition involves much more than that.

I believe what it means to be a composer you could find out when you have carefully studied all the riches inherent in the musical legacy which has been left to us from the great masters of the past. I hope we'll have a chance to meet and talk about it, though I must warn you that I'm not a great conversationalist. Your pieces display something which makes me get assured of your great composition talent. I'm afraid that I would fail to analyze it somehow. I rely on my flair, or to be more precise, on my perception of your music. Nonetheless, I would like to give my opinion about your compositions.

Gavotte. A very nice composition. The instrumentation is not bad. Shows a great and refined taste. As for myself, I don't like music of such light character, though I don't deny the right to its existence.

The song "Once upon a Time There Lived a Severe King". I did not like it. It is poor both in melody and harmony.

The song "On the Faraway Horizon". A bit better. The vocal part has big errors because of the senseless use of high notes. The resultant useless squeal is not justified by either musical or poetic content. Generally speaking, it is a piece of salon music.

The song "I Love You". Quite weak. A typical piece of salon music, in a not very good taste.

"Ante Lucem". This song is better than the two previous ones. In my view, here you make an abusive use of the elementary 'gloomy' sounds. The vocal part is quite poor. It is not a melody in the high sense of the word, but in Riemann's clumsy stereotyped definition ("A melody is a set of sounds in different size and different duration").

"You with Your Blue Eyes". A piece of salon music, pleasing to the ear.

"Tufts of the Falling White Snow". Not bad, but too lengthy and monotonous.

"Full Moon O'er the Meadow". I believe it is the best song of all (you've sent me). I liked it very much. A very good piano part.

"Autumn". A bad introduction. The ... is not bad.

I did not like very much the next two settings of Yesenin's poems.

"The Altai Collective-Farmers Song". Not bad, though I see nothing interesting in it.

"The Sea Song". The same.

"Failure". It is good by the very fact that you have a sense of humour. Regrettably, the vocal parts are not sufficiently impressive throughout.

Minuet for Oboe and Piano is very good.

Suite for Orchestra and Chorus astonished me with your skill in orchestration. As a whole, I liked it, though I don't think much of its first movement.

Here is a cursory account of my first impressions from your compositions. Don't be cross with me because I've failed to provide a detailed analysis and well-grounded criticism. I just can't do it. But here arises the question I've already posed at the beginning of this letter: what is your musical education? If you are a beginner with no sufficient musical training behind you, then everything you have sent to me is striking and worth of admiration. For a person lacking a solid musical education is incapable of writing such scores as your 'Suite' and 'Gavotte'. In case you have not got any musical education, I must admit that you are an extraordinary phenomenon.

In case you do have some musical training, I must tell you the following: you are endowed with a composition gift, but it is still to manifest itself in the future. All of your compositions you have sent to me are not yet sufficiently modern and profound. They are marked more for the outward euphony than for depth and pithiness. The same, but to a lesser degree, is valid of your 'Suite'. Then, if you are an experienced composer, I must tell, first, that your pieces show quite a number of professional drawbacks (bad voice-leading, etc.). Second, your personal style is almost indiscernible in your compositions: there is no composition individuality (for God's sake, don't look for it in the employment of false notes). An individual style is not to be found in this. It will come to you, if you are a budding composer, with the years and experience. I have no doubts about your gift. And if you regard your creative work honestly and chivalrously, everything will come. So to make a long story short: answer promptly all my questions I've posed before you. But the main point is what is your musical education and how long you have been composing.

Shaking your hand firmly,

D.Shostakovich

April 5, 1950. Moscow

Dear Edik, I've been very pleased to receive your two letters: one with your personal particulars and the other containing your response to my remarks about your compositions. I felt gratified to read how you are arguing to protect your works against my critical remarks. It means that you love them. It is another point in your favour, i.e., it shows that you are sure to become a composer. A true artist loves his creations. Nevertheless, I stick to my own opinion and find a number of forgivable shortcomings in your compositions which are undoubtedly to disappear in the future. You are asking for my advice about your future career. Your unquestionable talent makes me insist on you becoming a composer. But if you have just one year to go before you graduate from the university, then finish it. The composer's path is thorny (excuse me for this trite phrase). I've broken my neck doing it and I still do. So, I believe, or to be more precise, I'm sure that you are capable of becoming a composer and even 'with your own face'. If you take the challenge don't curse me in the future. I repeat: the composer's path is thorny. I tell it from my own experience. As for the university, don't hesitate to graduate from it.

I would like to meet your personally and have a talk. Perhaps, I'll find time and come to Tomsk for the purpose. Or maybe you'll be able to come to Moscow. In this case inform me beforehand about your coming and put down my telephone number: G 1–22–56.

Shaking your hand firmly,

D.Shostakovich

P.S. Let me know whether I should send your compositions back to you or I can keep them for some time more.

D.S.

April 22, 1950. Moscow

Dear Edik, first of all I must answer your questions. You are asking whether I'm teaching composition at the conservatoire. The answer is negative. So your second question (whether I could take you into my class) no longer arises. As for whose class I would advise you to enroll into, I must say that, as far as I know, composition at the conservatoire is taught now by Bogatyrev, Shaporin, Golubev and Fere. Probably there are some other teachers. I don't know for sure. I would advise you to take Bogatyrev for your tutorship. Semyon Semyonovich Bogatyrev has not established a reputation for himself as a composer. I don't know his compositions. But he is a remarkable musician and a fine connoisseur of the 'musical metier'. And for a start I would advise you to take up his classes. There is some talk about Vissarion Shebalin coming back to the conservatoire to teach, though the rumours have not yet been confirmed. If he comes back, I not only advise you but even insist that you should enroll himself into his class. I believe that V.Ya.Shebalin is the best teacher in composition in the Soviet Union. In a few days I'll know everything for sure and then I'll write to you. I'll also learn about all the formalities you'll have to go through to enter the conservatoire; whether it is possible to be admitted to the conservatoire upon finishing a music college or they require something else. At any rate I know that one can be easily transferred from the Moscow to the Leningrad Conservatoire and vice versa. In any other cases you have to pass the entrance exams.

And now about the everyday matters. It is extremely difficult to find lodgings in Moscow. I'm afraid you'll have a lot of troubles with this matter, if you decide to come to Moscow. The conservatoire hostel is overcrowded. You could hardly count on it. At any rate, I'll try to find out the current situation with the hostel accommodations as well.

I'm firmly convinced that any composer must be a fairly good pianist. Therefore, I advise you to enter two departments at once: composition and piano playing. If you like your selection of my piano preludes, play them. A pedal-point there is mine. But if it does not suit you, you may change it as you like.

I'm finishing this letter a bit worried. I wouldn't like you to be cross with me in case of some future troubles in your life. One day you may feel like saying: "my life was so quiet and peaceful and then, because of him, I went to Moscow, got myself involved with the conservatoire, and now the student's grant is so small and I have no place to live in, and the like..."

D.Shostakovich

P.S. Today or tomorrow I'll be sending you my Sixth Symphony and in addition my third quartet. I consider my third string quartet to be one of my most successful works. When you look through it, keep in mind that the first movement should be played not too lively but gently.

D.S.

May 6, 1950. Moscow

Dear Edik, I'm very sorry that my last letter so upset you. I didn't mean it. I just decided to inform you about the possible difficulties that might arise from your coming to Moscow (housing, the formalities, etc.). All these businesslike, prosaic matters don't dispose to lyrical reflections. In my last letter I forgot to mention that Anatoly Alexandrov is also a professor at the conservatoire. I have the following idea: I want to show your compositions to some Moscow musicians, namely to Shebalin, Bogatyrev, Alexandrov et al. Let them size you up and it will be sort of tentative examination for you. If you decide to enter the conservatoire you would be sure in advance that you are admitted. Personally I don't doubt it, but as far as I remember, the examiners have proved wrong in several cases.

As soon as you receive this letter, cable me whether I can show your compositions to anybody. I can't do it without your permission. In any case you must graduate from the university. Your letters make me glad. I'm happy about your trust in me.

The other day I looked through your compositions. Your talent is obvious. But you have the following weak points: your melodic material is weak. Besides, you are too restrained. You have to slacken the reins and give vent to your emotions. It seems to me that you are currently too anxious to 'smooth' your ideas. Try to write more boldly, vividly and substantially. But the main point: work hard on your melodic lines. Awaiting your cable.

Yours truthfully,

D.Shostakovich

May 20, 1950. Moscow

Dear Edik, I acknowledge the receipt of your cable, letter and music. I showed your compositions to S.S.Bogatyrev and V.Ya.Shebalin. Unfortunately, their opinion about your compositions does not coincide with mine. They see in your music the general musical capacity, a fairly high level of professionalism but fail to discern in you the hallmarks of genuine gift for composition. They explain it by the poorness of melody and uninteresting harmony. They attribute your ability to compose music to your intellect, versatile and unquestionable. They also point to a lack of heartfelt warmth and creative inventiveness. To my question about a possibility of you entering the conservatoire, they responded very indefinitely. Bogatyrev said that it was worth to keep contact with you, but on learning that you are residing in Tomsk, he expressed his doubts about the necessity, in view of your modest abilities, in his opinion, for making such drastic changes in your life (to give up your studies at the university, transfer to the conservatoire, move to Moscow and so on). Shebalin is also inclined to think so. Their judgements proved to be quite unexpected for me. When I think all this over and consider the pros and cons, I'll write to you more. Meanwhile don't be angry with me for such unpleasant letter. It is unpleasant for me too, so I end this letter at this point.

Yours sincerely,

D.Shostakovich

June 15, 1950. Komarovo

Dear Edik, I have been away in the Crimea. Upon my return to Moscow I found your cable and your letter. First of all, about my attitude to you. Under the influence of Bogatyrev and Shebalin I have not changed my opinion about you as a man endowed with a great gift. Your 'Classical Suite' is another evidence that I have been right. I had no chance to meet Anatoly Alexandrov and show him your compositions. Probably soon I'll have to go for a few days to Moscow and then I'll try to contact him and show him your works. You ought to pay serious attention to your shortcomings (melody!). A theme, melody, is the soul of music. And if this soul has a flaw, you may say that there is no composition as it were.

It would be useful for you to study at the conservatoire. I think you will be admitted. And in case of a failure, try once more, say, in a year or two. It is very difficult for me to give advice, especially as the road from Tomsk to Moscow is so long. Such a trip will involve a lot of expenses.

I'm finishing my letter at this. I repeat: I believe in your gift. Give more thought to melody and thematic arrangement. Melody doesn't come easily. You have to work on it as on polyphony, instrumentation, harmony, etc.

Yours faithfully,

D.Shostakovich

July 2, 1950. Komarovo

Dear Edik, thank you for your photograph. Now I have some idea how you look. Today I'm leaving for a few days for Moscow. And then I'll come back here again, to Komarovo. I'll get all your compositions together, fold them and put them in some fixed place. If you come to Moscow and call at my place, anybody who is to open the door will hand them over to you personally. You have just to name yourself. I advise you once more to think it over before you come to Moscow and enter the conservatoire. As I have already written to you, S.S.Bogatyrev, one of the influential conservatoire professors, gave a lukewarm response to your composion endeavours. It may so happen that his colleagues will be also sour in their attitude to you. In that case you'll have to make off and go back to Tomsk. By that time your contacts with the university would be severed and you'll have to settle your affairs somehow. The trip to Moscow will incur a lot of expenses. At any rate, I've done my best to give you most sensible advice. But let God help you. Inform me when you are coming to Moscow. I'll come down to meet you.

Yours faithfully,

D.Shostakovich

P.S. As for your compositions, don't neglect melody and keep it in mind that your music should be "expressive" of something.

D.S.

August 10, 1950. Cable

I'm in Moscow. Give me a call.

Shostakovich

August 22, 1950. Komarovo

Dear Edik, because of my illness I have been late with my answer. Don't take it hard that you've suffered a setback in Moscow.[1]

Yours sincerely,

D.Shostakovich

September 24, 1950. Moscow

Dear Edik, I have not heard from you for some time now. Where are you? Write to me, please. I hope everything is well with you. What was the end of your trials in Moscow? I've come back to Moscow and will be waiting for some news from you.
  Yours sincerely,

D.Shostakovich

February 21, 1951. Moscow

Dear Edik, I have not heard from you for a long time. Where are you? Are you in Moscow or in Tomsk? How do you feel, what about your studies and your plans? Write to me without fail.

D.Shostakovich

April 29, 1951. Moscow

Dear Edik, today I've received your letter which made me happy. I'm glad that you are passing your exams successfully. I'm very sorry that you are not in Moscow now. When are you coming here? I'll stay in Moscow up to the mid-July and then I'm going to Komarovo. Keep me informed about your life. Don't forget to write. If you have some spare time, apply yourself to the piano, especially at sight-reading.
  Yours sincerely,

D.Shostakovich

July 26, 1951. Moscow

Dear Edik, I often recall our last meeting. Your excellent university diploma makes me think of you much. It seems to me that at the current moment you are going through a very complicated period in your life. You have every opportunity to get involved in research work. You can take up the postgraduate courses; and after three years (as far as I know) to become a candidate of sciences. And some time later you may become a doctor of sciences and so on. And you can achieve it all within the forthcoming 5–10 years. On the other hand, your talented nature gravitates towards music. You aspire to become a composer and you have the potentialities for it. But you'll have to start from the scratch. It will take five years to study at the conservatoire. Will your gift for composition manifest itself if not fully but at least to a great extent within this short span of time, or upon graduation from the conservatoire you are going to make just another composer on the statistics list? When I think about you the biographies of some composers come to my mind. Borodin was a chemist all his life. He wrote music only in his spare time which was not very much, Rimsky-Korsakov was a naval officer up to his mature years and took up music only when he was firmly established in his musical career. Cui, quite a mediocre composer, was a scientist all his life. Liszt, Chopin and Paganini were the outstanding interpretative musicians. Glinka was a rich landowner. And there are a lot of other examples. Think about this. Do you feel yourself capable enough to give up science and take up composition? Perhaps, it would be more wise to follow Borodin's example. You could master the musical metier (harmony, instrumentation, polyphony, etc.) without the conservatoire. And for the present to take up a scientific career. Don't be cross with me for this letter. It is dictated by my best regards for you.

Let you be always healthy and happy. Hoping to hear from you,

D.Shostakovich

August 4, 1951. Komarovo

Dear Edik, thank you for your letter. I think that you should study under Shebalin at the conservatoire. I fully understand your worries about A.N.Alexandrov. Of course, he may be offended by your attitude. But he is a very decent person and for this reason he wouldn't put a spoke in your wheel. But you must study only in Shebalin's class, for nowadays he is the only one who can teach the 'musical metier', or to be more precise, the 'composition metier'. And this is the most important for you now. If anybody is going to ask you whether you know anything about my letters to Bogatyrev and Shaporin, say that you know nothing about them. Though I don't see any reason for you to deny this, nevertheless, to be on the safe side let us agree between ourselves that you know nothing about my letters to these musical figures. Don't give up science altogether. Certainly it would be better to enter the postgraduate courses at Moscow University, but if it is very difficult, apply to Tomsk University.

Here is my advice. I don't know how much it is practical and useful for you. I believe in your talent and want you to become a true composer.

Wishing you all success.

Yours sincerely,

D.Shostakovich

August 17, 1951. Komarovo

Dear Edik, from your last letter I've learned that you've passed your exam in composition. My hearty congratulations. I hope you won't fail in the other exams and will be admitted to the conservatoire. As for the other matters, do as you like. I think that you ought to become a composer. But don't drop science altogether. Very likely, it will all come right in the end. Don't forget to send me your photograph. But send it not to Komarovo but Moscow. I'm coming back soon to Moscow. This summer was spent in confusion. I've composed nothing new. It is quite distressing. I hope to see you often in Moscow.

Yours sincerely,

D.Shostakovich

July 27, 1952. Komarovo

Dear Edik, thank you for your letter. I congratulate you on you becoming a second-year student. So it is one year less before you graduate. As for me, this past year was not very prolific. I've brought down a lot of music paper which is still as pure as a virgin bride. I'm afraid it (I mean the paper) will remain an old maid. We are coming back to Moscow by September 1. Give me a call and show me your new compositions. It would be very interesting to see how you are getting on. Generally speaking, the summer is passing too fast. The autumn is just around the corner. And then winter will come in no time.
    Yours faithfully,

D.Shostakovich

August 6, 1954. Moscow

Dear Edik, I was so happy to get both your letter and your cable. I feel envious of you that you have been and heard so many interesting things during your expedition.[2] When you return I would ask you to show me the results of your work.
    Yours sincerely,

D.Shostakovich

August 1, 1956. Komarovo

Dear Edik, thank you for your letter. I've been very glad to learn that you have a lot of interesting work to do and that you are going to enter the postgraduate courses. I'm also happy that you have firmly embarked on the composer's career and make progress with each new composition.

D.Shostakovich

July 22, 1957. Komarovo

Dear Edik, I have been so happy to receive your letter. Thank you for remembering me. It is the more so pleasant since now you are going through the happiest period in your life[3] and God bless you to remain so happy for the rest of your life.
    After your departure it got unbelievably hot in Moscow. Down in Komarovo it is also very hot but somehow you can stand it here much more easily. And on the evenings and at night it is even cool. The storms are thundering every day, sometimes even roaring. The heavy rain is downpouring on the roof, with lightning flashing and cleaving the sky. Peals of thunder are booming while I sit all day long in my 'creative laboratory' writing a symphony. Soon I'll be finishing it. And then apparently I'll experience what was so inspiredly expressed by that 'modernist' and 'formalist' A.N.Scriabin in the finale of his First Symphony in which (I mean the finale) he occupied the realistic positions.[4] Meanwhile I sit all day long composing.

We liked your Galya[5] very much. And we wish her great happiness and good luck. Maxim has entered the conservatoire. A week before the exams he came down with the flu and had a high temperature, nevertheless, he managed to overcome all the obstacles and got excellent marks in the speciality and history. During the exam he played very well and I believe that he will make a good musician.

We all wishing you the best of luck,

Yours truly,

D.Shostakovich

P.S. Tell Galya that we wish her and you to be always well and happy and we approve of her choice very much.

D.S.

January 25, 1959. Moscow.[6]

Dear Galya and Edik, come today to see *Moscow-Cheryomushki*.[7] It starts at 7.30 p.m. I enclose the tickets herewith.

Yours truly,

D.Shostakovich

Notes to Appendix 1

1. Shostakovich implies here Denisov's failure to enter the Conservatoire.
2. Here Shostakovich implies the folkloristic expedition on which Denisov went within the framework of his student practice.
3. Shostakovich means Denisov's marriage.
4. Here Shostakovich is being sarcastic about the official 'ideological' appraisals of music during the years following the adoption of the Resolution of the CC CPSU in 1948. "To occupy the realistic positions" was a cliche of the ideological praise bestowed on a 'reliable' composition.
5. Denisov's first wife.
6. The last letter sent by Shostakovich to Denisov.
7. Shostakovich's operetta.

PIERRE BOULEZ ABOUT EDISON DENISOV

PIERRE BOULEZ

from an interview given in German to Yuri Kholopov on February 20, 1990, Moscow

Q. Mr Boulez, will you share your views about Edison Denisov?

A. I personally met Edison Denisov in 1967 when I came here for the first time, though we had been in correspondence before. Earlier he wrote to me in Germany and sent me his score of *The Sun of the Incas*. This was his first score I had ever seen. I played it, first in Paris, then in London. Together with the BBC Orchestra we went on a tour to Germany, to the Berlin Festival and played Denisov's composition there. That was the first time we came into contact, I think, it was in 1965 or 1966, shortly before I arrived here. So in this way we came to know each other.

Naturally, he captured my sympathy and since then we have been in constant contact. Denisov sent us his scores and we performed them quite regularly. We were not the sole sponsors of his concerts. He is now well known to the musical community in Paris. His opera, *L'écume des jours,* had its première in Paris, which I failed unfortunately to attend since I was in Los Angeles at the time. As far as I know, Daniel Barenboim commissioned Denisov to write a large symphony, which was first performed in Paris. We also played his latest piece for chamber ensemble approximately three years ago. So I'm fully able to trace his creative career.

In my opinion Denisov is first and foremost a very good and highly original composer. In his style he differs from Western composers, for instance, in his colours and his musical ideas. I believe, for one, his colours to be purely

Russian. Perhaps, I'm wrong and they are not so for you, I don't know, but I perceive them as typically Russian. Once we invited Denisov to the I.R.C.A.M. to meet his wishes to work there. We wanted to invite him for six months. During the period between 1978 and 1980 we repeatedly tried our best to make this project go through. A real war was waging to get a permission for his trip. But all our attempts proved in vain. We got very upset over the frustration of our plans. But this story is not finished yet. We still intend to 'win' Denisov and let him write some composition at the I.R.C.A.M.

Q. Which of Denisov's compositions do you like best?

A. I would call, for instance, his *Requiem*. I like it very much because it reveals great power and I feel that it is typical of what this composer has to say. It is a kind of religious ritual, soaring music. I believe the originality of his thinking lies in the contrast between the greatest activity and utter calmness. The slow passages are ritualistic in the religious sense.

Q. Which features in Denisov's music do you distinguish as Russian?

A. In the first place, there is this ritualism inherent in his music. You see, for instance, his musical messages are never delivered in the tone of the romantic *espressivo*. For me this is like an icon. The same features are encountered, for example, in some pieces by Stravinsky. I find the same ritualization in the old paintings; similar things occur in music too. But it has nothing in common with the 19th century orientalism, even with Mussorgsky's premediated Russian characteristics. With Denisov it is more imperative.

ABOUT SOME MUSICAL WORKS

3.1. A PLOT OF THE OPERA
L'ÉCUME DES JOURS

Act One

Scene One. At Colin's Place

Colin shares his room with La Souris, a household pet mouse. Colin is waiting for his friend, engineer Chick whom he has invited for a dinner. Nicolas, Colin's new cook, is reading outloud the recipes from a cookery book. When Chick comes, Colin explains to him the structure of an instrument he has invented — "pianock-tail", a piano which under the effect of music can produce various cocktails. Chick sits at the instrument playing an improvisation on a theme from Duke Ellington's song. Then he tells Colin about his meeting Alise, Nicolas's niece, at a conference arranged by Jean-Sol Partre. He invites Colin to accompany him tomorrow to the skating-rink.

Intermezzo. The street. Colin is dreaming about meeting a girl who will love him. On his way he picks up two orchids.

Scene Two. The Skating-Rink Molitor

Chick introduces Colin to Alise. On the skating-rink they meet Isis who invites everybody to be her guests at the birthday of her dog. One of the skaters crashes against the wall. The attendant fixes an icy cross on the site of the accident and conducts a liturgy service, with Alise, Colin and Chick taking part in it. Eight cleaners take away the fragments of the corpse.

Intermezzo. The street. The strong wind is blowing. Colin running conjugates the phrase: "Je voudrais être amoureux, tu voudrais être amoureux, Il voudrait...."

Scene Three. At Isis's Place

Isis greets the coming guests. Alise tells Colin that Chick is not willing to marry her because he spends all his money on collecting Jean-Sol Partre's books and things. The entry of Chloé. Colin feels at once that this is the girl he has been dreaming of. Everybody dances à "Chloé", a song by Duke Ellington.

Scene Four. The Square

Colin is waiting for Chloé thinking where to invite her. They decide to walk around the city but the absurdist horror of the urban window-cases scares them off and they wander into the woods. The pink-coloured cloud envelops them making them invisible for the rest of the world.

Act Two

Intermezzo. Colin is running to Chloé dreaming about the wonderful wedding they are going to have.

Scene Five. The Preparations for the Wedding

Two scenes unfold simultaneously. On the left side of the stage the Desmaret brothers, a pair of "honorary pederasts", are dressing for the wedding ceremony; Pégase accusing Coriolan of seeing him with a girl.

On the right side, Chloé, Alise and Isis are also preparing themselves for the wedding.

Intermezzo. The church. The marriage ceremony of Colin and Chloé. The sounds of a hymn to love.

Scene Six. The Wedding Tour

Colin and Chloé are in a car, with Nicolas at the wheel. On their road there arise strange visions frightening Chloé: the scaly beasts at the telegraph-posts and the dirty smoke of the coal-mines Colin and Chloé get engaged in a conversation about the working people, how work wears out a man and reduces him to the level of a mechanical machine.

Scene Seven. At Colin's Place

Colin and Chloé are in their bed. Colin awakes and starts telling about his dream. Chloé complains that she has a pain in her breast. Nicolas brings in La Souris in his hands. Because of Chloé's illness the window glasses turned darker and La Souris has hurt herself trying to scratch them to make light penetrate the room. Chloé asks Colin to switch on a gramophone record. As the music sounds, the room changes its shape turning into a balloon.

The doctor examines Chloé and writes out a prescription.

Intermezzo. The medical quarter. Pieces of blooded cotton wool are swimming in the canal. All of a sudden there emerges an eye looking at Colin and Chloé.

Scene Eight. The Pharmacy

Colin comes here together with Chick. The shop exhibits many weird things such as a guillotine for prescriptions and a mechanical rabbit producing pills. Colin tells Chick about Chloé's illness: a water-lily is growing in her lung and the best medicine for it are flowers.

Scene Nine. At Colin's Place

Chloé is lying surrounded by flowers. The room became smaller, the windows let virtually no light in. Colin is reading a love story for Chloé — the novel *Tristan et Isolde*. Colin has spent all his money on Chloé's operation and now he has to look for a job.

Act Three

Intermezzo. Colin is walking along the road. The hot soil is vibrating under his feet. Behind the heaps of excavated earth one could see the strange glass blocks piled up in an unstable equilibrium with dark shadows moving occasionally inside them.

Scene Ten. The Munition Factory

Here Colin finds a job for himself. Directeur explains to him that munitions are grown out of grains through the heat of a human body. He has to undress himself and lie still on the earth for 24 hours waiting for the canon to grow out.

Scene Eleven. At Colin's Place

Chloé is sleeping surrounded by flowers. Alise comes and says that Chick has spent all his money on his collections of Partre and wants to part with her. Colin is comforting her.

Intermezzo. The eight policemen headed by the *sénéchal* are going to confiscate Chick's property for his default of payment.

Scene Twelve. At Chick's Place.

Chick defending his books from the policemen dies. The *sénéchal* sees through the window the neighbourhood houses on fire.

Intermezzo. Alise is running around Paris setting fire to the bookshops selling Partre's books and herself perishes in fire.

Scene Thirteen. Chloé's Death

The church. In the centre is the coffin with Chloé's dead body. Colin asks Jesus hanging on the cross: "Why has Chloé died? She was so kind and never harmed anybody..."

Intermezzo. The empty city. A little girl is singing about the dead city.

Scene Fourteen. Epilogue

A dialogue of Le Chat (*cat*) and La Souris. La Souris is telling about Colin's despair and asks Le Chat to help her die. Le Chat agrees: "Put your head into my mouth and as soon as anybody steps on my tail my reflex will snap into action".

A group of the blind little girls from the orphanage de Jules l'Apostolique are coming along the street singing about Jesus Christ. One of them treads on Le Chat's tail.

3.2. A PLOT OF THE OPERA
LES QUATRE FILLES

Scene 1
   The girls are singing, dancing and playing in the garden watching its inhabitants — a cat, a bird, flowers and trees.
Scene 2
   The sacrifice of the Goat to the gods. The girls decapitate the Goat and pull out her heart.
Scene 3
   The girls sit talking in a large cage standing in the centre of the stage.
Scene 4
   At nightfall the girls are spreading on the earth a big blue lake surrounded by the flowers and bathe in it. They are speaking about love, life and death.
Scene 5
   The girls are reading a letter received from an old housemaid.
Scene 6
   The night; the girls lie down on the earth and fall asleep. The opera concludes with the chorus on poems by Henri Michaux "Dans la brume tiède d'une haleine de jeune fille, je me suis retiré" (I've retired into the tepid haze of a young girl's breath).

3.3. *BLUE NOTEBOOK*

Edison Denisov's annotation on the score

The performance of *Blue Notebook* may involve some of the following theatrical elements:
   The Introduction (Part One) is played in complete darkness. Only the bulbs on the control panels are on, and a weak shaft of white light illuminates the keyboard of Piano I. In the second part, with the first chord of Piano II, a narrow beam of orange colour is directed on the recitalist and a shaft of yellow light illuminates the keyboard of Piano II. At Figure 1 a ray of soft white light (less intensive than the orange light) spotlights the soprano. At Figure 5 the bright red light illuminates the entire centre of the stage (only three groups of bells are to remain in dark). At the end of the item the red light is gently removed and, shortly before the third part, a shaft of the bright white light is directed on the soprano, and a softer and wider beam of this light — on Piano I. In Part Four the singer sits on the chair and the light is removed from her. The violin and the cello are playing with only the bulbs on the control panels on. A shaft of the dark blue light is directed on Piano I while a yellow beam illuminates Piano II. The recitalist illumines himself with a lantern which he holds in his hands so as to light up his face from below. Beginning with bar 27 there starts a slow circular motion of light around the stage (the direct motion is preferable), and in bars 29–35 there arise sharp and intensive flashes of light (active and rhythmically free; part of them may be directed on the auditorium). At bar 36 the motion of light stops and there remain only shafts of dark blue and yellow light. At bar 46, simultaneously with the entry of the cello and the violin, the stage is flooded with gentle green light (the dark blue and yellow beams remain).

In the fifth part the light is exclusively white. Narrow rays illuminate the soprano (sitting on the chair), the recitalist (in the arm-chair) and the player at Piano II who with the beginning of the item stands up and takes a wooden hammer (used for striking the bells). A narrow, pistol-like, ray of light is directed on a big log lying near the soprano (birch wood preferable) with a large hammer on it. The soprano puts on a pince-nez, stands up and takes hold of the hammer. There is no writing-desk. The right-side door in the background of the stage is lighted up only for the exit of Yevdokim Osipovich.[1] Simultaneously with the opening bars of this part the slide depicting a horse with a gipsy man in its teeth is projected in the background of the stage.[2] The soprano strikes the log with the hammer noiselessly with the sound delivered only by Piano II (the movements of the performers are to be synchronous). At Figure 6 the spotlight is on the violin and the cello (more intensive than on Piano I and Piano II). The performers play this passage with great expressiveness (but seriously, without parodying). Their playing is only visible but almost inaudible; the soundscape is created exclusively by two pianists.

In Part Six the light is ordinary (like in Part Three). The recitalist stays behind the scene. Before the seventh part the recitalist comes out onto the stage. The whole stage is illuminated by the quiet white light (it is desirable to keep three groups of bells in darkness up to the last part). The soprano sits motionlessly on her chair. At bar 12, simultaneously with the entry of Piano I, the soprano starts moving her right hand in a slow mechanical rotary motion, stopping it at bar 17 (simultaneously with Piano II). In bars 65–69 the recitalist comes up to the soprano, puts a cigarette into her mouth, lifts her left hand and gives her a mushroom. At bar 70 the white light is being changed for the green light which becomes more and more intensive. The soprano (bars 72–73) closes one eye, opens the other eye widely and sits absolutely still. The light is gradually concentrated on her.

Part Eight is performed under the same light as in Parts Three and Five. In Part Nine the stage is illuminated by the ordinary white light (Parts Seven and Nine begin under the identical light). The initial statement of the bells (after the words "and suddenly has disappeared") gives a signal to change lights: the entire stage is flooded with the gentle blue light (only the recitalist is slightly lighted in white). In this item the part of Piano II may be played by the player on Piano I.

In Part Ten the blue light remains on the stage (but it gets softer). The white spotlight is on the soprano and Piano I. In bars 79–82 the three groups of bells are illuminated by shafts of light in different colours (red, yellow and green). The stage is still in the soft blue light. The white light remains only on the keyboard of Piano I. The violin and the cello are playing with the bulbs on the control panels switched on. In bars 93–94 the coloured beams of light directed on the bells are gradually removed. There remains only the blue light (and a slight shade of the soft white light on the keyboard of Piano I).

3.4. REQUIEM

Musical Forms

Part 1

Part One fulfils a two-fold function in the development of the Requiem's generalised plot line of its imagery. First, it is the "first variation" — the birth, i.e., the initial stage in the "variational" chain representing a human life. Second, Part One proper expresses in a condensed form the content of the whole composition serving as a prologue to the entire cycle. It already incorporates the main landmarks of a human life and it turns out to be closed like the permanent circle of life.

The multilayered level of its content determines its compositional structure, multidimensional and polyphonic. Let us consider the division of its form by various parameters such as the text, the cast of performers, dynamics, and thematic elements.

The text and its vocal part divide its form into three large sections: two choral sections based on Tanzer's poems frame up the tenor's solo singing the text from the Sermon on the Mount (bars 1–55, 56–59, 60–91).

The instrumental part and dynamics divide its form also into three sections, but not coinciding with the previous division at the beginning of the third section. The sounds of the organ and vibraphones in loud dynamics, starting with bar 56, spread up to bar 68 forming one extensive section (bars 1–55, 56–68, 69–91).

Finally, the division according to its thematic elements reveals the features of the ternary form the first section of which in its turn falls into three sections. The thematic material in this first section of the form (bars 1–55) emerges on the principle of renovation. Six thematically self-contained elements can be distinguished in it. Four of them make a kind of thematic exposition. The element "a" is an instrumental introduction (bars 1–10), the elements "b", "c" and "d" follow the semantic division of the text: "b" — the word "birth" in three languages (bars 11–20), "c" — the word "breath", which is separated from the previous element by an instrumental intermezzo (bars 21–33), and "d" — "cry", also separated by an instrumental intermezzo (bars 33–36). Each sub-division introduces a new thematic element: "a" — a solo of oboe d'amore with its expressive chromatic melodic line; "b" — the gently dissonant chords of the chorus alternating with "tearing" chromatic lines; "c" — consonant triads, and "d" — a polychord. The next thematic element is "e" (bars 37–44). On the one hand, it retains the renovation principle (there appears a new triple figure in the harp, which is associated with a lullaby), on the other hand, it incorporates some thematic and timbre elements of the previous section (arpeggio triads in the harp, a chromatic melody of the flute and the sounds of vibraphones). Such synthesis of thematic elements, as well as the unstable character of tonal motion, lend this section the features of development. And the final element "f" (bars 45–55) represents a cadence progressing for 11 bars and made up of 3 chords in D major. This progression harmony accords with the concluding section.

Thus, on the whole, the first extensive section of ternary form is logically completed consisting of three classical stages in the unfolding of a musical idea — exposition, development and the finale. In the terms of imagery this section constitutes the initial stages in a human life — the birth, breath, cry and the first light in the eyes.

The second large section in Part One (bars 56–58) includes two new thematic elements. These are the tenor's solo (bars 56–59) and the chorus following it (bars 60–68). This is a culmination section both in semantic and musical terms (the highest point of dynamic development, the use of the most spectacular instrumental tone-colours).

The radically modified recapitulation (from bar 69) reinstates some thematic elements from the first section: chromatic lines in the organ (from the sections "a", "b" and "c"), the harp's triads (section "e"), the movement of the strings from a high to a low register (the section "e", bars 42–44), and a cadence at the note "D" and at the end — an instrumental finale reminiscent of the beginning of this part.

Below is the layout of the form:

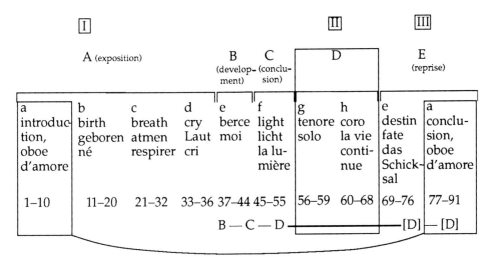

Part 2

This part, small in size and swift in character, occupies the place of Scherzo in the cycle. It represents a duet of two solo voices — the soprano and the tenor. This choice of the performers is determined by the main message of this part dealing with the fundamental "reality of opposite sexes" — man and woman.

The layout of the form:

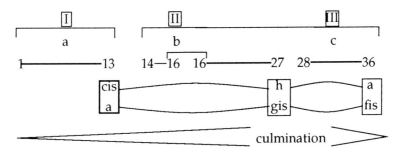

Part 3

The content of the poem which makes the basis of this part and conveys the idea of two extremes of life ("the budding passions of permanent variation" and "the wish to break out of the skin prison") determines its singular dramatic pattern: starting from the highest dynamic point, from a climax (this is one extreme of human life), this part seems to develop along the descending dynamic line; it has no climaxes in the middle section and ends in the gentle and soft sounds (the other extreme).

The layout of the form:

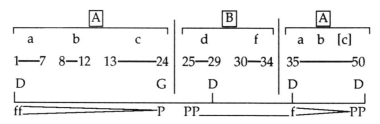

Part 4

This part is a kind of chamber intermezzo before the finale. A small body of instrumentalists (flute, clarinet, trombone, trumpet, harp, violin and cello), a lucid treatment of the chorus, a great number of pauses in the choral part, and the overall quiet and mellow character of music — all this reflects "the subdued soundscape of our time".

The layout of the form:

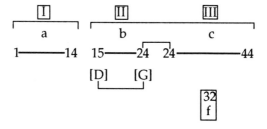

Part 5

This part is the most extended and complex in content and form: it incorporates several sections contrasting in content and musical material and merged together in one larger form (a kind of condensed cycle having no inner repetitions).

Two culmination zones, emotionally opposite but identical in their intensity, are identified in this part. To the first culmination zone at the words "exceptional variation" (bars 45–47) there extend the lines from Parts One and Three of the Requiem. This is the highest point in the development of the dramatic idea, a complete failure and disintegration of a human life, the destruction of all human aspirations. The antithesis is presented in the soprano's Aria (from bar 91), the second, lyrical culmination encompassing the lines of the imagery rooted in the episodes of the lullaby in Part One, and Parts Two and Four of the cycle. It is self-realisation, concentration of lyricism, warmth, light and hope.

In the tentative terms the finale may be defined as a form of sacred cantata comprising several sections, each with its own character, thematic material and definite orientations in the development of its imagery:

1. The initial chorus
2. The tenor's aria with chorus. The chorus
3. The soprano's aria. The chorus
4. The tenor's recitative
5. The choral requiem
6. The tenor's recitative with chorus
7. The final chorus

All the sections of the finale (for the exception of two connecting, fourth and sixth, episodes), despite their self-sustained structure, turn out to be regarded as separate elements of one larger entity. Therefore, the finale is characterised, on the one hand, by the compositional independence of each section and, on the other hand, by smooth flowing of one section into another. Thus, for instance, the soprano's Aria is singled out by its own tempo (Andante) and its ternary form. The chorus imperceptibly joins in the Aria's refrain (from bar 129) leading to the following section.

The structure of the choral requiem involves polyphonic forms such as imitation and fugato on a theme deliberately close to the theme of *Kyrie* from Mozart's *Requiem*.

The final chorus based on the lengthy organ point is fading away with the soft sounds of a major triad.

3.5. ROMANTIC MUSIC

Below are some extracts from the children's letters sent by M.-P. Faucher and M. Leger, schoolteachers, Paris, to Edison Denisov (March 28, 1984):
— *The music is so extraordinary. I've noticed that one instrument was playing so gentle and then gradually it became more and more violent. The composition ends not in silence but in resonance.* Marion, eleven-year-old
— *This music is so adventurous! You seem to find yourself in a fairy forest permeated with a sweet melody.* Véronique, eleven and a half years old
This music is wonderful for it conveys for me all the moments of life: the sentiments, joys and sorrows of the young. Vincent, ten-year old
— *I had the impression that somewhere in the middle of the composition there appeared a certain eerie personage on the scene.* Elise, eleven-year-old
— *I think this music is lingering, very mysterious and very disquieting. Most compositions end sharply while your finale is so gentle.* Alexandre, eleven-year-old

3.6. SOME SETS
Music for Eleven Wind Instruments and Kettledrums

Variations for piano

Sonata for violin and piano

"Sun of incas"

"Italian songs"

"Wails"

"Fünf Geschichten von Herrn Keuner"

I.

2.

3.

4.

Three pieces for piano four hands

Three pieces for cello and piano

Notes to Appendix 3

1. A character of this scene acted out by the recitalist.
2. The picture depicting a horse with a gipsy man in its teeth is hanging on the wall in this scene.

CHRONOLOGY

MAJOR BIOGRAPHICAL DATA

April 6, 1929	Born in Tomsk
1945	Began studying music at the General Music Courses (GMC)
1946	Finished a general-education school
1946	Entered the Physics & Mathematics Department at Tomsk University
1946	Entered the Music College at Tomsk
June 1948	Started his correspondence with Shostakovich
1950	Finished the Music College
1950 (summer)	The first unsuccessful attempt to enter the Moscow Conservatoire
1951	Graduated from Tomsk University, entered the postgraduate courses there
1951 (summer)	The second successful attempt to enter the Moscow Conservatoire (into the class of V.Ya.Shebalin)
1954 (summer)	The folkloristic expedition to the Kursk Region
1955 (summer)	The folkloristic expedition to the Altai
1956 (spring)	Graduated from the Conservatoire
1956 (summer)	The folkloristic expedition to the Tomsk Region and the Altai
June 1956	Became a member of the USSR Union of Composers
August 1956	Entered the postgraduate courses at the Moscow Conservatoire
1957	The first marriage

1959	Finished the postgraduate courses
1959	Started teaching at the Moscow Conservatoire
September 9, 1960	The birth of the son Dmitry
November 30, 1964	The performance of the cantata *The Sun of the Incas* in Leningrad
1965	The performance of the cantata *The Sun of the Incas* in Darmstadt and Paris
July 7, 1965	The birth of the daughter Yekaterina
August 1966	Publication of the article "New Technique Is Not a Fashion" in the journal *Il contemporaneo*
July 1978	The performance of the Violin Concerto in Milan
October 1980	The performance of the Requiem in Hamburg
1982	The release of the book *Percussion Instruments in a Modern Orchestra*
November 1984	The production of the ballet *Confession* in Tallinn
1986	The release of the book *Modern Music and Some Problems Arising in the Evolution of Compositional Techniques*
1986	Awarded the order for his contributions to literature and arts (France)
March 1986	The production of the opera *L'écume des jours* in Paris
September 1986	The performance of the Viola Concerto in Berlin
March 1988	The performance of the Symphony in Paris
1987	The second marriage
February 9, 1988	The birth of the daughter Anna
January 1990	Secretary of the Composers Union
January 1990	President of the Association of Modern Music
March 7, 1990	The birth of the daughter Maria
September 1990 – March 1991	Research work at I.R.C.A.M. (Paris) on the invitation of Pierre Boulez
March 19, 1991	The birth of the grandson Nikolai
July 21, 1992	The birth of the grandson Fyodor

COMPLETE CATALOGUE OF WORKS

I. STAGE MUSIC

1. OPERAS

L'écume des jours. Lyric drama in 3 acts and 14 scenes after Boris Vian (libretto by E.Denisov). 1981
    Première: March 15, 1986, Paris. "Opéra de Paris", John Burdekin, conductor
    Duration: 160'
Les quatre filles. Opera in 6 scenes after Pablo Picasso (libretto by E.Denisov). 1986
    Première: May 24, 1990, Moscow. "Forum", Mikhail Yurovsky, conductor
    Duration: 56'

2. BALLET

Confession. Ballet in 3 acts and 16 scenes, based on Alfred de Musset's novel *La confession d'un enfant du siècle* (libretto by Alexander Demidov). 1984
    Première: November 30, 1984, Tallinn, "Estonia", Paul Mägi, conductor
    Score. Moscow, Sovetsky Kompozitor Publishers, 1989
    Duration: 85'

II. WORKS FOR ORCHESTRA

1. SYMPHONIES

Symphony for two string orchestras and percussion (in 3 movements). Dedicated to Gennady Rozhdestvensky. 1962
    Première: November 29, 1963, Moscow. Gennady Rozhdestvensky, conductor

Score. Moscow, Sovetsky Kompozitor, 1974
Duration: 15'

Chamber Symphony (in 3 movements). Dedicated to Paul Mefano and the 2e2m ensemble. 1982
   Première: March 7, 1983, Paris. 2em Ensemble, Luca Pfaff, conductor
   Score. Paris, Le chant du monde, 1983
   Duration: 21'

Symphony for full orchestra (in 4 movements). Dedicated to Daniel Barenboim. 1987
   Première: March 2, 1988, Paris. Daniel Barenboim, conductor
   Duration: 57'

2. CONCERTOS. WORKS FOR SOLO INSTRUMENTS AND ORCHESTRA

Concerto for Flute, Oboe, Piano and Percussion (in 3 movements: Overture, Cadenza, Coda). Dedicated to Kazimierz Serocki. 1963
   Première: September 24, 1964, Warsaw. "Musica viva pragensis"
   Score. Vienna, Universal edition, 1968
   Duration: 12'

Concerto for Cello and Orchestra (in one movement). 1972
   Première: September 25, 1973, Leipzig. Wolfgang Weber, soloist; Herbert Kegel, conductor
   Score. Leipzig, Peters, 1973
   Duration: 18'

Concerto for Piano and Orchestra (in 3 movements). 1974
   Première: September 5, 1978, Leipzig. Günter Philipp, soloist; Wolf-Dieter Hauschild, conductor
   Score. Leipzig, Peters, 1978
   Duration: 27'

Concerto for Flute and Orchestra (in 4 movements). Dedicated to Aurèle Nicolet. 1975
   Première: May 22, 1976, Dresden, Aurèle Nicolet, soloist; Hans-Peter Frank, conductor
   Score. Leipzig, Peters, 1980
   Duration: 24'

Concerto Piccolo for 4 saxophones (1 performer) and percussion. 1977
   Première: April 28, 1979, Bordeaux. Jean-Marie Londeix and "Les percussions de Strasbourg"
   Score. Paris, Leduc, 1982
   Duration: 21'

Concerto for Violin and Orchestra (in 2 movements). Dedicated to Pavel Kogan. 1977
   Première: July 18, 1978, Milan. Gidon Kremer, soloist; Hubert Soudant, conductor
   Score. Moscow, Sovetsky Kompozitor, 1984
   Duration: 22'

Concerto for Flute, Oboe and Orchestra (in one movement). Dedicated to Aurèle Nicolet and Heinz Holliger. 1978.

Première: March 24, 1979, Cologne. Aurèle Nicolet and Heinz Holliger, soloists; Andrzej Markowski, conductor

Duration: 32'

Partita for Violin and Orchestra (in 6 movements). Dedicated to Leonid Kogan. 1981

Première: March 23, 1981, Moscow. Leonid Kogan, soloist; Pavel Kogan, conductor

Score. Moscow, Muzyka, 1990

Duration: 29'

Concerto for Bassoon, Cello and Orchestra (in one movement). 1982

Première: November 22, 1990, Moscow. Valery Popov and Alexander Sudzilovsky, soloists; Alexander Vedernikov, conductor

Duration: 32'

Chamber Music for viola, harpsichord and strings. 1982

Première: May 7, 1983, Moscow. Yuri Bashmet, soloist; Saulius Sondeckis, conductor

Duration: 12'

Tod ist ein langer Schlaf. Variations on a Haydn theme for cello and orchestra. Dedicated to Ivan Monighetti. 1982

Première: May 30, 1982, Moscow. Ivan Monighetti, soloist; Pavel Kogan, conductor

Score. Hamburg, Hans Sikorski, 1983

Duration: 12'

Concerto for Two Violas, Harpsichord and Strings (in one movement). 1984

Première: June 24, 1991, Amsterdam. Nobuko Imai and Petra Vahle, soloists; Lev Markiz, conductor

Duration: 32'

Happy End for two violins, cello, double-bass and strings. 1985

Première: December 4, 1989, Kaliningrad. "Amadeus" Ensemble. Valentin Zverev, conductor

Duration: 12'

Five Caprices of Paganini for violin and strings. 1985

Première: February 5, 1986, Moscow. Oleg Kagan, soloist; Saulius Sondeckis, conductor

Duration: 15'

Concerto for Oboe and Orchestra (in 3 movements). 1986

Première: March 4, 1988, Cologne. Heinz Holliger, soloist; Mathias Bamert, conductor

Duration: 26'

Concerto for Viola and Orchestra (in 4 movements). Dedicated to Yuri Bashmet. 1986

Première: September 2, 1986, Berlin. Yuri Bashmet, soloist; Charles Dutoit, conductor

Score. Moscow, Sovetsky Kompozitor, 1990

Duration: 38'

Concerto for Clarinet and Orchestra (in 2 movements). Dedicated to Eduard Brunner. 1989

Première: July 8, 1989, Lubek. Eduard Brunner, soloist; Udo Zimmermann, conductor

Duration: 26'

Concerto for Guitar and Orchestra (in one movement). Dedicated to Christopher, Thomas and Marie-Christina Wehrmann. 1991
  Première: November 30, 1991. Stuttgart. Reinbert Evers, soloist; Alexander Winterson, conductor
  Duration: 26'
Concerto for Flute, Vibraphone, Harpsichord and Strings (in one movement). Dedicated to Heinz A. Herrtag. 1993
  Première: August 17, 1993. Lucerne. Dmitry Denisov, Vladimir Goloukhov, Ivan Sokolov, soloists; Rudolf Baumhartner, conductor
  Duration: 18'

3. OTHER WORKS FOR ORCHESTRA

Peinture for full orchestra. Dedicated to Boris Birger. 1970
  Première: October 30, 1970, Weiz. Ernest Bour, conductor
  Duration: 11'
Aquarelle for 24 strings. 1975
  Première: June 12, 1975, Paris. Daniel Chabrun, conductor
  Score. Moscow, Sovetsky Kompozitor, 1989
  Duration: 12'
Epitaph for chamber orchestra. 1983
  Première: September 11, 1983, Reggio Emilia. Giorgio Bernasconi, conductor
  Duration: 6'
Confession. Suite from the ballet (in 8 movements). 1985
  Première: October 22, 1985, Moscow. Vasily Sinaisky, conductor
  Duration: 35'
Bells in the Fog for full orchestra. 1988
  Première: August 19, 1988, Moscow. Leonid Nikolayev, conductor
  Duration: 15'

III.   CHAMBER INSTRUMENTAL MUSIC

1. WORKS FOR PIANO. PIANO ENSEMBLES

Bagatelles. Seven pieces. Dedicated to Mikhail Voskresensky. 1960
  Leipzig, Peters, 1971
  Duration: 8'
Variations. 1961
  Première: March 28, 1965, Copenhagen. Torben Peterson, soloist
  Cologne, Gerig, 1968
  Duration: 5'
Three Pieces for piano four hands. Dedicated to Susan Bradshaw and Richard-Rodney Bennett. 1967
  Première: February 16, 1968, London. Susan Bradshaw and Richard-Rodney Bennett, soloists
  Vienna, Universal edition, 1968
  Duration: 11'

Signes en blanc. Dedicated to Adam Fellegi. 1974
   Première: September 26, 1974, Warsaw. Adam Fellegi, soloist
   Cologne, Gerig, 1978
   Duration: 16'
Variations on a Handel Theme. Dedicated to Felix Gottlieb. 1986
   Première: March 26, 1987, Leningrad. Felix Gottlieb, soloist
   Moscow, Sovetsky Kompozitor, 1990
   Duration: 23'
Points and Lines for two pianos eight hands. Dedicated to "Orgella-Kwartet", 1988
   Première: October 2, 1988, Amsterdam. The "Orgella-Kwartet"
   Duration: 12'
Pour Daniel. Dedicated to Daniel Barenboim. 1989
   Duration: 2'
Reflections. 1989
   Première: November 23, 1989, Glasgow. Susan Bradshaw, soloist
   Duration: 6'

2. WORKS FOR OTHER SOLO INSTRUMENTS

Solo for Flute. Dedicated to Aurèle Nicolet. 1971
   Première: April 29, 1973, Witten. Aurèle Nicolet, soloist
   Cologne, Gerig, 1973
   Duration: 3'
Solo for Oboe. Dedicated to Heinz Holliger. 1971
   Première: Helsinki, Heinz Holliger, soloist
   Cologne, Gerig, 1973
   Duration: 4'
Sonata for Solo Clarinet (in 2 movements). Dedicated to Lev Mikhailov. 1972
   Première: January 24, 1974, Moscow. Lev Mikhailov, soloist
   Cologne, Gerig, 1973
   Duration: 6'
Solo for Trumpet. 1972
   Duration: 3'
Sonata for Solo Violin (in 3 movements). Dedicated to Leonid Kogan. 1978
   Première: October 19, 1978, Hamburg. Yoshiko Nakara, soloist
   Hamburg, Hans Sikorski, 1978
   Duration: 13'
Dead Leaves for harpsichord. 1980
   Première: October 8, 1983, Berlin. Ruth Zechlin, soloist
   Leipzig, DVFM, 1984
   Duration: 6'
Sonata for Solo Guitar (in 3 movements: Toccata, Lullaby, Reminiscence About
Spain). Dedicated to Reinbert Evers. 1981
   Première: December 14, 1981, Moscow. Nikolai Komolyatov, soloist
   Hamburg, Hans Sikorski, 1982
   Duration: 14'

Sonata for Solo Bassoon (in 3 movements). Dedicated to Valery Popov. 1982
   Première: November 1, 1982, Moscow. Valery Popov, soloist
   Paris, Leduc, 1985
   Duration: 13'
Sonata for Solo Flute (in 3 movements). 1982
   Première: February 15, 1984, Münster. Paul Meisen, soloist
   Paris, Leduc, 1985
   Duration: 16'
Five Studies for solo bassoon. Dedicated to Valery Popov. 1983
   Leipzig, DVFM, 1986
   Duration: 15'
Two Pieces for solo flute (Pastorale, Motion) 1983
   Leipzig, DVFM, 1987
   Duration: 8'
Winter Landscape for harp. 1987
   Leipzig, DVFM, 1990
   Duration: 7'

3. WORKS FOR A SOLO INSTRUMENT AND PIANO

Sonata for Flute and Piano (in one movement). Dedicated to Alexander Korneyev. 1960
   Première: March 27, 1962, Moscow. Alexander Kozlov and Galina Rubtsova, soloists
   Moscow, Muzyka, 1967
   Duration: 11'
Sonata for Violin and Piano (in 3 movements). 1963
   Première: April 1, 1972, Moscow. Gidon Kremer and Oleg Meisenberg, soloists
   Leipzig, Peters, 1971
   Duration: 12'
Three Pieces for cello and piano. Dedicated to Natalia Gutman. 1967
   Première: May 11, 1968, Moscow. Natalia Gutman and Boris Berman, soloists
   Vienna, Universal edition, 1972
   Duration: 7'
Sonata for Alto Saxophone and Piano (in 3 movements). Dedicated to Jean-Marie Londeix. 1970
   Première: December 14, 1970, Chicago. Jean-Marie Londeix and Henriette Puig-Roget, soloists
   Paris, Leduc, 1973
   Duration: 12'
Sonata for Cello and Piano (in 2 movements: Recitative, Toccata). Dedicated to Natalia Gutman. 1971
   Première: April 8, 1971, Royan. Pierre Penassou and Marie-Elena Barrientos, soloists
   Leipzig, Peters, 1973
   Duration: 10'

Two Pieces for alto saxophone and piano. Dedicated to Lev Mikhailov. 1974
   Première: June 1974, Bordeaux. Lev Mikhailov and Igor Katayev, soloists
   Paris, Leduc, 1978
   Duration: 5′
Choral Variations for trombone and piano. Dedicated to Anatoly Skobelev. 1975
   Première: August 27, 1976, Venice. James Fulkerson, soloist
   Paris, Leduc, 1979
   Duration: 8′
Four Pieces for flute and piano. Dedicated to Aurèle Nicolet. 1977
   Première: April 21, 1978, Paris. Aurèle Nicolet and Jurg Wittenbach, soloists
   Paris, Leduc, 1978
   Duration: 9′
Prelude and Aria for flute and piano. 1978
   Paris, Leduc, 1979
   Duration: 6′
Es ist genug. Variations on a Bach theme for viola and piano. 1984
   Leipzig, DVFM, 1991
   Duration: 10′
Paysage au clair de lune for clarinet and piano. 1985
   Paris, Billaudaut, 1987
   Duration: 3′
Variations on a Schubert Theme for cello and piano. 1986
   Première: March 8, 1986, Moscow. Alexander Rudin and Vladimir Skanavi, so-
loists
   Hamburg, Hans Sikorski, 1988
   Duration: 15′

4. WORKS FOR TWO SOLO INSTRUMENTS
   (without piano accompaniment)

Sonata for Flute and Guitar (in 3 movements: Dialogue, Nocturne, Serenade). 1977
   Première: December 25, 1978, Moscow. Irina Lozben and Nikolai Komolyatov,
soloists
   Hamburg, Hans Sikorski, 1978
   Duration: 15′
Sonata for Violin and Organ (in 2 movements). Dedicated to Mikhail Fichtengolz.
1982
   Première: March 26, 1983, Leningrad. Mikhail Fichtengolz and Yevgenia Lisitsi-
na, soloists
   Duration: 23′
Sonata for Flute and Harp (in 2 movements). 1983
   Première: January 7, 1984, Moscow. Marina Vorozhtsova and Olga Eldarova, so-
loists
   Paris, Leduc, 1985
   Duration: 10′

Duet for Flute and Viola. 1985
   Première: March 28, 1990, Moscow. Dmitry Denisov and Igor Boguslavsky, soloists
   Paris, Leduc, 1989
   Duration: 5'

5. WORKS FOR A SOLO INSTRUMENT AND ENSEMBLE

Three Pictures by Paul Klee ("Diana in autumnal wind", "Senecio", "A child on a platform") for viola and ensemble (Ob., Cor., Vibr., Piano, Cb.). Dedicated to Igor Boguslavsky. 1985
   Première: January 27, 1985, Moscow. Igor Boguslavsky, soloist
   Leipzig, DVFM, 1986
   Duration: 23'
Es ist genug. Variations on a theme of Bach's chorale for viola and ensemble (Fl., Ob., Celesta, 2 V-ni, V-la, Vc, Cb.). 2nd version. 1986
   Première: September 3, 1989, Lucerne. Christoph Schiller, soloist; "Camerata" Ensemble, Heinz Holliger, conductor
   Moscow, Muzyka, 1991
   Duration: 14'

6. WORKS FOR TWO SOLO INSTRUMENTS AND ENSEMBLE

Romantic Music for oboe, harp and string trio. Dedicated to Heinz and Ursula Holliger. 1968
   Première: May 16, 1969, Zagabria. Heinz and Ursula Holliger, soloists; Trio à cordes français
   London, Universal edition, 1970
   Duration: 11'
Dedication for flute, clarinet and string quartet. Dedicated to "Nash-ensemble". 1991
   Première: February 6, 1992, London. "Nash-ensemble"
   Duration: 15'

7. TRIOS

String Trio (in one movement). Dedicated to Trio à cordes de Paris. 1969
   Première: October 23, 1969, Paris. Trio à cordes de Paris
   Score. Vienna, Universal edition, 1972
   Duration: 10'
Piano Trio (in four movements). 1971
   Première: October 30, 1972, Moscow. Valery Vilker, Mark Drobinsky and Victor Derevyanko, soloists
   Leipzig, Peters, 1975
   Duration: 20'

Trio for Oboe, Cello and Harpsichord (in three movements). 1981
  Première: November 1981, Donaueschingen. "Aulos Trio"
  Leipzig, Peters, 1984
  Duration: 30'

8. QUARTETS

String Quartet No. 2 (in three movements). In memory of Béla Bartók. 1961
  Moscow, Sovetsky Kompozitor, 1981
  Duration: 13'
Quartet for Flute, Violin, Viola and Cello (in two movements). 1989
  Première: November 7, 1989, Trento. Dmitry Denisov, Yevgenia Alikhanova,
  Tatiana Kokhanovskaya and Olga Ogranovich, soloists
  Duration: 26'
Four Pieces for string quartet. 1991
  Première: June, 1991, London. "Arditti-quartet"
  Duration: 6'

9. QUINTETS

Quintet for Flute, Oboe, Clarinet, Bassoon and Horn (in two movements). 1969
  Première: October 10, 1970, Amsterdam. "Danzi-Quintett"
  London, Universal edition, 1971
  Duration: 6'
Quintet for Two Violins, Viola, Cello and Piano (in three movements) 1987
  Première: May 24, 1987, Bristol. "Chameleon"
  Duration: 24'
Quintet for Clarinet, Two Violins, Viola and Cello (in three movements). Dedicated to
Eduard Brunner. 1987
  Première: May 30, 1987, Saarbrücken. Eduard Brunner and SDR quartet
  Hamburg, Hans Sikorski, 1991
  Duration: 19'
Quintet for Four Saxophones and Piano (in three movements). Dedicated to Claude
and Odile Delangle. 1991
  Première: February 20, 1993, Paris. "Quintette Delangle"
  Paris, Leduc, 1992
  Duration: 25'

10. SEXTET

Sextet for Flute, Oboe, Clarinet, Violin, Viola and Cello (in two movements). 1984
  Première: July 15, 1985, Cheltenham. "Capricorn"
  London, Boosey & Hawkes, 1988
  Duration: 14'

11. OCTET

Octet for Two Oboes, Two Clarinets, Two Bassoons and Two French Horns (in two movements). Dedicated to "Bläserensemble Sabine Meyer". 1991
　　Première: July 19, 1991, Wotersen. "Bläserensemble Sabine Meyer"
　　Hamburg, Hans Sikorski, 1991
　　Duration: 18'

12. VARIOUS ENSEMBLES

Music for Eleven Wind Instruments and Kettledrums (in three movements). Dedicated to Gennady Rozhdestvensky. 1961
　　Première: November 15, 1965, Leningrad. Gennady Rozhdestvensky, conductor
　　Leipzig, Peters, 1972
　　Duration: 7'
Crescendo e diminuendo for harpsichord and 12 strings. 1965
　　Première: May 14, 1967, Zagabria. Igor Gjadrow, conductor
　　Vienna, Universal edition, 1972
　　Duration: 6'
Ode for clarinet, piano and percussion. 1968.
　　Première: January 22, 1968, Moscow. Lev Mikhailov, Boris Berman, Valentin Snegirev, soloists
　　Moscow, Sovetsky Kompozitor, 1976
　　Duration: 8'
DSCH for clarinet, trombone, cello and piano. 1969
　　Première: September 26, 1969, Warsaw. "Atelier de musique"
　　Vienna, Universal edition, 1972
　　Duration: 5'
Silhouettes for flute, two pianos and percussion (in five movements: Donna Anna, Ludmila, Liza, Loreley, Marie). 1969
　　Première: October 5, 1969, Baden-Baden. Tomasz Sikorski Ensemble
　　Moscow, Sovetsky Kompozitor, 1983
　　Duration: 10'
Canon in Memory of Igor Stravinsky for flute, clarinet and harp. 1971
　　Première: 1972, London
　　London, *Tempo*, No. 97, 1971
　　Duration: 3'
　　Three Pieces for Harpsichord and Percussion (Reflections, Coincidences, Isolated Points in Space). 1972
　　Première: October 8, 1983, Moscow. Valery Kamyshev and Mark Pekarsky, soloists
　　Duration: 5'
Two Pieces for three instruments. 1978
　　Première: July 3, 1984, London. "Capricorn"
　　London, Boosey & Hawkes, 1987
　　Duration: 5'

Prelude for four harps. 1972
  Moscow, Sovetsky Kompozitor, 1983
  Duration: 5′
In Deo speravit cor meum for violin (flute), guitar and organ. 1984
  Première: November 1, 1984, Kassel. Otfried Nies, Reinbert Evers and Klaus
Martin Ziegler, soloists
  Duration: 12′
Hommage à Pierre for chamber ensemble (2 Fl., 2 Cl., Cor., Vibr., Arpa, Piano, V-no,
V-la, Vc.). Dedicated to Pierre Boulez. 1985
  Première: September 31, 1985, Baden-Baden. "Intercontemporain"
  Paris, Leduc, 1987
  Duration: 10′
Three Pieces for Percussion (Black Clouds, Appearances and Disappearances, Rays
of Distant Stars in Twisted Space). 1989
  Première: April 14, 1989, Moscow. Mark Pekarsky, soloist
  Leipzig, DVFM, 1990 (the first piece only)
  Duration: 25′
Variations on a Mozart Theme for eight flutes. 1990
  Première: January 25, 1991, Munich. Soloists: Andras Adorján, William Bennett,
Michel Debost, Peter-Lukas Graf, Hiroshi Hari, Maxence Larrieu, Wolfgang
Schulz, Ransom Wilson
  Paris, Billaudaut, 1992
  Duration: 10′

IV. CHORAL WORKS

1. WORKS FOR CHORUS, SOLOISTS AND ORCHESTRA

Requiem for soprano, tenor, chorus and orchestra on poems by Francisco Tanzer
and liturgical texts (in 5 parts). 1980
  Première: October 30, 1980, Hamburg. Eva Csapo and Lutz Michaels Herder, so-
loists; Francis Travis, conductor
  Score. Hamburg, Hans Sikorski, 1983
  Duration: 36′
Colin and Chloé. Suite from the opera *L'écume des jours* for soprano, mezzo-sopra-
no, tenor, chorus and orchestra (in 8 movements). 1981
  Première: October 17, 1983, Moscow. Nelly Li, Nina Terentyeva and Nikolai
Dumtsev, soloists; Vasily Sinaisky, conductor
  Duration: 36′
Kyrie for chorus and orchestra. In memory of Mozart. 1991
  Première: August 25, 1991, Stuttgart. Rupert Huber, conductor
  Duration: 10′
The Story of Life and Death of Our Lord Jesus Christ for tenor, bass, chorus and or-
chestra (in 7 parts) based on New Testament and Orthodox liturgical texts. (1. The
Birth of Jesus Christ, 2. The Worship of the Magi, 3. Sermon on the Mount, 4. The
Vision, 5. The Garden of Gethsemane, 6. The Calvary, 7. The Resurrection). 1992
  Duration: 60′

2. WORKS FOR A CAPPELLA CHORUS

Spring Coming (in 5 parts) on poems by Afanasy Fet. 1984
Première: November 7, 1986, Moscow. Valery Polyansky, conductor
Duration: 8'
Gladsome Light ("Svete tikhy") on Russian liturgical texts. 1988
Première: January 30, 1989, Tallinn
Duration: 17'

V. WORKS FOR VOICE

1. WORKS FOR VOICE AND PIANO

Merry Time for voice and piano on verses by 18th-century Russian poets (in 5 parts). 1961
Première: December 12, 1971, Moscow. Mikhail Ryba, soloist
Duration: 10'
Two Songs on Poems by Ivan Bunin for soprano and piano. 1970
Première: April 3, 1971, Halle. Roswitha Trexler, soloist
Moscow, Sovetsky Kompozitor, 1987
Duration: 5'
At the Turning Point for voice and piano on poems by Osip Mandelstam (in 4 parts). 1979
Première: January 28, 1980, Moscow. Lydia Davydova and Vasily Lobanov, soloists
Duration: 7'
Five Poems by Yevgeny Baratynsky for voice and piano. 1979
Première: January 28, 1980, Moscow. Irina Muratova and Vasily Lobanov, soloists
Moscow, Sovetsky Kompozitor, 1987
Duration: 9'
Your Charming Image for voice and piano on poems by Alexander Pushkin (in 10 parts). 1980
Première: December 8, 1980, Moscow. Alexei Martynov and Vasily Lobanov, soloists
Moscow, Muzyka, 1984
Duration: 19'
To Flore for voice and piano (in 3 parts) on poems by Attila Josef. 1980
Première: November 1, 1982, Moscow. Alexei Martynov and Vasily Lobanov, soloists
Moscow, Sovetsky Kompozitor, 1987
Duration: 6'
On Snow Bonfire for voice and piano on poems by Alexander Blok (in 24 parts). 1981
Première: April 12, 1982, Moscow. Alexei Martynov and Aristotle Konstantinidi
Moscow, Sovetsky Kompozitor, 1990
Duration: 57'

Light and Shade for bass and piano on poems by Vladimir Solovyov (in 3 parts). 1982
    Première: October 31, 1983, Moscow. Anatoly Safioulin and Georgy Fedorenko, soloists
    Moscow, Sovetsky Kompozitor, 1987
    Duration: 7′

2. WORKS FOR VOICE AND INSTRUMENTAL ENSEMBLE

Canti di Catullo for bass and three trombones (in 4 parts). 1962
    Première: March 18, 1982, Moscow. Anatoly Safioulin, soloist, and the Bolshoi Theatre trombone trio
    Moscow, Sovetsky Kompozitor, 1982
    Duration: 8′
The Sun of the Incas for soprano and ensemble (Fl., Ob., Cl., Tr- ba, Cor., V-no, Vc., 2 pianos, percussion) on poems by Gabriela Mistral (in 6 parts). Dedicated to Pierre Boulez. 1964
    Première: November 30, 1964, Leningrad. Lydia Davydova, soloist; Gennady Rozhdestvensky, conductor
    London, Universal edition, 1971
    Duration: 21′
Italian Songs for soprano, violin, flute, horn and harpsichord on poems by Alexander Blok (in 4 parts). 1964
    Première: May 10, 1966, Leningrad. Lydia Davidova, soloist; Igor Blazhkov, conductor
    Budapest, *Muzsika,* 1973
    Duration: 19′
Wails for soprano, piano and percussion on folk Russian texts (in 6 parts). 1966
    Première: December 17, 1968, Brussels. Basia Retchitska, soloist
    Vienna, Universal edition, 1972
    Duration: 29′
Fünf Geschichten von Herrn Keuner for tenor and seven instruments (Cl. picc., Sax. alto, Tr- ba, Tr- ne, Piano, Cb., Perc.) on texts by Bertold Brecht. 1966
    Première: February 20, 1968, Berlin. Horst Histermann, soloist; Joachim Freyer, conductor
    Moscow, Muzyka, 1978
    Duration: 14′
La vie en rouge for voice, flute, clarinet, violin, cello, piano and percussion on poems by Boris Vian (in 7 parts). 1973.
    Première: May 1973, Zagabria. Roswitha Trexler, soloist
    Duration: 24′
Merry Time for voice and piano trio on verses by 18th-century Russian poets. 2nd version. 1975
    Duration: 10′

Blätter for soprano and string trio on poems by Francisco Tanzer (in 5 parts). Dedicated to Roswitha Trexler. 1978.
    Première: January 28, 1980, Moscow. Lydia Davydova, soloist
    Hamburg, Hans Sikorski, 1979
    Duration: 9'
Pain and Silence for mezzo-soprano, clarinet, viola and piano on poems by Osip Mandelstam (in 4 parts). 1979
    Première: January 28, 1980, Moscow. Yelena Druzhenkova, soloist
    Moscow, Sovetsky Kompozitor, 1988
    Duration: 11'
Wishing Well for voice, clarinet, viola and piano on poems by Francisco Tanzer. 1986
    Première: March 1, 1986, New York. "Continuum"
    Duration: 6'
Four Poems by Gérard de Nerval for voice, flute and piano. 1989
    Première: July 22, 1989, Davos. Ernst Haefliger, Aurèle Nicolet and Andreas Haefliger, soloists
    Duration: 10'

3. WORKS FOR VOICE AND ORCHESTRA

Chant d'automne for soprano and full orchestra on poems by Charles Baudelaire (in 4 parts). 1971
    Première: May 16, 1971, Zagabria. Dorothy Dorow, soloist; Samo Hubad, conductor
    Score. Vienna, Universal edition, 1972
    Duration: 13'
Your Charming Image for voice and orchestra on poems by Alexander Pushkin (in 10 parts). 2nd version. 1982
    Première: October 30, 1984, Moscow. Alexei Martynov, soloist; Gennady Rozhdestvensky, conductor
    Duration: 19'
Au plus haut des cieux... for voice and chamber orchestra on poems by Georges Bataille (in 12 parts). 1986
    Première: May 11, 1987, Paris. Marie Angel, soloist; "Intercontemporain", Peter Eötvös, conductor
    Paris, Le Chant du monde, 1992
    Duration: 20'
Christmas Star for voice, flute and strings on poems by Boris Pasternak. 1989
    Première: December 28, 1989, Moscow. Yelena Bryleva and Dmitry Denisov, soloists; Yuri Bashmet, conductor
    Duration: 10'

4. VOCAL ENSEMBLES

Autumn for 13 solo voices on poems by Velimir Khlebnikov (in 3 parts). 1968
    Première: March 30, 1969, Royan. Marcel Couraud, conductor

Moscow, Sovetsky Kompozitor, 1985
Duration: 6'
Trois fragments du Nouveau Testament for contratenor, two tenors, baritone, flute and campane (bells). 1989
Première: December 7, 1990, Basel. "Hilliard-Ensemble"
Duration: 8'
Légendes des eaux souterraines for 12 solo voices on poems by Ives Bergeret (in 8 parts). 1989
Duration: 15'

VI. SPECIAL GENRES

1. INSTRUMENTAL THEATRE

Blue Notebook for soprano, recitalist, violin, cello, two pianos and three groups of bells on poems by Alexander Vvedensky and texts by Daniil Kharms (in 10 parts). 1984
Première: April 11, 1985, Rostov-on-Don. Yelena Komarova, soloist
Duration: 45'
The Ship Steams Past the Harbour ("Parokhod plyvet mimo pristani"). Music for sound orchestra. Dedicated to Mark Pekarsky and his ensemble. 1986
Première: April 1, 1987, Moscow. Mark Pekarsky Ensemble
Duration: 10'

2. ELECTRONIC AND CONCRETE MUSIC

Birdsong for prepared piano and tape. 1969
Première: December 20, 1970, Dubna. Alexei Lyubimov, soloist
Duration: 7'33"
Sur la nappe d'un étang glacé... for 9 instruments (Fl., Ob., Cl., Tr-ba, Cor., Tr-ne ten., Piano, Arpa, Vibr.) and tape. 1991
Première: February 24, 1993, Paris. David Robertson, conductor
Duration: 16'

VII. ORCHESTRATIONS

Yuri Kochurov. *Don Juan.* Suite from the ballet for full orchestra. 1960
Leningrad, Muzyka, 1967
Modest Mussorgsky. *The Nursery* for soprano and orchestra. 1976
Moscow, Muzyka, 1984
Modest Mussorgsky. *Sunless* for bass and orchestra. 1981
Alexander Mosolov. *Three Children Scenes* for voice and chamber orchestra. 1981
Alexander Mosolov. *Four Newspaper Announcements* for voice and chamber orchestra. 1981
Franz Schubert. Walzer Op. 9a for chamber orchestra. 1981

Franz Schubert. Walzer Op. 9a for full orchestra. 1982
Franz Schubert. Walzer Op. 9b for chamber orchestra. 1982
Ludwig van Beethoven. *Marcia alla turca* for chamber orchestra. 1982
Franz Schubert. *Ave Maria* for chamber orchestra. 1982
Franz Shubert. Grätzer Walzer Op. 91a for chamber orchestra. 1983
Franz Schubert. Walzer Op. 18a for chamber orchestra. 1983
Modest Mussorgsky. *Songs and Dances of Death* for bass and orchestra. 1983
Franz Schubert. *Hommage aux belles Viennoises* Op. 67 for chamber orchestra. 1983
Franz Schubert. Letzte Walzer Op. 127 for chamber orchestra. 1984
Franz Schubert. Walzer Op. 9b for full orchestra. 1984
Frederic Chopin. Etude cis-moll Op. 10 No. 4 for piano and orchestra. 1984
Franz Schubert. Walzer Op. 18a for full orchestra. 1986
Claude Debussy. *Rodrigue et Chimène*, opera in 3 acts. 1992

VIII.   MISCELLANEOUS

1. THE EARLIEST WORKS (1947–1951)

Preludes for piano (21). 1947–1949
Classical Suite for two pianos in D major (in five movements: Prelude, Gavotte, Minuet, Intermezzo, Gigue). 1948–1949
Gavotte (from *Classical Suite*) for chamber orchestra. 1949
Songs for voice and piano on poems by H. Heine, A. Mickiewicz, A. Blok, S. Yesenin and M. Lermontov. 1948–1949
Failure ("Neudacha"). Comic scene after Anton Chekhov. 1949
Suite for orchestra and chorus. 1949
Minuet for oboe and piano. 1949
Songs for voice and piano on poems by A. Blok and H. Heine. 1950–1951

2. WORKS WRITTEN DURING
THE CONSERVATOIRE YEARS

Five Settings of Robert Burns for voice and piano. 1951
Moscow, Sovetsky Kompozitor, 1980 (Nos 2 and 3 only)
Evening for voice and piano on poems by Fyodor Tyutchev. 1951
Two A Cappella Choruses on poems by Avetik Isahakian. 1952
Three Songs for voice and piano on poems by Avetik Isahakian. 1952
You Like Spring for voice and piano on poems by Sandor Petöfi, 1952
Winds Blow for soprano and piano on poems by Alexei Koltsov. 1952
Behind the River, Behind the Mountain ("Za rekoi, za goroi"). Russian folk song for chorus. 1953
Nocturnes. Song-cycle for mezzo-soprano and piano (8 settings) on poems by Bo Tzu-i. 1954
Music supplement to the *Sovetskaya Muzyka* magazine, No. 4, 1954 (two songs only); Moscow, Sovetsky Kompozitor, 1980 (the whole cycle)

Piano Trio (in four movements). Dedicated to Dmitry Shostakovich. 1954
   Moscow, Sovetsky Kompozitor, 1960
Symphony for full orchestra (in four movements). 1955
Blacksmith, You Blacksmith ("Kuznetsy, vi kuznetsy"). Russian folk song for voice and piano. 1955
Boriska Is Walking ("Khodit Boriska"). Russian folk song for voice and piano. 1955
Ivan the Soldier ("Ivan-soldat"). Opera, one scene. 1956
String Quartet No. 1 (in three movements). 1957 (the score is missing)
Sinfonietta on Tajik Themes (in three movements). 1957
Trio for Violin, Clarinet and Bassoon (in two movements). Dedicated to Nikolai Peiko. 1957
   Moscow, Muzyka, 1965
Youth Sufferings ("Stradaniya yunosti"). Song-cycle for voice and piano (10 settings) on poems by H. Heine. 1958
   Moscow, Sovetsky Kompozitor, 1980
Sonata for Two Violins (in three movements: Introduction, Variations on Two Folk Themes, Fugue). 1958
   Moscow, Muzyka, 1967
Little Suite for orchestra (in five movements: Melody, Divertimento, Landscape, Intermezzo, Play). 1958
Children Suite for orchestra (in five movements: March, Russian Song, Joke, Request, Finale). Dedicated to Nikolai Litvinov. 1958
   Moscow, Muzyka, 1965
Musical Pictures. Suite for orchestra (in six movements: Early in the Morning, Merry Song, Quarrel, Clowns, Dance, Lullaby). 1958
   Moscow, Sovetsky Kompozitor, 1963[1]
Three Pieces for Violin and Piano (Improvisation, Adagio, Dance). 1958
   Moscow, Sovetsky Kompozitor, 1962 (Nos 2 and 3)
Ivan the Soldier. Opera in 3 acts and 5 scenes after a Russian fairy tale. 1959
Native Land. Song-cycle for middle voice and piano (four settings) on poems by Alexander Prokofiev. 1959
   Moscow, Sovetsky Kompozitor, 1978
Chamber Symphony for clarinet, bassoon, piano and strings (in three movements: Overture, Basso ostinato, Toccata). 1960
Siberian Land. Oratorio for recitalist, bass, mixed chorus and orchestra (five settings) on poems by Alexander Tvardovsky. 1961
Divertimento in classical style for piano four hands (in five movements: Prelude, Chorale, Minuet, Aria, Fugue on BACH). 1961
   Moscow, Sovetsky Kompozitor, 1989[2]

3. ARRANGEMENTS

Three arrangements for guitar and voice (P.E. Phontso, V. de Meglo, Neapolitan serenade)
   Moscow, Muzgiz, 1956
Saint Saëns. Tango; Mexican folk song. Arrangement for two mandolins (domras) and guitar

Moscow, Muzgiz, 1958
Ravel. *Chanson espagnole*. Arrangement for voice and two guitars
  Moscow, Muzgiz, 1958
Album of easy arrangements for piano four hands. Issues 1, 2 and 3. Compiled and arranged by E.Denisov
  Moscow, Muzgiz, 1961, 1962, 1963
Works by French Composers. Easy arrangements for piano four hands by E. Denisov
  Moscow, Muzyka, 1965

IX. INCIDENTAL SCORES TO FILMS, PLAYS, TV AND RADIO PRODUCTIONS

Over 60 film scores (features, popular science, cartoons), among them *I'll Present You with a City, Lebedev Versus Lebedev, The Strong in Spirit, The Anonymous Star, An Ideal Husband, A Blue Cup, Born Twice, Prishvin's Paper Eyes, The Body, The Feast of Balthazar or Night with Stalin,* and *Love Fervour;*
  More than 30 incidental scores to plays, among them:
  At the Taganka Theatre: *Listen!* (Vladimir Mayakovsky), *The Living One* (Boris Mozhayev), *The Exchange* (Yuri Trifonov), *The Master and Margarita* (Mikhail Bulgakov), *Crime and Punishment* (Fyodor Dostoyevsky), *The Three Sisters* (Anton Chekhov), *A Theatre Romance* (Mikhail Bulgakov), *Phèdre* (Marina Tsvetayeva);
  At the Sovremennik Theatre: *The Cabal of Hypocrites* (Mikhail Bulgakov), *The Turbins' Days* (Mikhail Bulgakov), *A Pet Cat Not Too Downy* (Vladimir Voinovich);
  At the Mayakovsky Theatre: *The Seagull* (Anton Chekhov);
  Staged in Helsinki: *A Raw Youth* (Fyodor Dostoyevsky).
  Scores to TV and radio productions, including *Gargantua and Pantagruel* (François Rabelais), Kiddy and Karlsson Who Lives on the Roof (Astrid Lindgren), *Mother Courage* (Bertold Brecht), *Aladdin's Magic Lamp* (from *Arabian Nights' Entertainments*).

Notes to Appendix 5

  1. Separate pieces from the last three cycles *Little Suite, Children Suite* and *Musical Pictures* appeared in various publications, e.g. *Six Pieces for Piano* (Moscow, Sovetsky Kompozitor, 1962), *Piano Pieces* (Moscow, Sovetsky Kompozitor, 1960) and *Canto russo* (Milan, Ricordi, 1980).
  2. The last three compositions — *Chamber Symphony, Siberian Land* and *Divertimento* were written after Denisov's graduation from the conservatoire, but stylistically they are related to this period.

DISCOGRAPHY

— "BIRDSONG" 1990
E.Denisov on "ANS" synthesizer
Melodia C 60 30721 000
— "CANON IN MEMORY OF IGOR STRAVINSKY" 1982
V.Samec, J.Luptacik, M.Vildner
Opus 9III 1277
— CHAMBER SYMPHONY 1989
Conductor A.Lazarev
Melodia C 10 28753 008
— "COLIN AND CHLOÉ". Suite from the opera "L'écume des jours" 1985
N.Li, N.Terentyeva, N.Dumtsev, conductor V.Sinaisky
"TOD IST EIN LANGER SCHLAF". Variations on a theme
of Haydn, I.Monighetti, conductor P.Kogan
Melodia C 10 24593 004
— CONCERTO FOR CELLO AND ORCHESTRA 1979
G.Georgian, conductor D.Kitayenko
Melodia C 10-13893-4
— CONCERTO FOR PIANO AND ORCHESTRA 1980
G.Philipp, conductor W.-D.Hauschild
PEINTURE
Conductor W.-D.Hauschild
Eterna 8 27 333
— "CRESCENDO E DIMINUENDO" 1967
Conductor L.Bernstein
Columbia MS 7052
— "LA VIE EN ROUGE" 1986
G.Hartman, G.Burgos, D.Simpson, U.Kneihs,
N.Tamestit, J.-L.Bergerard
"COLIN AND CHLOÉ"
N.Li, N.Terentyeva, N.Dumtsev, conductor V.Sinaisky
Le chant du monde LDX 78 806

— ODE   1969
R.Annunsiata, V.Voskoboinikov, A.Lanzi
Fratelli Fabri Editori mm IIIO
— ODE   1972
J.J.Junco, P.Ortiz, L.A.Barrera
Egrem LD-3653
— ODE   1985
"Modern Music Trio" (Bulgaria): I.Glavanov,
L.Getova-Raikova, T.Kyrparova
Balkanton BKA 11542
— PEINTURE   1970
Conductor E.Bour
Amadeo C VSTX 1408
— PEINTURE   1983
Conductor V.Verbitsky
Opus 9110 1448
— PEINTURE   1983
Conductor G.Rozhdestvensky
Melodia C 10-18757-62
— PIECES FOR PIANO: "Merry Song", "Russian Song"   1978
R.Bobritskaya
Melodia C 50-09933-34
— QUINTET FOR WIND INSTRUMENTS   1991
V.Kudrya, V.Tambovtsev, I.Panasyuk, L.Melnikov, V.Sazykin
Melodia C 10 31057 000
— REQUIEM   1989
N.Li, A.Martynov, conductor V.Katayev
SPRING COMING
Conductor B.Tevlin
Melodia C 10 29277 007
— "ROMANTIC MUSIC"   1975
A.Lyubimov, N.Tolstaya
Melodia C 10-10983-4
— SOLO FOR OBOE   1975
H.Holliger
Denon OX 7031-ND
— SONATA FOR ALTO SAXOPHONE AND PIANO   1974
J.-M.Londeix, P.Pontier
EMI C 065-12805
— SONATA FOR ALTO SEXAPHONE AND PIANO   1976
Ph.Dehibero, M.Smellie
Open Loop Records XPL-1059
— SONATA FOR ALTO SAXOPHONE AND PIANO   1976
T.Kynaston, Ph.Rappeport
Coronet LPS 3044
— SONATA FOR ALTO SAXOPHONE AND PIANO   1983
I.Roth, G.Wyss
Colosseum Colos SM 640

— SONATA FOR ALTO SAXOPHONE AND PIANO   1984
  M.Shaposhnikova, S.Solodovnik
  Melodia C 10 20849 004
— SONATA FOR ALTO SAXOPHONE AND PIANO   1985
  J.-M.Londeix, C.Picard
  SNE-517
— SONATA FOR SOLO CLARINET   1976
  K.-I.Stewensson
  BIS LP-62
— SONATA FOR FLUTE AND GUITAR   1987
  SONATA FOR SOLO FLUTE
  SONATA FOR SOLO GUITAR
  P.Meisen, R.Evers
  Digital MD+G 61249
— SONATA FOR VIOLIN AND PIANO
  G.Feigin, V.Poltoratsky
  Melodia C 10-07283-4
— SONATA FOR VIOLIN AND ORGAN   1983
  M.Fichtengolz, Ye.Lisitsina
  Melodia C 10 24483 002
— "SPRING COMING"   1990
  Conductor B.Tevlin
  Melodia C 10 30499 008
— "THE SUN OF THE INCAS"   1983
  N.Li, conductor A.Lazarev
  Melodia C 10-18403-4
— THREE PIECES FOR CELLO AND PIANO   1978
  I.Monighetti, A.Lyubimov
  Melodia C 10-10167-68
— TRIO FOR VIOLIN, CELLO AND PIANO   1980
  SONATA FOR VIOLIN AND PIANO
  "SIGNES EN BLANC" for piano
  J.-P.Armengaud, D.Erlih, A.Meunier
  Le chant du monde CM 480 LDX 685
— TRIO FOR OBOE, CELLO AND HARPSICHORD   1989
  "Aulos-trio"
  Eterna 7 29277
— TWO SONGS ON POEMS BY IVAN BUNIN   1977
  D.Dorow, R.Jansen
  Caprice CAP 1112
— VARIATIONS FOR PIANO   1974
  L.Majlingova
  Opus 9111 0342
— "KIDDY AND KARLSON WHO LIVES ON THE ROOF"   1969
  Music to the story by A.Lindgren
  Melodia D 25415-20
— "GANGARTUA AND PANTAGRUEL"   1981
  Music for TV play from F.Rabelais
  Melodia C 40-14703-04

— "MAGIC LAMP OF ALADDINE"   1984
  Music to radio production of the Arabian fairy tale
  Melodia C 50 20833 001
— M.Mussorgsky. "Songs and Dances of Death"; "Sunless "   1985
  Orchestrations by E.Denisov
  E.Nesterenko, conductor G.Rozhdestvensky
  Melodia A 1000105 004
— A.Mosolov. "Three Children Scenes",   1987
  "Four Newspaper Announcements"
  Orchestrations by E.Denisov
  N.Li; conductor G.Rozhdestvensky
  Melodia C 10 25177 003
— A.Mosolov. "Three Children Scenes",   1987
  "Four Newspaper Announcements"
  Orchestrations by E.Denisov
  N.Li, conductor A.Lazarev
  Melodia C 10 25031 009

COMPACT DISCS

— Chamber symphony
  Conductor A.Lazarev
  Melodia, SUCD 10-00061
— Chamber symphony
  Conductor V.Ponkin
  VIST, MK-417036
— Chorale Variations for trombone and piano
  B.Sluchin, P.-L.Aimard
  ADDA 581087
— "Colin and Chloé"
  Concerto for cello and orchestra
  "Tod ist ein langer Schlaf" for cello and orchestra
  N.Li, N.Terentyeva, N.Dumtsev, conductor V.Sinaisky
  C.Georgian, conductor D.Kitayenko
  I.Monighetti, conductor P.Kogan
  Melodia, SUCD 10-00107
— Concerto for two violas, harpsichord and strings
  Chamber music for viola, harpsichord and strings
  "Es ist genug" for viola and ensemble
  "Epitaph" for chamber orchestra
  N.Imai, P.Vahle, A.de Man, conductor L.Markiz
  BIS, CD-518
— Five poems by Yevgeny Baratynsky
  E.Vasilyeva, J.Schab
  Le chant du monde, LDS 278973
— "La vie en rouge" for voice and ensemble
  G.Hartman, ensemble "Kaleidocollage"
  Le chant du monde, LDC 278806

— "Peinture" for orchestra
Conductor G.Rozhdestvensky
Melodia, MLD-32113
— Quintet for piano, two violins, viola and cello
Quintet for clarinet, two violins, viola and cello
Quartet for flute, violin, viola and cello
T.Alikhanov, A.Ivanov, D.Denisov, "Moscow Quartet"
Art Electronics, AED-10430
— "Romantic Music"
Piano trio
String trio
Quintet for clarinet, two violins, viola and cello
A.Lyubimov, N.Tolstaya
T.Alikhanov, E.Alikhanova, V.Tonkha
O.Krysa, A.Bobrovsky, I.Monighetti
A.Ivanov, "Moscow Quartet"
Mobile fidelity, MFCD 917
— Sonata for alto saxophone and piano
A.Bornkamp, J.Janssen
Globe, GLO 5032
— Sonata for alto saxophone and piano
Three pieces for percussions
Three pieces for piano four hands
Concerto piccolo
C.Delangle, O.Delangle, J.-L.Haguenauer, M.Soveral
"Percussions de Strasbourg"
Pierre Verany, P.V. 790112
— Sonata for cello and piano
A.Karttunen, T.Hakkila
Finland, FACD 362
— Sonata for solo clarinet
A.Damiens
ADDA 581066
— Sonata for solo clarinet
R.Wehle
EMI, CDC 7-49709-2
— Sonata for solo flute
P.Meisen
Dabringhaus, MD+GL 3370
— Sonata for flute and piano
Four pieces for flute and piano
M.Wiesler, R.Pöntinen
BIS, CD-419
— "The Sun of the Incas" for soprano and ensemble
N.Li, conductor A.Lazarev
Mobile fidelity, MFCD 869
— Symphony for orchestra
Conductor D.Barenboim
ERATO, 2292-45600-2

— Symphony for orchestra
  Conductor G.Rozhdestvensky
  Melodia, SUCD 10-00060
— Three pieces for piano four hands
  A.Grau, G.Schumacher
  Deutsche Harmonia Mundi, HM/DMR 2039-2
— Three pieces for piano four hands
  Piano trio
  Sonata for violin and piano
  "Signes en blanc" for piano
  J.-P.Armengaud, J.-C.Pennetier, D.Erlih, A.Meunier
  Le chant du monde, LDC 2781057
— Two songs on poems by Ivan Bunin for voice and piano
  "To Flore"
  "On Snow Bonfire"
  E.Vasiljeva, J.Schab
  Le chant du monde, LDC 278951
— Variations on a theme of Handel for piano
  F.Gottlieb
  Art Electronics, AED-10144
— A.Mosolov. "Three Children Scenes",
  "Four Newspaper Announcements"
  Orchestrations by E.Denisov
  N.Li, conductor A.Lazarev
  OLYMPIA, OCD-170
  Melodia, SUCD 10-00077

MUSICOLOGICAL WORKS BY EDISON DENISOV

EDISON DENISOV: MUSICOLOGICAL WORKS

1. Research Papers. Books

Title	Publication
Alexander Goedike's Symphonies	*A.F.Goedike*. Collected Articles and Memoirs. Moscow: Sovetsky Kompozitor, 1960
Music in the Technological Age	*Slovenska hudbá*, Issue 4, 1964
Béla Bartók's String Quartets	Collection *Music & Modern Times*, Issue 3. Moscow: Muzyka, 1965 Collection: E. Denisov. *Modern Music and Some Problems Arising in the Evolution of Compositional Techniques*. Moscow: Sovetsky Kompozitor, 1986
A Few Words About Anton Webern	*Hudebni rozhgledy*, Issue 3, 1966
Whence Goes Music?	Collection *In the World of Hypotheses*. Moscow: APN, 1967
On Dmitry Shostakovich's Orchestration	Collection *Dmitry Shostakovich*, Moscow: Sovetsky Kompozitor, 1967 Collection: E.Denisov. *Modern Music and Some Problems Arising in the Evolution of Compositional Techniques*. Moscow: Sovetsky Kompozitor, 1986
New Music and Jazz	*The World of Music*. Berlin, 1968, No.3 Collection: E.Denisov. *Modern Music and Some Problems Arising in the Evolution of Compositional Techniques*. Moscow: Sovetsky Kompozitor, 1986

Title	Publication
Dodecaphony and Some Problems in Modern Compositional Techniques	Collection *Music & Modern Times*, Issue 6. Moscow: Muzyka, 1969
Anton Webern's Variations Op.27 for Piano	*Collage 9*, Palermo, 1970; *Res facta*, No.6, 1972 Collection: E.Denisov. *Modern Music and Some Problems Arising in the Evolution of Compositional Techniques*. Moscow: Sovetsky Kompozitor, 1986
Stable and Mobile Elements in Musical Form and Their Interaction	Collection *Theoretical Problems of Musical Forms and Genres*. Moscow: Muzyka, 1971 Collection: E.Denisov. *Modern Music and Some Problems Arising in the Evolution of Compositional Techniques*. Moscow: Sovetsky Kompozitor, 1986
The Compositional Process and Some Possibilities of Its Formalisation in the Analysis	Collection *Exact Methods and Musical Art*. Rostov, 1972
Der Kompositionprozess und einige Möglichkeiten seiner Formalisierung bei der Analyse	*Beiträge zur Musikwissenschaft*. Heft 4, 1976
Sonata-Form in Sergei Prokofiev's Works	Collection *Sergei Prokofiev. Articles & Research Studies*. Moscow: Muzyka, 1972 Collection: E.Denisov. *Modern Music and Some Problems Arising in the Evolution of Compositional Techniques*. Moscow: Sovetsky Kompozitor, 1986
Music & Mechanical Devices	Collection *Artistic & Scientific Creativity*. Leningrad: Nauka, 1972 Collection: E.Denisov. *Modern Music and Some Problems Arising in the Evolution of Compositional Techniques*. Moscow: Sovetsky Kompozitor, 1986
Percussion Instruments in Igor Stravinsky's Music	Collection *Igor Stravinsky. Articles & Some Other Materials*. Moscow: Sovetsky Kompozitor, 1973
The Compositional Process	*Tempo*. A Quarterly Review of Modern Music. 1973, June, No. 105 Collection *Essays on Aesthetics*. Issue 5. Moscow: Muzyka, 1979
Witold Lutoslawski	*Music Encyclopedia*, Vol.3. Moscow: Sovetskaya Entsiklopedia, 1976
Percussion Instruments in Béla Bartók's Music	Collection *Béla Bartók*. Moscow: Muzyka, 1977

Title	Publication
Some Specific Features of Claude Debussy's Composition Technique	Collection *Some Questions of Musical Form*, Issue 3. Moscow: Muzyka, 1977 Collection: E.Denisov. *Modern Music and Some Problems Arising in the Evolution of Compositional Techniques*. Moscow: Sovetsky Kompozitor, 1986
Percussion Instruments in a Modern Orchestra	Moscow: Sovetsky Kompozitor, 1982
Some Melodic Types in Modern Music	Collection: E.Denisov. *Modern Music and Some Problems Arising in the Evolution of Compositional Techniques*. Moscow: Sovetsky Kompozitor, 1986
Arnold Schoenberg's Opera *Von Heute auf Morgen*	Collection: E.Denisov. *Modern Music and Some Problems Arising in the Evolution of Compositional Techniques*. Moscow: Sovetsky Kompozitor, 1986

Modern Music and Some Problems Arising in the Evolution of Compositional Techniques:
Collected articles:
  1. The Compositional Process
  2. Béla Bartók's String Quartets
  3. Sonata-Form in Sergei Prokofiev's Works
  4. Some Notes on Dmitry Shostakovich's Orchestration
  5. Some Specific Features of Claude Debussy's Composition Technique
  6. Stable and Mobile Elements in Musical Form and Their Interaction
  7. Some Melodic Types in Modern Music
  8. Music & Mechanical Devices
  9. New Music and Jazz
10. Arnold Schoenberg's Opera *Von Heute auf Morgen*
11. Anton Webern's Variations Op.27 for Piano
	Moscow: Sovetsky Kompozitor, 1986

2. Prefaces and Annotations

Title	Publication
Béla Bartók. Selected Easy Pieces for Piano. Prefaced, compiled and edited by E.Denisov	Moscow: Muzyka, 1963

Title	Publication
Béla Bartók. The Second Piano Concerto. Preface to the piano score	Moscow: Muzyka, 1964
Béla Bartók. The Second Violin Concerto. Preface to the piano score	Moscow: Muzyka, 1964
Igor Stravinsky. *The Firebird.* Preface to the full score	Moscow: Muzyka, 1964
Béla Bartók. String Quartets / Vols 1 and 2/. Preface to the full score	Moscow: Muzyka, 1965, 1966
Andrei Volkonsky. *Suite of Mirrors.*	Commissioned by Sovetsky Kompositor, Moscow, 1970, but remained unpublished

3. Memoirs

My Meetings with Dmitry Shostakovich	MSS, 1952–1958
A Subtle Musician and Remarkable Teacher (about V.Ya.Shebalin) (in coauthorship with Alexei Nikolayev)	*Sovetskaya Muzyka* magazine, No.6, 1962
Shebalin the Teacher (in coauthorship with Alexei Nikolayev)	In the book: *In Memory of Vissarion Yakovlevich Shebalin.* Memoirs and Some Other Materials. Moscow: Sovetsky Kompozitor, 1984

4. Some Publicistic Writings. Reviews

Songs of Kursk Collective-Farmers (in coauthorship with Alexander Pirumov)	*Sovetskaya Muzyka,* No.12, 1954
Around the Altai. Contemporary Essays (in coauthorship with Alexei Nikolayev and Alexander Pirumov)	*Sovetskaya Muzyka,* No.12, 1955
Once More on the Youth Education	*Sovetskaya Muzyka,* No.7, 1956
Siberian Songs (in coauthorship with Alexei Nikolayev)	*Sovetskaya Muzyka,* No.12, 1956
Early Music	*Sovetskaya Muzyka,* No.6, 1957
Evening of German Chamber Music	*Sovetskaya Muzyka,* No.8, 1957
New Programme of Chamber Orchestra	*Sovetskaya Muzyka,* No.5, 1959
The Concert of the Borodin String Quartet	*Sovetskaya Muzyka,* No.8, 1960

Symphonic Repertoire Should Be More Freely Renewed	*Sovetskaya Muzyka*, No.2, 1962
Mahler's Second Symphony	*Sovetskaya Muzyka*, No.4, 1962
Igor Stravinsky's *L'histoire du soldat*	*Vechernaya Moskva* (Evening Moscow) newspaper, May 11, 1963
The New Technique Is Not a Fashion	*Rinàscita*, August, 1966
Some Questions to a Music Critic	*Sovetskaya Muzyka*, No.8, 1989

5. Some Texts for Radio Programmes

Luigi Dallapiccola's Opera *Ulisse*	MSS, the late 1960s
Bernd Alois Zimmermann's Opera *Die Soldaten*	
Luigi Dallapiccola's Opera *The Prisoner*	
The Evolution of Expressive Media in Music	

APPENDIX 8

REFERENCES

REFERENCES

Barce,R. Edison Denisov. *Ritmo*, No. 605, Madrid, December 1989

Bradshaw,S. The Music of Edison Denisov. *Tempo*, No.151. December 1984

Gojowy,D. Sowjetische Avantgardisten. *Das Orchester*, Heft I, 1970

Gojowy,D. Kunst als kategorischer Imperativ. Notizen zu Edison Denissow. *Musica*, No.1, 1975

Grabovsky,L. Two Versions of 'The Nursery' (orchestrations of Mussorgsky's song-cycle for voice and orchestra by Edison Denisov and Rodion Shchedrin). *Sovetskaya Muzyka*, No.3, 1989

Kholopov,Yu. The Music of Edison Denisov. *Teater. Muusika. Kino*, No.8, 1985, Tallinn

Kholopov,Yu. Text in the prospectus on the opera *L'écume des jours* in 'Opera de Paris'. 1986

Kholopov,Yu. The Search for a New Kind of Beauty. Composer Edison Denisov: Music and Ideas. *Music in the USSR*, January-March, 1988

Kholopov,Yu. Edison Denissow. *Kammermusik* (A-G). DVFM, Leipzig, 1988

Kholopov,Yu. Striving for High Beauty. *Muzykalnaya Zhizn*, No.12, 1988

Kholopov,Yu. Edison Denisov. "Profiles of Composers: Reference Book". Moscow, Muzyka, 1990

Kholopova,V. Nowe kompozycje E.Denisowa (1968–1969). *Res facta*, No.6, 1972, Kraków

Kholopova,V. Rhythmische Organisation in der Musik Edisson Denissows. *Sowjetische Musik. Betrachtungen und Analysen*. Akademie der Künste der DDR, Arbeitsheft 37, 1984, Berlin

Rozhdestvensky,G. and Lyubimov,Yu.: Interview on the occasion of the 60th birth anniversary of Edison Denisov. *Sovetskaya Kultura* newspaper, April 6, 1989

Schnittke,A. Edison Denisov. *Res facta*, No.6, 1972. Kraków

Sjoqvist,G. Edison Denisov — en instrumentationens müstare. *Rysk musik*, No.5, 1991

Tsenova,V. Die Oper 'Der Schaum der Tage' von Edison Denissow. *Sowjetische Musik im Licht der Perestroika*. Laaber, 1990

Tsenova,V. Edison Denisov and Boris Vian. The opera *L'écume des jours*. *Moscow Musicologist*, Issue 1. Moscow, Muzyka, 1990

Dmitri Schostakowitsch. Briefe an einen Studenten. *Neue Zeitschrift für Musik*, Marz-April, 1981 (publication by D.Gojowy)

Dmitri Schostakowitsch. Briefe an Edison Denissow. *Musik des Ostens* 10, Kassel-Basel-London, 1986 (publication by D.Gojowy)

A Love Story. Edison Denisov's opera *L'écume des jours*. Reviews. *Music in the USSR*, April-June, 1987

SOME INTERVIEWS GIVEN BY EDISON DENISOV

1. In the Russian press

L'écume des jours. *Music in the USSR* (Moscow), October–December, 1984

'Music Which I Love'. *Melodia* (Moscow), No.4, 1984

Talks on Craftsmanship. *Sovetskaya Kultura* newspaper (Moscow), September 15, 1987

Variations on Familiar Themes. Dialogue: Edison Denisov and Yuri Nagibin. *Literaturnaya Gazeta* (Moscow), August 2, 1989

'One Must Sing in Opera'. *Teatr* (Moscow), No.3, 1989

'I Don't Like Formal Art'. *Sovetskaya Muzyka* magazine (Moscow), No.12, 1989

A New Facet of Edison Denisov. *Sovetskaya Kultura* (Moscow), February 17, 1990

Crossing the Doorstep of the Study. *Ogonyok* magazine (Moscow), No.31, 1990

"In Boris Birger's Pictures I Hear a Purely Musical Expression of Art..." *Music in the USSR*, January–March, 1990

"One Can't Exist Without Faith". *We and Culture Today*, Collection (Sverdlovsk), No.3, 1991

"I'm Too Linked with My Country". *Vechernaya Moskva* (Evening Moscow) October 24, 1991

"Perhaps Music Will Save Our Souls?" *Pravda* newspaper (Moscow), December 12, 1991

2. In the foreign press

Interview mit einem jungen sowjetischen Komponisten. *Musica* (Kassel) No.4, 1970

Il compositore Edison Denisov. *Rassegna sovietica* (Roma), No.2, 1973

Mühelybeszélgetes Egyiszon Gyenyiszovval. *Muzsika* (Budapest), No. 1, 1978

Muzsikportrek. *Zenemükiadó Budapest*, 1979

Genese einer Oper. *Neue Zeitschrift für Musik* (Mainz), No.12, 1986

"People don't change, only things change..." *Russkaya Mysl* (Paris), May 2, 1986

"Für mich ist Oper lyrische Kunst". *Theater der Zeit* (Berlin), Heft 6, 1987

"Differing Tastes Should Not Prevent Mutual Respect". *Muzikalni horizonti* (Sofia), No.5, 1989

Edison Denissow und Udo Zimmermann in Gespräch. *Jahrbuch 3*, Bayerische
    Akademie der Schonen Künste, *Oreos Verlag* (München), 1989
'Musik skal give lys'. *Dansk musik tidsskrift*, No.3, 1991
Der Komponist Edison Denissow: Interview// Thüring Bräm. *Bewahren und
    öffnet*. Musikedition Nepomuk 4. Aarau Schweiz. 1992

Name Index

Index of Denisov's Compositions